Preparation of Inexpensive Teaching Materials

Third Edition

JOHN E. MORLAN and LEONARD J. ESPINOSA
San Jose State University

Fearon Teacher Aids
a division of
David S. Lake Publishers
Belmont, California

ISBN 0-8224-5606-0

Library of Congress Catalog Card Number: 87–50618

Printed in the United States of America

1. 9 8 7 6 5 4 3 2 1

Contents

Preface

Teachers in all subject areas and at every grade level need to use a variety of approaches and techniques to assist students in reaching educational objectives. Lessons must be vital and alive. Whether preparing for a lesson, developing materials for a presentation, designing a learning center, or working with students in small groups, teachers find that locally produced instructional media of all kinds lend meaning, depth, and variety to the learning situation.

Teachers who use this manual should consider involving students in preparing materials. Teachers and students may use these materials to summarize ideas, interpret information, and communicate with others.

The contents of this manual are directed toward teachers who have had little or no technical background in materials preparation. Many of the processes may be accomplished without special materials or equipment, and all may be completed with little expense in relation to the usefulness of the finished product. Each chapter and each process within the chapter may be treated as an independent unit. When alternatives are available for preparing materials, the approach requiring no special equipment and utilizing readily available materials will appear first, followed by the more complex procedures requiring special equipment. Teachers and students may prepare many of the materials they need at home or they may be able to use special equipment at school or in an instructional materials center to do a more professional job.

The procedures in this book have been tried and tested over a period of several years. The book has been used as a textbook for university media production classes and as a reference tool for teachers. In addition to procedures usually included in university courses in instructional materials preparation, many new and unique classroom-tested ideas are included here. Teachers at every grade level and in every subject area will find information in this book useful to them. In a book of this length, however, it is impossible to include all the possible procedures for preparing instructional materials. Teacher ingenuity and student creativity will enhance the application of the ideas presented here.

We are greatly indebted to colleagues and students who have shared their ideas and suggestions for this book with us. Professors Cochern, Marcyes, Hailer, McBeath, Kemp, and Brown of San Jose State University have given many useful comments and suggestions. Karen Hoffman, Marvin Harmon, and many other students have given us encouragement and important suggestions. Our wives, Gwen Morlan and Barbara Espinosa, have provided invaluable assistance in typing and editing the manuscript. It is to them, and to all the teachers who have taught us so very much, that this book is dedicated.

JOHN E. MORLAN
LEONARD J. ESPINOSA

Planning and Developing Communications Media

I

1.1 The Communications Process

An understanding of the communications process may help you develop instructional materials to enhance your teaching. One communications model developed by Shannon and Weaver is widely accepted as an appropriate explanation of the communications process.[1] Figure 1.1 illustrates this model, modified to suit educational settings.

- The sender develops and structures the content of the message.
- The sender encodes the message using the appropriate transmittable form—lecture, film, computer, prints, audio, or other media.
- The message is then transmitted to the receiver.
- The receiver takes in the message through the appropriate senses.
- The receiver decodes the message depending upon his or her perception of the message. Our perception of what we receive from our senses depends on our previous knowledge and experiences. A student who has flown in a plane through and above clouds, for example, will have a different perception of clouds than a student who has never been in an airplane.
- Interference is anything that hinders the transmission of the message. Interference may originate with the sender or the receiver of the message, or it may be caused by environmental conditions. Examples of interference originating with the sender might include misconceptions about the audience, poor selection of media, poor use of media, language difficulty, and cultural differences. Examples of interference originating with the receiver might include cultural differences, language difficulty, and lack of prerequisite knowledge. Environmental interference might include poor lighting, poor air circulation, distracting sounds, or poor seating arrangements.

[1]Claude Shannon and Warren Weaver, *The Mathematical Theory of Communication*, pp. 4–7.

Figure 1.1
The Communications Process

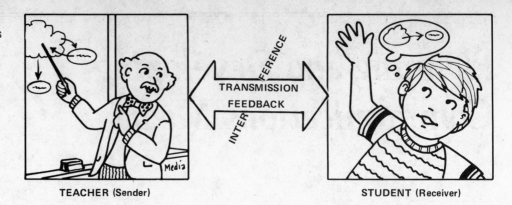

TEACHER (Sender)   STUDENT (Receiver)

- Feedback from the receiver to the sender is necessary for the sender to measure the message's effect on the receiver. Did the message get to the receiver? Did the receiver understand it? Feedback to the sender might be an evaluation in the form of a written or oral test, project, or report.

Planning and preparing your graphics and lessons carefully can help you overcome interference. In the pages that follow, you will learn how to design and produce instructional materials to help transmit your message effectively.

1.2   Guidelines for Designing Instruction

To ensure that the communication process is successful, consider a systematic approach to designing instructional experiences. A systematic method for designing effective instructional materials should include the following elements:

> Statement of Purpose
> Audience Identification
> Performance Objectives
> Learning Activities
> Instructional Modes
> Instructional Resources
> Learning Environment
> Human Resources
> Evaluation

Statement of Purpose

The first step in designing instructions is to briefly state the topics or tasks you intend your lessons to teach.

EXAMPLES
1. To teach students how to use a vacuum tube voltmeter.
2. To teach trainees studying electricity how to solder.
3. To teach new employees fire safety.
4. To teach students how to tell time.

Audience Identification

A brief statement describing the audience will help you select appropriate teaching methods.

EXAMPLES
1. All students taking the course "Electricity I."
2. All vocational instructors.
3. Fifth- through seventh-grade students.

Performance Objectives

Performance objectives help both the student and the teacher understand what is to be learned and what criteria will be used to evaluate performance. When you ask for support or approval of a project or lesson, your performance objectives will help the administrator or other evaluator understand the purpose of the project or lesson.

A well-written performance objective will contain:

1. A statement about the audience for which your lesson is intended.
2. An exact statement that describes the behavioral change you expect to *observe* and *measure* as a result of your lesson.
3. A statement of the conditions and limitations under which the student must perform during observation or measurement.
4. A statement of the degree to which the student must master the objective.

The following are samples of performance objectives that have the necessary characteristics:

- (1) All students in "Electricity I" (2) will operate the vacuum tube voltmeter to measure voltage and resistance (3) on a given electrical circuit while being observed by the teacher. (4) The measurement must be made with 90% accuracy.
- (1) The student (2) will identify the elements of design (3) on a given poster (4) with 100% accuracy.
- (1) The student (2) will make a hot solder connection (3) using no. 22 rubber-coated stranded copper wire, a Weller solder copper, 60/40 solder, long nose pliers and a wire stripper. (4) The completed connection will be considered hot if the wire cannot be pulled from the terminal.

Terminal and Enabling Objectives

Terminal objectives state the behavior you expect your students to demonstrate after thay have successfully completed the lesson. Enabling objectives form the steps of knowledge the student must achieve to reach the terminal objective. Depending on the complexity of the content to be taught, peformance objectives may be organized in a hierarchy of increasing specificity. One method for sequencing performance objectives is to write each objective on a 3" × 5" card, and then rearrange them, by adding or deleting cards until the correct sequence is achieved. Once you are comfortable with the sequence, ask for input from someone who knows the topic or subject matter.

Each student, orally or in writing, will describe, with 80% accuracy, the founding of the Jamestown colony, including a description of its people, crops, and location.

EXAMPLES OF ENABLING OBJECTIVES
1. Each student will be able to locate the Jamestown colony on a map of the colonies.
2. Each student will be able to name the company that started the Jamestown colony and give the one main reason why the owners of the company sent the settlers to the New World.
3. Each student will be able to state the main crop that was grown in Jamestown and explain in one sentence or more why the crop was easy to sell in Europe.
4. Each student will be able to describe, orally or in writing, the type of government started in the Jamestown colony.

Learning Activities

Learning activities provide the experiences the student will need to attain the desired behavior described in the objectives. Learning activities include: reading, writing, discussing, listening, interviewing, experimenting, constructing, developing, producing, photographing, displaying, graphing, presenting, teaching, researching, collecting, watching, recording, videotaping, computing, visualizing, organizing, experiencing, and evaluating.

Instructional Modes

There are three basic modes of instruction: large group, small group, and individualized instruction.

Large group instruction appears to be very cost effective, but in fact it is not usually as effective as other modes. The main disadvantage with large group instruction is that the teacher has very little, if any, interaction with the audience. This mode usually consists of verbal presentation and does not account for individual differences. However, large group presentations can be improved with appropriate nonprint media, good display techniques, and well-planned use of the chalkboard.

Small group instruction is an ideal method for facilitating learning when teacher and students need to interact. This mode allows the teacher to address the needs of individual students. Small group instruction permits face-to-face interaction between student and teacher, student and student, or student and various forms of media.

Individualized instruction provides for students' differences in abilities, knowledge, and readiness by offering a sequence of learning experiences designed to meet students' individual needs.

Instructional Resources

Tools available to teachers are constantly increasing in number. At one time the ability to lecture, to use a chalkboard, and to give reading assignments were considered the basic teaching tools. Today, a teacher who is interested in presenting a topic should be familiar with the selection and use of audio-visual materials and support equipment.

Examples of such materials include: motion picture film; television and radio programs; tape and disc recordings; slides; displays; filmstrips; overhead transparencies; sound-filmstrips; mock-ups; models; realia; computer programs; and flannel and magnetic board programs.

Examples of equipment include: motion picture, overhead, slide, and filmstrip projectors; television and radio receivers; videotape and record players; computers and computer terminals; cameras; video recorders; graphic production equipment; and interactive video equipment. Teachers should know how to select appropriate instructional resources and, at times, how to produce instructional materials.

Learning Environment

As a teacher, you should be familiar with the facilities required for each mode of instruction. Consider the following questions:

- What should a lecture hall, classroom, seminar room, or independent study facility contain to make it a good learning facility?
- What support facilities will you need?
- Will the instruction be most effective in the classroom, laboratory, media center, library, or some other facility?

Human Resources

Librarians, teaching assistants, technicians, graphic artists, clerks, custodians, other teachers, and administrators may all be considered support staff. Teachers need to know who is available to provide assistance and support. For example, when you give a research assignment to your students, inform the librarian at your school and at the local public library so they may be prepared to assist the students.

Evaluation

The instructional process requires continuous evaluation. This evaluation may include pretesting to determine the students' level of knowledge, and posttesting to determine if students have met the objectives of the lesson. Judgments of the teacher's effectiveness by students, administrators, and other teachers are also useful forms of evaluation that may help the teacher become more effective.

1.3 Planning Media Productions

Designing and producing high-quality media productions requires careful planning if your message is to be communicated clearly. Take the time to sit down with paper and pencil to consider the following steps.

1. *Audience Identification.* Describe the audience in terms of socioeconomic background, ethnic background, age, grade level, motivation, and prior knowledge.
2. *Assessment of Needs.* Decide what you and your audience need most. Consider time, budget, and production skill constraints.
3. *Statement of Purpose.* State the general purpose of your production.
4. *Objectives.* Translate your statement of purpose into performance objectives that will state exactly what the student will know or be able to do as a result of your production project.
5. *Content Outline.* Make a content outline listing the content needed to meet each objective. Share your outline with another person and revise as necessary.
6. *Media Selection.* Select a media format. Consider costs, production facilities, available equipment, required materials, and the time necessary to complete the project.
7. *Production.* Following a detailed schedule, apply your media design and production skills.

1.4 Guidelines for Planning a Presentation

The steps involved in planning a presentation are similar to those involved in planning media productions.

Topic Selection

As you choose your topic, consider the following questions:

- How much material will you be able to include in the time provided for your presentation?
- What presentation and equipment operation skills are necessary for each of the topics you are considering?

Audience Identification

If at all possible, know who your audience will be and prepare your presentation for them. Ask questions such as:

- Who will be in the audience? (*Consider sex, grade level, reading level, language proficiency, and other characteristics.*)
- How many people will be in attendance?
- What is their interest in the topic?
- What prior knowledge do they have of the subject?

Statement of Purpose

Write a statement that describes the purpose of the presentation. Ask for input from others who are interested in the topic. Once you are sure your

Planning and Developing Communications Media

statement of purpose is clear, write objectives that will inform the audience of the presentation's content, and then make a content outline of what should be included for each objective. Ask for input and revise as necessary.

Media Format Selection

Choose the media format that best suits your presentation. Consider your time, budget, skills, and available support services. One important guideline is: keep it simple.

Production

If you are planning to produce materials, or have them produced, you must establish a time schedule for each element of the project and make sure that all parties involved stick to the schedule. Be certain to specify the quality of the product and services you expect.

Rehearsal

Rehearsal is vital to a presentation's success. Rehearse with someone who will give you honest feedback. If possible, videotape your presentation.

Check the facility, support equipment, and materials prior to giving the presentation. Some questions to ask yourself about facilities and equipment are presented below:

Facility

- What is the size of the room?
- Will you be able to control the lighting? How is it controlled?
- If the temperature in the room needs adjusting, do you know how to do it?
- What kinds of classroom furniture will you need?
- Will all members of the audience be able to see the presentation?
- If you require electricity, will you have the needed outlets? Do you need extension cords, or three-wire adaptors? Will you need tape to fasten down the cord to prevent tripping?
- If you intend to read a script with the lights out, will you need a flashlight?

Equipment

PROJECTORS
- Will the equipment be checked for proper operation before you get it?
- Will spare lamp(s), fuses, and other backup equipment be available if needed?
- Will you be able to place the projector in a position that allows the projected image to fill the screen?
- Do you need a technical assistant to help with the equipment?
- Do you need projection or other equipment tables?
- If you are using a projection screen, will it be set up for you?

PUBLIC ADDRESS SYSTEM

- Will your microphone and speaker be placed in a position to eliminate feedback?
- Will all equipment be checked for proper operation after it is set up, and before your presentation?
- Will your presentation require a special type of microphone?
- Will you need a technician to help with the equipment?

DISPLAY

- Will you display materials?
- Do you need felt, magnetic, hook-and-loop, or other display surfaces?
- Will you need chalk, tacks, tape, or pins?

Planning Graphics

II

2.1 Guidelines for Graphic Layout and Design

Layout and design refer to the graphic elements that are arranged within a given space to *attract attention*, *create interest*, and *convey a message*.

A *layout* is a drawing that represents how a finished printed page, poster, or display will look. A good layout will follow basic design guidelines and will add visual interest to the material.

Layout elements may contain:

1. Headline
2. Copy
3. Illustration
4. Logo
5. White space

Figure 2.1 identifies each layout element by number. Layouts need not contain all of these elements.

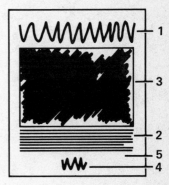

Figure 2.1
Layout Elements

Types of Layout

Graphic layout is usually accomplished in three stages, moving from the simple to the complex, as follows:

1. Thumbnail sketch
2. Rough
3. Comprehensive

Each stage will help you to plan your graphic layout by providing a way to visualize the piece as it develops.

Figure 2.2
Thumbnail Sketch

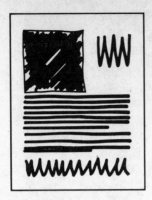

Thumbnail Sketches

Thumbnail sketches are small, quick drawings. They contain the elements of design and layout in different arrangements. The purpose of the thumbnail sketch is to experiment with different visual arrangements (Figure 2.2). Figure 2.3 shows one method of identifying the elements of the layout.

Rough Layout

A rough layout is a full-size drawing of the best thumbnail sketch. Headlines are lettered, illustrations are sketched, and the location of the elements are as close as possible to the final product so the printer or artist can use this rough layout to produce a comprehensive layout. The first thumbnail sketch in Figure 2.2 was selected for this rough layout, which is shown in Figure 2.4.

Comprehensive

The comprehensive is an exact representation of what the finished product will look like. Headlines are precise, and the body type can be lined or pasted into position.

For the printed page, comprehensive layout shows exactly what the final printed page will look like. If a graphic piece such as a single poster will not be reproduced, the comprehensive may be the finished piece.

Design Guidelines

In our everyday lives, we are accustomed to arranging items in space, selecting colors to emphasize certain items, and placing items in order. Our eyes are also accustomed to looking at pictures in a certain way. Research on how people tend to look at visuals indicates that people in Western cultures

Figure 2.3
Layout Symbols

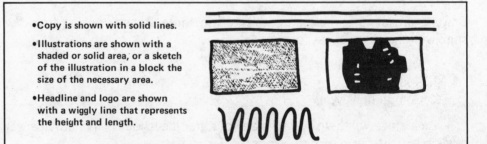

- •Copy is shown with solid lines.
- •Illustrations are shown with a shaded or solid area, or a sketch of the illustration in a block the size of the necessary area.
- •Headline and logo are shown with a wiggly line that represents the height and length.

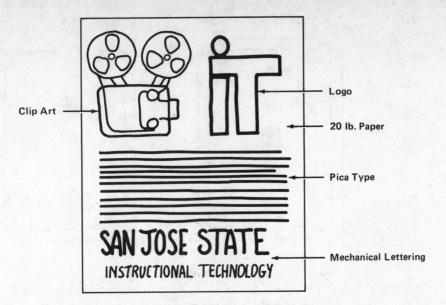

Figure 2.4
Rough Layout

Clip Art

Logo

20 lb. Paper

Pica Type

Mechanical Lettering

SAN JOSE STATE
INSTRUCTIONAL TECHNOLOGY

Figure 2.5
Eye Movement Direction

41%	20%
25%	14%

usually look at the upper left-hand area of a picture first.[2] In Figure 2.5, the picture area has been divided into quadrants. The percentage in each quadrant represents the frequency with which people look at that particular section first. This information can be helpful in graphic design. If you want to emphasize or attract attention to important items in a graphic layout, you may wish to place them in the upper left-hand area of the arrangement.

Other elements in a design can also help direct the eye. In Figure 2.6, the texture of the logo and the overlapping planes guide the eye to the logo. In this way, selected elements of a graphic layout can be emphasized.

To produce an effective layout, remember how the viewer's eye will scan the layout, and consider the following six design criteria:

Simplicity
Balance
Proportion
Contrast
Rhythm
Unity and Harmony

Figure 2.6
Directing the Eye

Simplicity

Keep your layout simple and don't clutter the copy. Use enough white space to emphasize the message and draw attention to the main ideas. Eliminate needless details in your drawings.

Balance

Balance can be *formal* (Figure 2.7)—one side of the layout appears to be a mirror image of the other. Or *informal* (Figure 2.8)—both sides have equal weight but are made up of different arrangements of the elements. Formal balance is static, but can be very effective. Informal layout can be dynamic and exciting.

Figure 2.7
Formal Layout

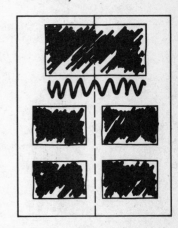

---

[2]Robert Heinich; Michael Molenda; and James D. Russell, *Instructional Media and the New Technologies of Instruction*, p. 71.

Figure 2.8
Informal Layout

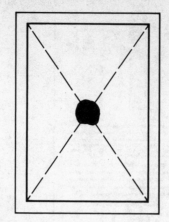

Figure 2.9　　Mathematical Center　　　　　Optical Center

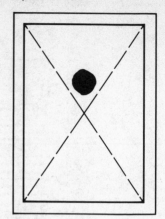

Both formal and informal layouts are positioned in relation to an invisible line that divides the layout. On both sides of the invisible line, the elements of the layout are arranged to achieve a balance of weight. It is generally agreed that the optical center of a picture, is slightly above the mathematical center (Figure 2.9).

Placing items in the optical center of a layout may be more pleasing to the eye than placing them in the mathematical center.

Proportion

Proportion reflects the overall visual effect of the layout and the size of the elements, both individually and in relation to each other. The rectangular format layout is the most common format and will be dealt with here. A layout with an equal division of space (Figure 2.10) does not seem to be as appealing as a layout with an unequal division of space (Figure 2.11). Figure 2.10 is divided in two equal divisions of space, and Figure 2.11 is divided into three divisions of space. In a layout, areas of space appear to be more appealing if they are divided into thirds or fifths.

Contrast

To direct attention to the message in the layout, use contrasting shapes, sizes, or textures.

Figure 2.10
Equal Division of Space

Figure 2.11
Unequal Division of Space

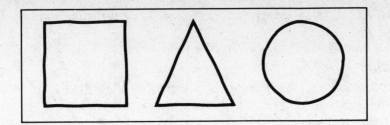

Figure 2.12
Geometric Shapes

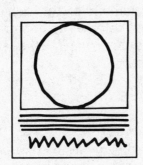

Figure 2.13
Sample Layouts

Figure 2.14
Equal Division Lacks Contrast

Figure 2.15
Size Adds Contrast

SHAPE

Geometric shapes, used individually or in combination, can make the layout interesting and direct the reader's eye (Figure 2.12). A shape can include line art, photography, and mounted pictures. It can also be formed by a solid color. Sample layouts are shown in Figure 2.13.

SIZE

The size of the illustration, logo, copy, or headline lettering can attract the interest of the viewer. Consider the amount of white space as well. The layout shown in Figure 2.14 has areas of copy and illustration of equal size. The layout in Figure 2.15 has a larger illustration with less copy. The illustration's size provides contrast and attracts attention.

TEXTURE

Texture is a visual element that can add interest to a design. Like color, texture can be used to attract and direct the viewer's eye. The layout in

Figure 2.16
Lacks Texture

Figure 2.17
Texture Adds Contrast

Figure 2.18
Eye May Be Distracted

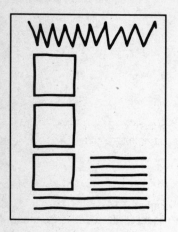

Figure 2.19
Rhythm Guides the Eye

Figure 2.16 lacks texture, and is therefore less interesting than the layout in Figure 2.17.

Rhythm

A successfully designed layout has a rhythm that guides the viewer's eye from element to element in a *predetermined* course. Line, shape, graphics, color, and pointers such as arrows may be used to achieve this end.

The viewer's eye will move from one element of the layout to the next, depending upon the placement of the various shapes. In Figure 2.18, the eye moves from one picture to the other before arriving at the message. It is possible that the viewer may not complete the series of pictures, and therefore, never read the message.

In Figure 2.19, the eye is directed to the message with little chance of being distracted.

Unity and Harmony

When a layout has unity and harmony, it conveys one central message and is visually pleasing. Each element should be satisfying to look at and should complement the whole if the layout is to produce a strong visual impact.

The paper should complement the ink, the typeface should complement the message, and the art should harmonize with the typeface. All elements work together.

COLOR

Color can be used to create a mood, achieve unity, give emphasis, and guide the viewer's eye through the display. The colors you use should complement each other. The *primary colors* are red, yellow, and blue. The *secondary colors* are green, orange, and violet. Red, orange, and yellow are warm colors that seem to jump out at you. Violet, blue, and green are cool, receding colors that often make a good background.

Complementary colors, opposite each other on the color wheel, go well with each other (Figure 2.20). *Analogous colors* are side by side on the color wheel. If the primary colors produce a busy display, consider using analogous colors. *Monochromatic colors*, shades and tints of the same color, may also be used for contrast. Use white, gray, and black with any color combination—complementary, analogous, or monochromatic.

Figure 2.20
Color Wheel

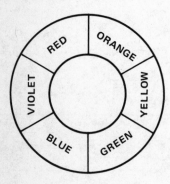

2.2 Layout Mechanics

Use the layout mechanics described below to produce visuals such as posters, charts, and transparencies. You can improve the quality of photocopies by applying layout skills to the original master. The master is also called a paste-up, a mechanical, or camera-ready copy. It is sometimes advisable to design your master larger than the size to be reproduced, and then to reduce the master before producing the copies. Reducing the master makes flaws less noticeable and sharpens the overall image. The layout procedure described below is specifically for material that you plan to photocopy. Using this method, you can also design other graphics.

Figure 2.21
Prepare the Drawing Surface

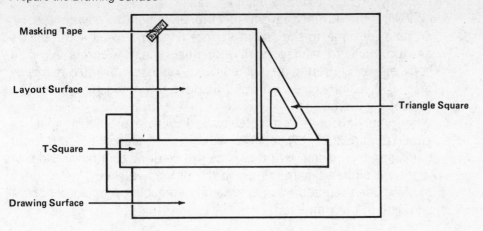

Masking Tape

Layout Surface

Triangle Square

T-Square

Drawing Surface

Materials and Equipment

- layout surfaces (cardboard, tracing paper, fade-out blue grid paper or white paper)
- white paper the same size as the layout surface
- triangle square
- rubber cement
- nonreproducible blue pencil
- T-square
- straight edge
- masking tape
- correction fluid
- art
- lettering
- tweezers
- drawing board

Procedure

1. Select a drawing surface that has a straight edge. A drawing board is designed for this purpose, but a kitchen table will do.
2. Mount the layout surface to the drawing surface (Figure 2.21) by pushing the T-square firmly against the edge of the drawing surface and placing the layout surface along the straight edge. Tape all four corners with masking tape. The T-square gives you a perfect horizontal edge, and the triangle provides a vertical edge and two angled edges.
3. Collect all of your copy, line art, and lettering. Copy may be typed on white paper and cut out.
4. On the layout surface, line in the image area that will contain the copy, art, and lettering. Use a nonreproducible blue pencil so that the lines you make will not be copied by a correctly adjusted photocopy machine. Next, locate the optical center of the layout surface by drawing a line from each corner of the layout surface (Figure 2.22). The optical center is just above the spot where the lines intersect. To help balance your layout, divide the image area in half by drawing a vertical line through the intersection (Figure 2.23). If you intend to use margins, line them in (Figure 2.24). Then line in your layout,

Figure 2.22
Determine the Optical Center

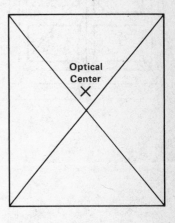

Optical Center
X

Figure 2.23
Divide the Image Area

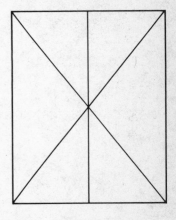

Figure 2.24
Line in the Margins

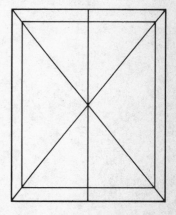

Figure 2.25
Line In the Design Elements

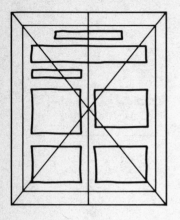

using graphic design considerations. Finally, line in the position of the copy, art, and lettering (Figure 2.25).

5. Following the outlined layout, use rubber cement to paste the copy, art, and lettering to the layout surface (Figure 2.26). If some pieces are too small to manage with your fingers, use tweezers. After all copy, art, and lettering are pasted down, remove unwanted marks by erasing or using correction fluid. Remove unwanted rubber cement by rubbing it off.

6. When your layout is complete, cover it with a protective sheet of paper (Figure 2.27). The paper will prevent marks and dirt from damaging the master. If further work will be done by a proofreader or a printer, add any instructions on the protective sheet. Instructions may include such items as paper weight and color, number of copies, and date to be completed.

Figure 2.26
Pasteup

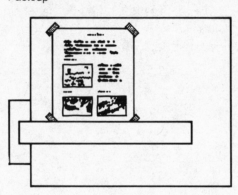

Figure 2.27
Cover Layout with Protective Paper

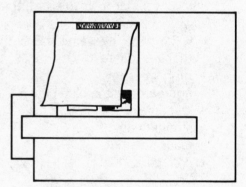

2.3 Computer Graphics

The complete layout and design of educational materials can be accomplished on a computer. You can design computer graphics for overhead transparencies, slides, printed pages, charts, posters, and bulletin board displays. Most personal computers with the appropriate software can produce graphics similar to those a graphic artist does. However, computer graphics may be limited by the sophistication of the computer program and by the computer operator's ability to apply graphic design skills to the layout and design.

A computer graphics system may include the following components (Figure 2.28):

1. The *keyboard* allows you to control the computer system.
2. The *graphic tablet* or *digitizer* is a sensitized surface that, when touched by a special pen, produces a symbol (a *cursor*) on the computer screen. The cursor's movement corresponds with the movement of the pen on the sensitized surface. This process can be used to produce images

Figure 2.28
Computer Graphics System

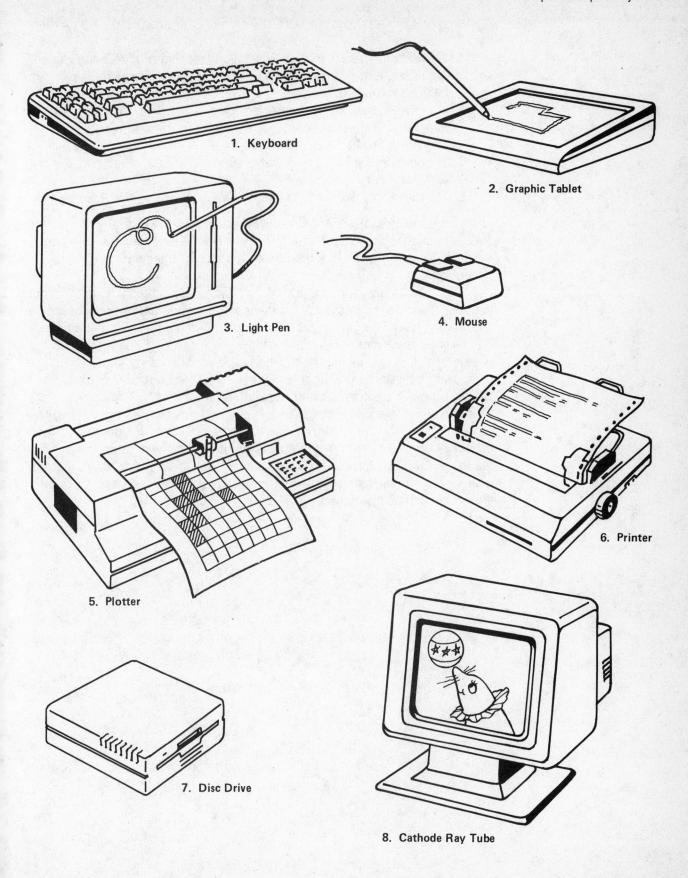

1. Keyboard

2. Graphic Tablet

3. Light Pen

4. Mouse

5. Plotter

6. Printer

7. Disc Drive

8. Cathode Ray Tube

on the screen. The computer stores the screen images, which can be recalled as needed.

3. A *light pen* lets you draw directly on the computer screen to produce an image.
4. The *mouse* is a device moved on a flat surface that produces corresponding movement of the cursor on the computer screen. The cursor can be used to draw or to point to a command.
5. The *plotter* uses the movement of one ink pen or more to produce images.
6. The *printer* produces an image on paper.
7. The *disc drive* provides an entry to and collection method for the computer system.
8. The *cathode ray tube* (CRT) produces a clear image on the screen.

Computer graphics systems can range greatly in price and in quality. Excellent quality equipment usually costs more, but inexpensive equipment may be all you need. The quality of a graphic image is judged by its resolution.

With reasonably priced graphic software available, you can create graphics in a fraction of the time it takes to do comparable work by hand. In addition to images, many of these programs also handle lettering and text. It is easy to experiment with different layouts, fonts, and image sizes on the computer before producing the finished product. You can create art with the computer, select art from libraries of electronic reproducible "clip art," or take a picture or photograph and translate it into a computer picture.

In summary, computer graphics systems range from the simple to the complex, but all systems provide useful graphics. You and your students can produce computer-generated graphics or purchase them from a computer graphics company. Although the resolution of your graphics will reflect the quality of your programs and equipment, your layout and design should always be technically correct.

Preparing Materials for Projection

III

Good illustrations will help students understand the information you present. This chapter explains how to make effective materials for projection. When projection materials are needed but unavailable, you can prepare your own transparencies and opaque projection materials by following the suggestions given in this chapter.

3.1   Transparencies for Overhead Projection

The overhead projector is used by teachers at all educational levels, from primary grades to university graduate courses, and in virtually all subject areas. Because the projector is versatile, a wide variety of materials can be used to present information vividly. All teachers should know how to use an overhead projector.

Many types of transparencies can be easily prepared by a teacher who has no previous technical training. An overhead projector transparency is a transparent sheet with information on it. When placed upon an overhead projector, the information on the transparency is projected onto a screen.

Overhead Transparency Design Guidelines

1. Keep your design simple.
2. Try to use a horizontal format.
3. Use graphics (pictures, sketches, symbols) whenever possible.
4. When using words, try to limit yourself to a maximum of six lines of six words each.
5. Letter size should be ¼" at the minimum.
6. If possible, use lowercase letters to increase visibility.

Figure 3.1
Placement of the Base Cell

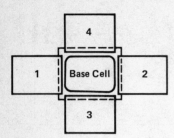

7. Present one major concept in each transparency.
8. Reduce glare by using tinted film.
9. Use graphic design principles in preparing your transparency master.
10. If a base cell with overlays is used, mount the base cell (the main transparency) on the underside of the frame and place the overlays on top of the frame (Figure 3.1). The frame is used to block unwanted light from the projected image.

Hand-Drawn Transparencies

Hand-drawn transparencies may be easily prepared with readily available and inexpensive materials. You may draw on clear, treated, or frosted plastic, usually cellulose acetate. These transparencies are produced in much the same way, although you may use a wider variety of materials and tools with the frosted plastic. Treated acetate is preferable to untreated acetate because it absorbs inks more readily. Reprocessed x-ray film works well and is inexpensive.

Materials and Equipment
- engineering tracing paper
- drawing inks (if color is important, use colored India inks, slide inks, plastic inks, or felt pens)
- sharpened, soft lead pencil
- drawing pen
- ruler with raised edge
- cardboard mounts (for overlay assemblies)
- pressure-sensitive tape such as masking tape
- acetate sheets (clear, treated, or frosted, in dimensions appropriate to the projector size)
- clear plastic spray

Procedure (Figure 3.2)

To prepare clear and treated acetate: Prepare the basic detailed drawing in pencil, on a sheet of tracing or drawing paper that fits the projector size. Place register marks in the upper left and lower right corners of the pencil drawing. Register marks are used to line up the overlays on top of the base cell.

1. Trace the base cell outline directly onto the acetate sheet with drawing ink suitable for drawing on plastic. Use *only* this type of ink. The additional cost is minimal and well worth the investment. Pelikan and Koh-i-noor inks are exceptionally fine. Add register marks, and lay the acetate aside to dry.
2. After the ink outline is completely dry, apply color in the desired areas. For each overlay, follow the same procedure.
3. If the transparency is complete on one sheet, protect the drawing from any damage by covering it with a second sheet of plastic before taping it to the frame (mount).

An overlay assembly should be mounted on commerically produced frames (mounts) or on cardboard mounts made by the teacher. Attach the base cell to the cardboard mount with pressure-sensitive tape. Mount

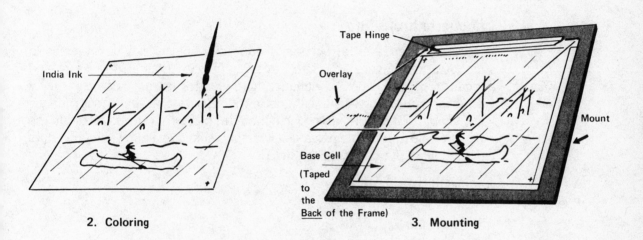

Figure 3.2
Hand-Drawn Transparencies

1. Outlining

2. Coloring

3. Mounting

successive overlays by hinging the plastic film with tape on one edge only, carefully matching the register marks on the overlays and the base cell. Cut the tape so it does not extend beyond the edge of the film. After all the overlays have been mounted, the overlay assembly is ready for projection.

Procedure

Follow the same procedure to prepare frosted acetate transparencies as you did to prepare clear or treated acetate transparencies; however, the finished transparency must be sprayed with a clear plastic spray to make the projected image appear bright on the screen. Do *not* use frosted acetate for overlays. You may use India inks suitable for plastics, plastic inks, felt pens, soft lead pencils, and slide crayons to draw on the acetate.

Draw only on the *dull* side of the plastic. Then coat the frosted surface of the completed transparency with a thin layer of plastic spray, *except* when felt pens have been used for color. Spraying the frosted plastic will make it more transparent and will protect the drawing from damage. If felt-tipped pens are used, protect the surface of the transparency with a sheet of clear plastic. Plastic spray on felt-tipped pen inks will often cause them to smear, which will ruin the transparency.

Take care to follow the manufacturer's directions when applying the coating of plastic spray to avoid smearing or bubbling.

Figure 3.3
Silhouette Projection

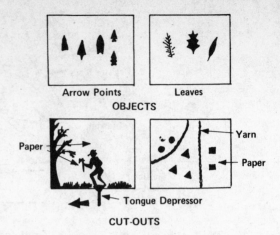

Iron Filings

Glass

Magnet

Overhead Projector

MAGNETIC FIELD

Arrow Points   Leaves
OBJECTS

Paper

Yarn

Paper

Tongue Depressor

CUT-OUTS

Silhouette Projection

Objects such as leaves, arrow points, and other objects may be projected in silhouette (see Figure 3.3). Use paper cutouts to dramatize a story and geometric paper shapes to enhance mathematics lessons. Use a piece of yarn and groups of objects in silhouette to illustrate concepts of set theory.

Magnetic field demonstration: One silhouette projection shows students the magnetic field around the poles of a horseshoe magnet. Follow the procedure below to illustrate this magnetic field.

Materials and Equipment

- magnet
- iron filings
- sheet of glass or plastic
- overhead projector

Procedure

1. Place the magnet on the projector stage.
2. Place the glass or plastic on top of the magnet.
3. Sprinkle iron filings on the glass. The filings will form a magnetic pattern.

Astronomy Punch-out Projection

Astronomy teachers often look for creative ways to introduce the constellations to their students, ways to develop students' interest in astronomy. The following project uses the overhead projector to present constellation forms easily and inexpensively.

Materials and Equipment

- star chart (an encyclopedia is a good reference)
- tracing paper
- pencil
- ruler

- nail or saddle punch
- lightweight cardboard (manila folder)

Procedure (Figure 3.4)

1. Draw a grid on the cardboard with lines 1" apart.
2. Draw a grid on a sheet of tracing paper with lines ½" apart. Clip this grid on top of the star chart.
3. Use the grid marks on the two grids as reference points and transfer the star pattern to the grid on the chalkboard.
4. With a saddle punch or nail, punch out holes where you wish stars to appear in projection. If you use a nail to make holes in the cardboard, be sure to use sandpaper to remove the raised cardboard around the holes so that the holes will not close in projection.

Suggestions for Use

Place the cardboard sheet on the overhead projector. Focus the light points on the screen and dim the room's lights. The constellation will appear dramatically in white against a darkened screen.

You can also project the constellation onto the chalkboard, then mark the place of each star with chalk. This is a quick, easy, and accurate way to transfer the illustration from the cardboard to the chalkboard.

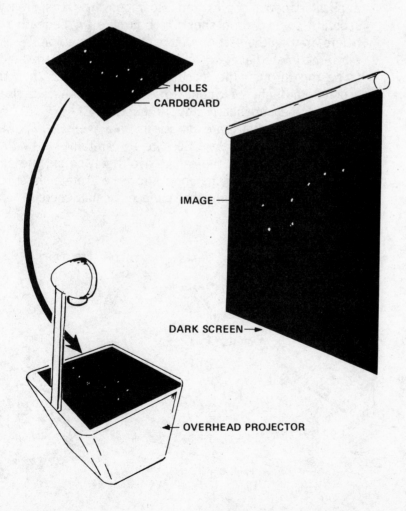

HOLES
CARDBOARD

IMAGE

DARK SCREEN →

OVERHEAD PROJECTOR

Figure 3.4
Astronomy Punch-Out
Projections

Spirit Duplicator Transparencies

Teachers may use the spirit duplicator to produce color transparencies suitable for projection. This process is especially useful for preparing transparencies to match duplicated materials handed out to the class. The materials projected on the screen, however, will *not* be as bright as material projected from a hand-drawn transparency.

Materials and Equipment

- spirit duplicator
- frosted acetate sheet
- duplication carbon master(s)
- drawing instrument(s)
- duplicator paper
- plastic spray
- cardboard mount
- pressure-sensitive tape

Procedure (Figure 3.5)

1. Prepare the duplication master. Use a primary typewriter, lettering pen, or stencil to do the lettering. Use a ballpoint pen or hard lead pencil to make drawings. For each color desired on the finished duplicated paper copies and accompanying transparency, insert a separate color carbon sheet, carbon side *up*, beneath the master, before drawing the section that is to appear in color.
2. Place the frosted acetate, sheet, *dull side up*, under the stack of paper to be run through the machine. Feed the paper, then the frosted acetate, through the duplicator. *Hand feed the acetate sheet* into the machine to ensure successful printing.
3. Place the printed acetate *dull side up* on a sheet of paper and coat it evenly with plastic spray. Be sure to carefully follow the spraying directions printed on the can to avoid getting an uneven finish on the surface of the transparency. Allow the acetate sheet to dry for at least two minutes, or until the surface has hardened.

Figure 3.5
Spirit Duplicator Transparencies

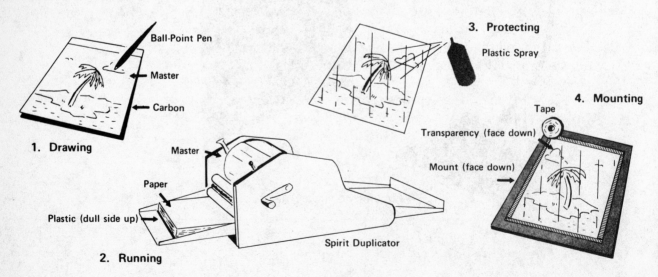

4. Mount the completed transparency on a cardboard mount with pressure-sensitive tape. A sheet of clear acetate may be placed on top of the spray-coated side of the transparency, and mounted simultaneously with it, in order to further protect the printed surface.

Thermal-Copy Transparencies (Thermo-Fax)

Newspaper reports, magazine articles, charts, graphs, pictures, and most typed, written, or drawn materials can be produced in transparency form for projection with Thermo-Fax copying machines and transparency films. No photographic developing solutions are necessary. People inexperienced in audio-visual production can make transparencies by the thermal copy method in a lighted room. Films that provide a black line or a colored line on a clear background, or a black line on a colored (tinted) background, are available as well as other specialized films.

When selecting material to copy or preparing an original, be sure the copy to be reproduced is *no larger* than 7½″ × 9½″, although it may be on an 8½″ × 11″ sheet of paper. Prepare hand-drawn materials in pencil (#1, #2, or IBM pencils), or better yet, with black drawing ink on *opaque* paper (ledger paper or Ditto paper rather than tracing paper). The lettering should be large enough to be easily read when projected. For example, primary-typewriter type is easy to read in projection, while pica and elite types are *not*.

Materials and Equipment
- original material to be copied
- Thermo-Fax copying machine
- Thermo-Fax transparency film (positive, negative, and five colors of film are available)
- clear acetate or plastic, the size of the transparency film
- cardboard mount
- pressure-sensitive tape

Procedure (Figure 3.6)
1. Place the original material to be copied face up on the table, and put a sheet of Thermo-Fax film *face down* on top of the material. The cut corner will be in the upper right-hand corner. Another type of thermal acetate requires a charging sheet along with the acetate. The charging sheet must be in the correct position on the acetate or the process will not work. The charging sheet and the acetate are arranged correctly in the box they come in. If they have become separated, place the dull side of the charging sheet against the heat-sensitive side of the acetate.
2. Set the dial to the *white* setting for originals drawn or printed with black ink. For drawings in pencil, move the dial about ½″ from the *white* toward the *buff* setting. Insert the material to be copied together with the transparency film into the copying machine. In approximately four seconds, the completed transparency and copied material will come from the machine.
3. It is usually best to mount the transparency on a substantial cardboard mount, for Thermo-Fax film weighs very little and can be

Figure 3.6
Thermal Copy Transparencies
(Thermo-Fax)

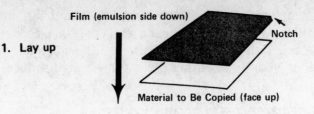

Film (emulsion side down)

Notch

1. **Lay up**

Material to Be Copied (face up)

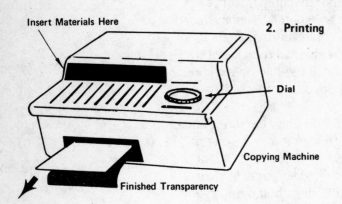

Insert Materials Here

2. **Printing**

Dial

Copying Machine

Finished Transparency

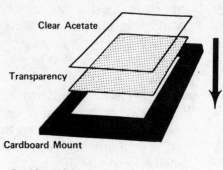

Clear Acetate

Transparency

Cardboard Mount

3. **Mounting**

handled better once it is mounted. Place the film on the mount and tape it into place with pressure-sensitive tape. The transparency may be covered with clear acetate to protect it from damage, especially if a grease pencil or water-soluble felt pen will be used to add further information during projection.

You may use several colors of film in combination with one transparency by overlaying several separately printed sheets. Material to be copied is easy to edit. Simply blank out unwanted sections with a sheet of plain white paper before placing the copy and film in the Thermo-Fax copy machine.

Plastic-Bag Transparencies

Ordinary clear plastic bags, such as small sandwich bags, may be used to prepare transparencies if minute details are not needed. Using this method, students may prepare inexpensive transparencies for creative writing or social studies projects. Heavyweight plastic bags will work even better than lightweight bags.

Materials and Equipment
- original material (drawn or printed in black)
- thermal copy machine
- plastic bag

Procedure (Figure 3.7)
1. Cut off the bottom and the sides of the bag to produce two pieces of acetate.
2. Set the dial on the copy machine to *white*.
3. Place one piece of plastic on the original and insert, plastic *up*, into the thermal duplicator. After printing, tape to the underside of a

Preparing Materials for Projection

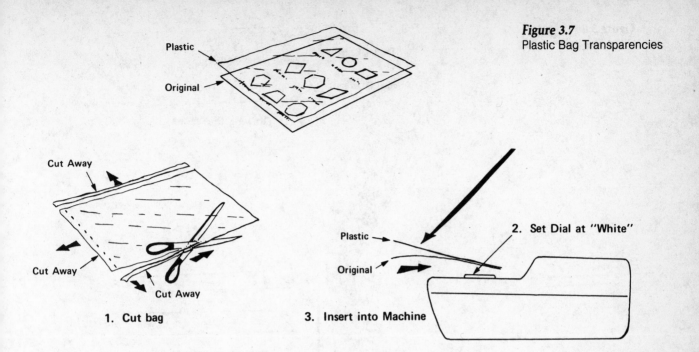

Figure 3.7
Plastic Bag Transparencies

Plastic

Original

Cut Away

Cut Away

Cut Away

1. Cut bag

Plastic

Original

2. Set Dial at "White"

3. Insert into Machine

frame with masking tape, if desired. Note: The black lines on the master will appear as a white etching on the acetate. This white image will appear *black* on the screen.

Diazo (Ammonia Process) Transparencies

The professional quality and permanence of diazo transparencies make them very popular with teachers. These tranparencies require special materials, so teachers interested in making diazo transparencies should arrange with the school audio-visual director or other media support person for a supply.

Three different kinds of equipment for transparency printing are described here. For directions on using other equipment, see the manufacturer's suggestions that accompany the machine. The instructions below explain how to produce an overlay assembly with a Beseler printer or printing frame.

Materials and Equipment

- plain white paper
- engineering tracing paper
- pens, ruler, and other instruments for drawing or tracing
- India ink
- One 1-gallon jar with screw top, or commercial developing unit
- sponge, to be placed in the bottom of the jar
- reflective foil sheet
- pressure-sensitive tape (masking tape)
- diazo film (several colors are available)
- transparency printer or printing frame
- cardboard mounts
- soft lead (graphite) pencil
- concentrated ammonia or household ammonia

Figure 3.8
Diazo Transparencies

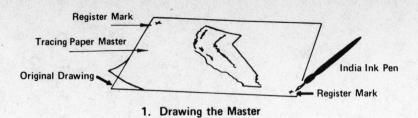

1. Drawing the Master

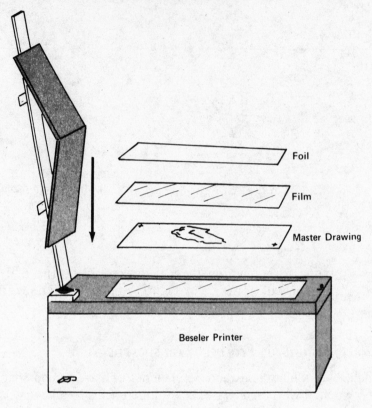

Foil

Film

Master Drawing

Beseler Printer

2. Exposing

or

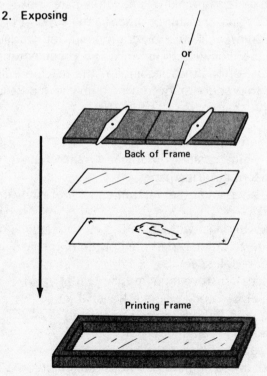

Back of Frame

Printing Frame

Preparing Materials for Projection

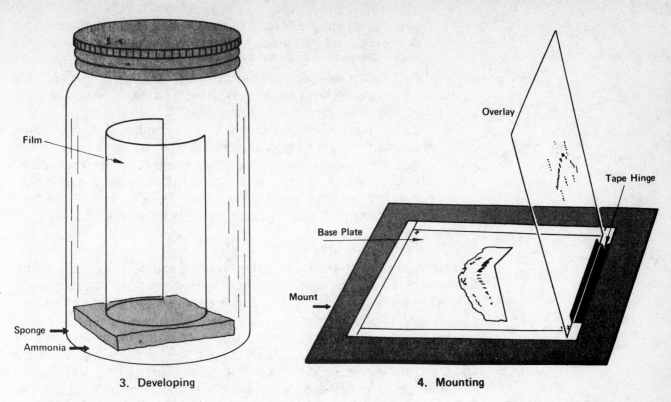

3. Developing

4. Mounting

Figure 3.8 (continued)
Diazo Transparencies

Procedure (Figure 3.8)

The procedure for making a simple single sheet transparency and the procedure for making a base cell for an overlay transparency are the same. Additional steps are necessary to produce an overlay assembly.

1. Outline the complete, detailed drawing in pencil on a sheet of plain white paper, keeping the drawing within a 7½" × 9" area. The finished pencil drawing will be a guide for successive drawings made on engineering tracing paper with India ink. Each drawing will be a master for an overlay. Place two register marks on the pencil drawings as illustrated.

2. Trace the outline of the base cell from the pencil drawing onto the registered tracing paper masters to check the alignment of all the elements in the transparency assembly. Choose a color film (usually black) for the base cell. Transparency film can be handled in a normally lit room without fear of light damage. Place the first tracing *face up* in the transparency printer; then place the plastic transparency film *face* (emulsion side) *down* on top of the tracing paper master, with the notch on the transparency film in the upper left-hand corner. Cover with a foil (reflective) sheet, and fasten the cover of the transparency printer in place. Set the timer of the printer according to the instructions printed on the film box (usually about 2½ minutes).

   If a printing frame is used instead of a transparency printer, place the tracing in it first, then the film, and close the frame. Expose the frame in direct sunlight according to the directions of the film manufacturer for the time and light intensity.

   For each plastic film overlay, repeat step two. Choose contrasting colors of film to make it easy to identify separate elements.

3. Place a sponge in the bottom of the jar. Pour in ¼ cup of ammonia, and screw the lid into place. Remove the exposed plastic film from the printer. Open the jar, drop the film into it, and then quickly screw the lid tightly into place. Allow the film to develop in the ammonia fumes until the lines are as dark as desired, and then remove the developed transparency film from the jar.
4. Tape the base cell to the underside of a cardboard mount. Mount successive overlays by taping the plastic film to make a hinge on one edge only. Carefully match the register marks on all elements of the assembly as each element is mounted. Cut the tape so that it does not extend beyond the edge of the film. After all overlays have been mounted, the transparency assembly is ready for projection.

Using Other Diazo Units

Several types of units are available for exposing and developing diazo film. Some of them have the light stage *above* the slot or tray for inserting materials. When using these units, you should reverse the order in which materials are stacked for the Beseler printer (Figure 3.9).

First, prepare the original (tracing paper master), following the directions above for making an overlay assembly using a Beseler printer. Next, select a film color, and assemble as follows: white paper; film on *top* of white paper, with notch in *upper right-hand corner*; and master *face down* on *top* of the film. Turn on the machine, set the timer as suggested by the manufacturer, and insert the film into the machine. When the film has been ejected, place it in a developing unit until the colors are as dark as desired. Mount the film on a cardboard frame.

Problems in Diazo Printing and Development

Occasionally teachers have difficulties with diazo printing. If you follow the directions, but find that the lines appear too light on the film, either the film has been exposed *too long* in the diazo printer (passed too slowly through the machine), or the developing unit needs recharging with ammonia, or the film

Figure 3.9
Diazo Printer

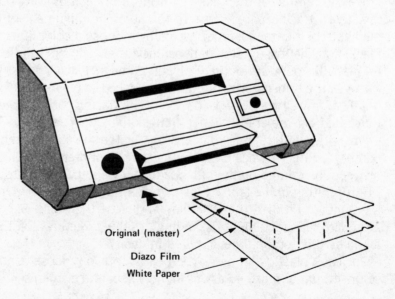

Original (master)

Diazo Film

White Paper

has *not* been left long enough in the developing unit. If the film looks cloudy, with color splotches, the film has *not* been exposed long enough. Adjustments in exposure and developing will result in good transparencies.

Heat-Lift Transparencies Made with a Dry-Mount Press

Full color transparencies for overhead projection may be made inexpensively with heat-sensitive plastic and a dry-mount press. Magazine illustrations printed on clay-coated paper may be transferred to a durable plastic through the procedures outlined below. Most illustrations in pictorial magazines lend themselves to this method. Lightweight heat-sensitive laminating plastic may be used in this process. This plastic is relatively inexpensive and does not require elaborate equipment.

Materials and Equipment
- picture or print to be transferred
- dry-mount press with a temperature control setting of 270 degrees Fahrenheit
- lightweight heat-sensitive laminating plastic
- pan or sink full of water
- household detergent
- plain white paper
- sheet of cardboard or masonite
- scissors
- clear plastic spray
- protective paper (wrapping or butcher paper)
- soft cloth
- newspaper
- old, large magazine
- tacking iron

Procedure (Figure 3.10)
1. Select pictures to be lifted (transferred). These must be printed on clay-coated paper. To check if the picture you plan to lift is printed on clay-coated paper, moisten a finger tip and rub it gently over the margin (white area) surrounding the print. A milky or gray liquid residue should be deposited on your finger tip if the paper is clay-coated. More residue generally indicates that the lift will be more successful. Each picture to be lifted should receive the wet-finger test since some pages in the same issue of a magazine may not be clay-coated. After selecting and testing, remove each picture from the magazine by cutting out the *entire page*. Do *not* trim the picture at this point.
2. Preheat the dry-mount press to 270 degrees Fahrenheit. Proper temperature and extreme pressure are necessary to produce a good quality transparency. To gain additional pressure, place a piece of masonite or heavyweight cardboard in the press on top of the rubber pad. Close the press so that it will heat up more rapidly.

    To remove any moisture from the picture, place it in the press under a piece of clean paper for about ten seconds. Remove the picture from the press, and place it on a flat, clean surface.

Figure 3.10
Heat-Lift Transparencies

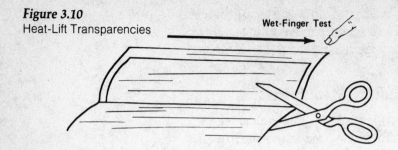

Wet-Finger Test

1. Print Selection

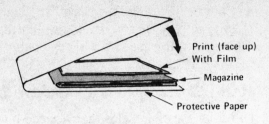

Print (face up)
With Film
Magazine
Protective Paper

5. Prepare to Place in Press

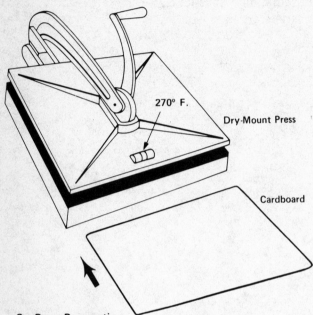

270° F.

Dry-Mount Press

Cardboard

2. Press Preparation

270° F.

Cardboard

Protective Paper

Film and Print

Magazine

6. Laminating, Lifting

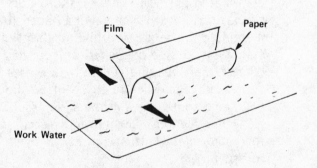

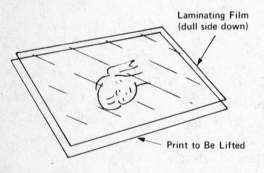

Laminating Film
(dull side down)

Print to Be Lifted

3. Cut Film to Size

Film   Paper

Work Water

7. Separating

Tacking Iron

4. Tack all Four Corners

Film (dull side up)

Tape   Tape

8. Cleaning

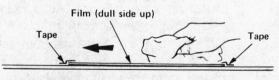

3. Cut the laminating plastic *slightly smaller* than the page the picture is on; the plastic should extend beyond the picture area if possible. Place the *dull* side *down* on the untrimmed picture page.

4. Turn the tacking iron up to the *high* setting. Tack the plastic to the picture at all four corners by touching the tip of the iron to the plastic. Heat from the iron will melt the adhesive on the underside of the plastic, causing it to stick to the paper as it cools.

5. Place the print with plastic attached *face up* on top of a large magazine. Take a piece of wrapping or butcher paper, cut it, and fold it around the print and magazine as illustrated. This will protect the plastic surface from any foreign matter which may be on the heated metal surface of the press.

6. Insert the pack into the press as shown. Close the press, and allow the material to remain in the press for about 30 seconds. Open the press, and remove the material. Do *not* try to keep the material from curling. It will slowly curl into a tube shape. After it cools, look at the material to see if there are any gray areas where the plastic may not have adhered to the picture. If necessary, reheat it to remove bubbles or gray spots.

7. Place the bonded material in a pan of water and add a little detergent. Soon the paper will begin to pull loose from the plastic. You will be able to separate the paper from the plastic after a few minutes of soaking. Test to see if the paper is ready to separate by trying one corner. The paper should separate from the plastic easily. The inks from the printed materials have now been transferred to the laminating plastic. Carefully wipe off clay and paper fibers with a soft, wet cloth. Blot off any excess moisture and allow the plastic to dry. Be sure no gray residue (clay) remains on the dull side of the plastic, for clay is opaque and will project *black* on the screen.

8. When the material is completely dry, lay it *dull side up* on a sheet of newspaper. Tape the corners to the sheet. Be sure that the tape does not cover anything that you plan to project when the transparency is completed. Spray the transparency with several thin coats of plastic spray, allowing each coat to dry before applying successive ones. Cut and trim the plastic so that it fits over the opening of a transparency frame or mount. Mask out any unwanted material by taping a piece of paper over the portion you do not wish to project. Then tape the transparency material to a frame.

Lift Transparencies Made with Adhesive Shelf Paper

Those unable to conveniently use a dry-mount press and heat-lamination film to prepare lift transparencies can use transparent adhesive shelf paper instead. Pictures printed on clay-coated paper may be lifted from the page through the steps outlined below.

Procedure (Figure 3.11)

1. Determine if the illustration is printed on clay-coated paper by rubbing a moistened finger along the edge of the page beside the picture to be lifted. If a gray residue comes off on your finger, cut out

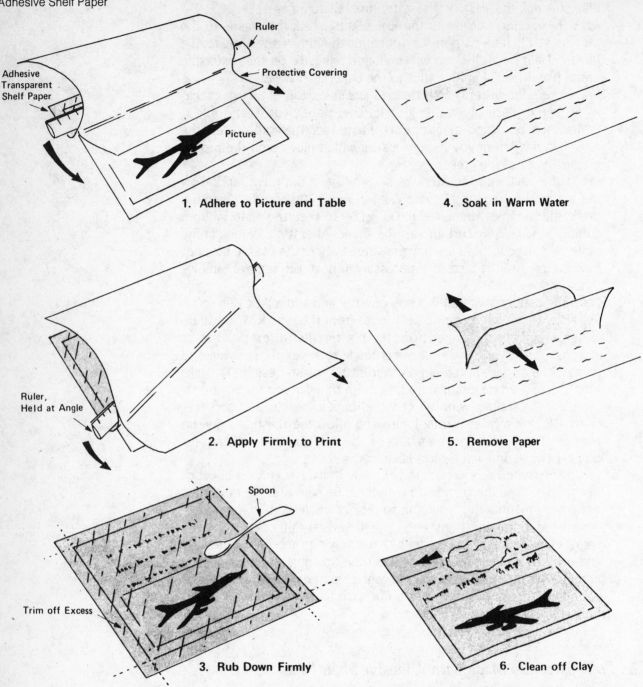

Figure 3.11
Lift Transparencies Made With Adhesive Shelf Paper

Ruler

Protective Covering

Adhesive Transparent Shelf Paper

Picture

1. Adhere to Picture and Table

4. Soak in Warm Water

Ruler, Held at Angle

2. Apply Firmly to Print

5. Remove Paper

Spoon

Trim off Excess

3. Rub Down Firmly

6. Clean off Clay

the entire illustration from the magazine, and place it *face up* on a clean, smooth surface. Cut the shelf paper *larger* than the picture to be lifted, peel back the protective covering at one corner, and adhere the transparent material to the table and picture as illustrated. Allow the plastic and the covering sheet to curl over as you work.

2. Move a ruler diagonally across the picture, smoothing out any bubbles which may occur. Hold the ruler at an angle as illustrated. Continue until the entire page area is covered.

3. Trim off excess shelf paper up to the edge of the magazine page. *Rub out any gray spots or bubbles with a spoon or with the back of a comb.*
4. Add a bit of soap or detergent to some warm water, and soak the bonded material in it.
5. When the paper begins to loosen from the plastic, gently peel the paper off. The inks have now been transferred to the plastic adhesive surface of the shelf paper.
6. Clean off clay and paper fibers by gently rubbing with a soft, damp cloth. Allow the plastic to dry. If there is still some gray residue (clay) on the plastic, clean it again with a damp cloth until all residue has been removed. Allow it to dry. Spray the sticky, dull surface with a plastic spray, and allow it to dry. Use several coats of spray to ensure good coverage, to make the transparency more durable, and to cover the sticky side of the plastic with a hard nonadhesive protective film. A clear piece of acetate placed over the sticky side will also make the transparency more durable. The transparency is now ready to trim and attach to a transparency mount with pressure-sensitive tape.

Photocopy Machine Transparencies

Making transparencies on a photocopy machine is also a common practice. Special acetates are used, but the procedure is easy. Check the instructions that came with the copy machine available to you.

Adhesive Acetate

Adhesive acetate, a transparent film with adhesive backing, is convenient for adding color tones, symbols, or patterns to transparencies. It is available in sheets or rolls.

Materials and Equipment
- adhesive acetate of the desired color or pattern
- base transparency
- stencil knife or razor blade
- scissors

Procedure (Figure 3.12)
1. Complete the transparency except for the color. Then use scissors to cut a section of adhesive acetate slightly larger than the area to be covered.
2. Peel off the protective backing sheet.
3. Press the adhesive acetate into place on the base transparency, working out all air bubbles and wrinkles. Carefully cut off all excess acetate with a razor blade. Use the outline of the area to be colored on the base transparency as a guide. After peeling off the excess acetate, rub the edges of the colored acetate firmly into place. The transparency is now ready to project. (Note: Adhesive acetate is especially useful in preparing graphs for projection. Cut the adhesive acetate into strips, remove the backing, and apply the strips directly to the surface of the transparency materials.)

Figure 3.12
Adhesive Acetate

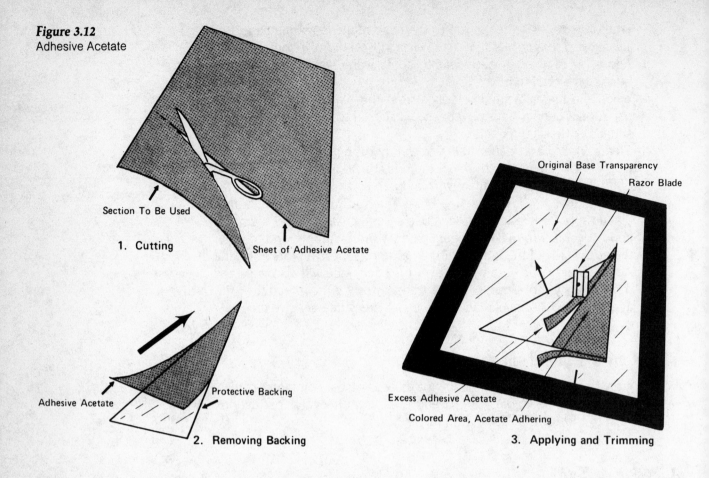

1. Cutting

Section To Be Used

Sheet of Adhesive Acetate

2. Removing Backing

Adhesive Acetate

Protective Backing

3. Applying and Trimming

Original Base Transparency

Razor Blade

Excess Adhesive Acetate

Colored Area, Acetate Adhering

Transparency Mounts

Acceptable cardboard mounts for overhead-projection transparencies may be easily made if commercial mounts are not available.

Materials and Equipment

- eight-ply cardboard (or poster board)
- razor blade or knife
- ruler, metal or metal-edged
- pencil
- scissors or paper cutter
- transparency to be mounted

Procedure (Figure 3.13)

1. With scissors or a paper cutter, cut the cardboard to 12″ × 10″.
2. Outline in pencil the area to be cut out on the cardboard, using the appropriate transparency as a guide.
3. Place the ruler along the lines drawn on the cardboard, and *carefully* cut out the desired area with a razor blade. Use caution to avoid slashing your fingers. Make a *shallow* cut first, and then repeat the cutting with *medium* pressure until the cut comes completely through the cardboard.

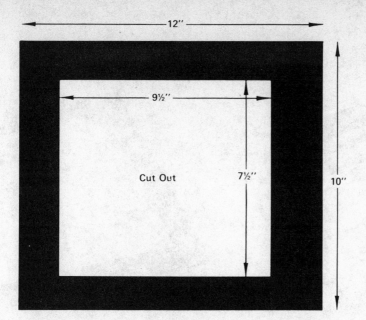

Figure 3.13
Transparency Mount

Transparency-Masking Techniques (Figure 3.14)

When you lead viewers through a step-by-step procedure, consider revealing only one step at a time. A transparency that might be confusing if revealed all at once may be clear and useful if portions are successively revealed and fully discussed. Instead of using a series of transparencies, consider using one base transparency to present several steps in a sequence.

Materials and Equipment

- base transparency
- cardboard
- pressure-sensitive tape
- scissors
- file folders or opaque plastic sheets

Procedure

1. Fasten the base transparency to a cardboard mount with pressure-sensitive tape.
2. Cut masking strips from light cardboard (file folders work well) or from opaque plastic sheets.
3. Make hinges for the masking strips from strips of tape, or use commercially prepared hinges. Strips of tape can be used to cover captions and then removed during the presentation. Also, place tape over captions and labels when using the transparency in testing situations.

Several examples of successful masking techniques for different purposes are shown in Figure 3.14. Select and use the technique which best meets your communication need.

Figure 3.14
Transparency Masking Techniques

Preparing Materials for Projection

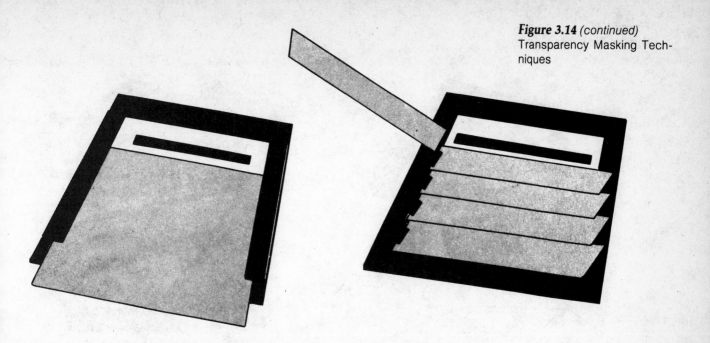

Figure 3.14 (continued)
Transparency Masking Techniques

3.2 Opaque Projection Materials

Using an opaque projector, you can project materials such as mounted prints, magazine or book materials, student work, small objects, materials embedded in plastic and Riker-mounted specimens (see Figure 3.15). Various materials suited for opaque projection and suggestions for using these materials are presented below. (*Caution*: Since opaque projectors typically focus a relatively great amount of heat on objects being projected, do not leave materials in the projector for prolonged periods of time, for heat damage may result.)

Mounted Prints

Printed images mounted by any of the techniques presented in this section can be projected in the opaque projector. For ease of handling, prints should not be larger than 8″ × 10″. If the opaque projector has a roll attachment, prints may be rolled in one side and out the other quickly and easily.

Accordion-Fold Mount

Mounted prints may be fastened together with tape to form sets that can be used in an opaque projector. To construct accordion-folded sets, line the prints up side by side, *face down*, on a clean, flat surface. Keep the *bottom* of the prints toward you, and allow a space of ⅛″ between prints. Hinge the prints together with pressure-sensitive tape, and then turn the prints over, *face up*. Apply strips of tape to the *top* side of the assembly to fasten the edges of the prints together. Fold the prints accordion style and label the set.

Roll Mount

Prints or drawings may be ironed to a strip of Chartex (an inexpensive, adhesive cloth) or permanently mounted on heavy paper strips for presentation in roll form. When positioning materials on the roll, be sure to allow

Figure 3.15
Opaque Projection Materials

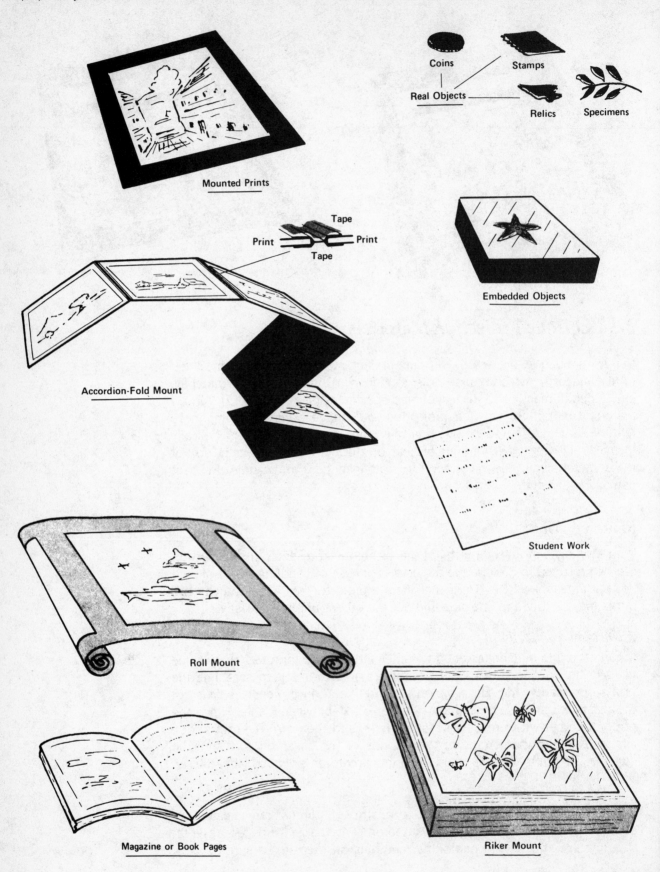

Mounted Prints

Coins

Stamps

Real Objects

Relics

Specimens

Tape

Print

Print

Tape

Embedded Objects

Accordion-Fold Mount

Student Work

Roll Mount

Magazine or Book Pages

Riker Mount

enough space between illustrations so only one complete illustration will be projected at one time. Write identifying information on the outside of the roll. The rolled prints curl and need a glass plate to hold them flat in the projector.

Student Work

Student work may be presented unmounted for analysis or criticism. It is a good idea to cover the student's name or fold the name under before presenting material for the class to see.

Magazine or Book Pages

Magazine or book materials may be presented in the opaque projector without being removed from their bindings. To facilitate focusing, place a sheet of heat-resistant glass over bound materials before inserting them into the opaque projector, unless a sheet of glass is built into the machine.

Solid Objects

Solid objects such as coins, small relics, and botanical specimens may be placed in the projector for presentation. Use a contrasting background sheet of paper or cardboard to help bring out the details of the objects more clearly.

Embedded Objects

Fasten objects embedded in plastic to card stock before projecting them; this protects the objects from being dropped and broken. Use a loop of transparent tape to hold the embedded material to the card stock.

Riker-Mounted Objects

Riker-mounted specimens can be projected in the opaque projector without any special physical preparations.

3.3 Worksheets to Accompany Projected Materials

Student learning is often enhanced and reinforced when handouts or worksheets accompany and complement projected materials. Spirit-duplicated materials may be easily prepared for such purposes. Two types of spirit-duplicator masters are presented here: multicolor spirit masters and thermal spirit masters.

Multicolor Spirit Masters

You may prepare spirit masters to duplicate materials in two or more colors, with only *one pass* of the paper through the duplicator. Use colors to emphasize important points or to break down a complex presentation into components for analysis.

Materials and Equipment

- spirit masters, two or more colors
- pencil
- ballpoint pen
- spirit duplicator
- duplicator paper
- material to be duplicated

Procedure (Figure 3.16)

1. Draw or trace the entire drawing in pencil on the white paper side of the master unit. Be sure the colored carbon is folded back and away, as illustrated.
2. When you have completed the drawing, fold the colored carbon back under. Draw or write with ballpoint pen, or type, *only* what you wish to have in that color. Tear off the carbon.
3. Slide the second colored carbon underneath the master and add the second color by drawing only over the pencil lines you wish to appear in the second color on the duplicated material.
4. Complete the master by adding the other colors as in step 3. The spirit master is now ready to run.

Thermal Spirit Masters

Use material printed, typed, or drawn with carbon-base or metallic-base inks to produce excellent thermal spirit masters. Articles from newspapers or magazines, or typewritten copy will work well. If you use a typewriter to

Figure 3.16
Multicolor Spirit (Ditto) Master

1. Original Drawing

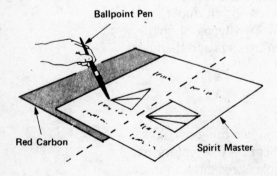

2. Drawing for First Color (Red)

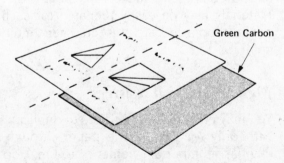

3. Adding Second Color (Green)

Preparing Materials for Projection

prepare the original, use a carbon ribbon or a medium-inked ribbon, and a backing sheet *behind* your paper.

Materials and Equipment

- thermal copy machine
- original material to be copied
- packing sheets (several sheets of paper)
- thermal spirit masters
- carrier (if required with your master)

Procedure (Figure 3.17)

1. Two types of thermal masters are available. One requires the use of a carrier while the other type does not. (A carrier is a plastic folder large enough to hold the thermal master and original as they are inserted into the thermal duplicator.) If your master carbon requires the use of a carrier, assemble the materials as follows: (a) Place the packing sheets on the table. (b) Place the original *face up* on the packing sheets. (c) Place the thermal master on the original, as illustrated. If you have a master that does *not* require a carrier, place the thermal master on the table, tissue up. Insert the original *face up*

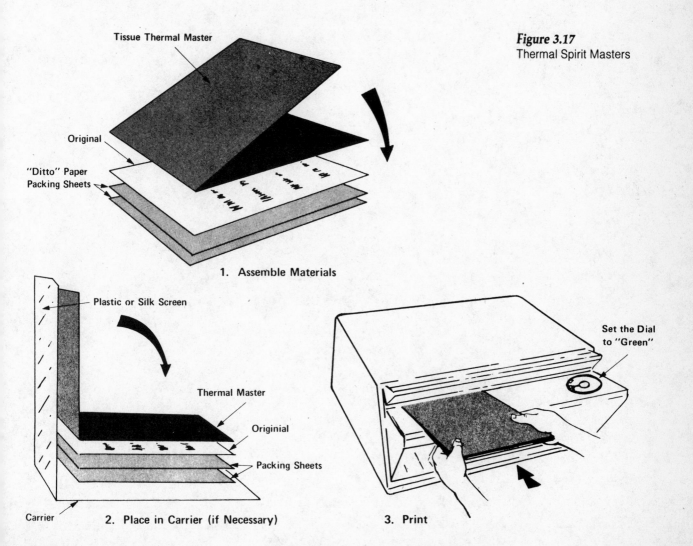

Figure 3.17
Thermal Spirit Masters

Tissue Thermal Master

Original

"Ditto" Paper Packing Sheets

1. Assemble Materials

Plastic or Silk Screen

Thermal Master

Originial

Packing Sheets

Carrier

2. Place in Carrier (if Necessary)

Set the Dial to "Green"

3. Print

under the carbon. Discard the brown paper which comes with the thermal master before proceeding.

2. If you need to use a carrier with your machine, place the assembled master into the carrier. The transparent side of the carrier should be face up. If you don't need to use a carrier, simply insert the assembled master directly into the thermal copy machine.

3. Set the control knob on the copying machine to the appropriate setting, usually the *green* setting. Run the loaded carrier or the master through. Open the carrier and remove the thermal master. Peel the carbon sheet from the master slowly and carefully. Discard the carbon. The master is now ready to use on the spirit duplicating machine.

Mounting and Preserving

IV

Teachers are often confronted with the problem of how to mount and preserve materials for repeated use as instructional tools. Techniques appropriate for mounting pictorial materials and techniques for mounting specimens such as coins, insects, and botanical materials are discussed in this chapter.

4.1 Mounting Pictorial Materials

Excellent methods of mounting materials include permanent and temporary rubber cement mounting, dry-mounting with photographic mounting tissue, adhesive paper mounting, wet-mounting on cloth, and dry-mounting on cloth.

Rubber Cement Mounting

Although mounting materials with rubber cement is more time-consuming than some other methods, you can achieve professional results by using this technique with materials readily available in most schools.

Temporary mounting with rubber cement is very simple. Its major advantage is the ease with which the item can be slipped into position.

Permanent mounting with rubber cement lasts much longer than temporary mounting. The mounting procedure, however, must be followed exactly as described here, for once the rubber-coated picture comes in contact with the rubber-coated mounting board, the picture cannot be repositioned.

Materials and Equipment
- item to be mounted, trimmed to final dimensions
- paper cutter or scissors

- rubber cement
- brush for spreading cement
- pick-up (a piece of tacky rubber to which the cement will cling; you can make one by rolling partially dried rubber cement into a small ball)
- mounting board, cut to size
- two sheets of waxed paper, large enough to cover the mounting board completely with some overlap
- soft lead pencil
- plastic spray or shellac (a brush is necessary if shellac is used), or laminating materials and equipment

Procedure for Permanent Mounting (Figure 4.1)

1. Center the print on the mounting board, leaving a margin at the bottom of the print slightly larger than those at the top and sides. With a soft lead pencil, register the placement of the picture on the mounting board, using the corners of the picture as a guide.
2. Turn the print over, place it on a newspaper or other work sheet, and apply rubber cement to the back of the print. Take care not to get rubber cement on the picture front because it may dissolve the inks.

   Apply rubber cement to the face of the mounting board. Be sure to cover the entire area the picture will occupy after mounting. Any cement on the edges of the mounting board can be easily rubbed off after the picture has been mounted.
3. When the rubber cement is completely dry and has lost its glossy appearance, cover the mounting board with two sheets of waxed paper, overlapping the paper near the center of the mounting board as illustrated. Position the picture on top of the waxed paper, taking care to align the picture with the register marks on the mounting board.
4. Slide out one of the wax paper sheets, smoothing the face of the print as the cement-coated surfaces touch. Repeat this procedure to remove the other wax paper sheet. Remove any excess cement by rubbing it with the tips of your fingers or with a pick-up. Preserve the mounted print by coating it with plastic spray, clear shellac, or laminating plastic (see pp. 54–59).

Procedure for Temporary Mounting

Follow steps 1 and 2 in the procedure for permanent mounting of prints. After coating the back of the print with rubber cement, place the print on the mounting board and rub it into position before the cement dries.

Dry-Mounting with Photographic Mounting Tissue

Dry-mount tissue is often used by professional photographers and artists when a smooth, wrinkle-free, uniform bond is needed for displayed materials. This tissue is available in sheets or rolls from photographic supply outlets. This material produces excellent results when graphics require mounting on card stock.

Figure 4.1
Rubber-Cement Mounting

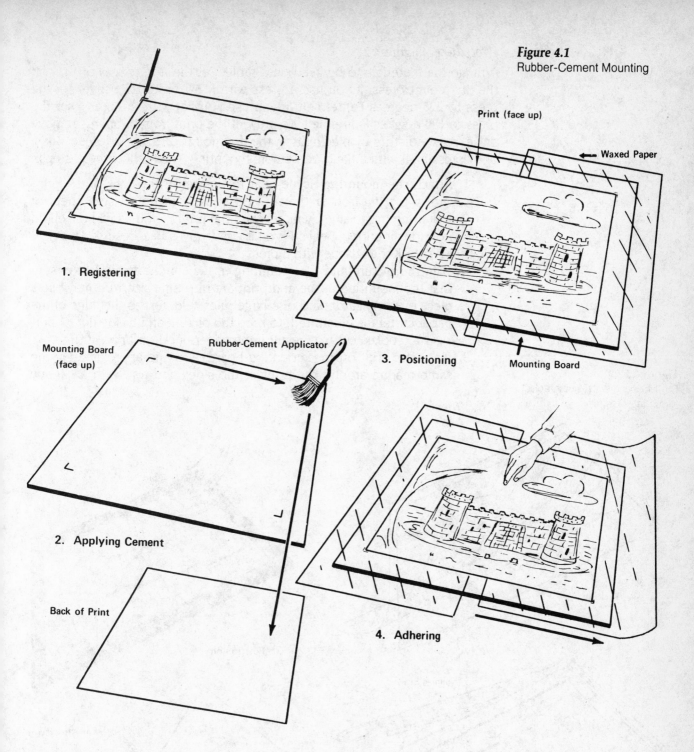

1. Registering

2. Applying Cement

Mounting Board (face up)

Rubber-Cement Applicator

Back of Print

Print (face up)

← Waxed Paper

3. Positioning

Mounting Board

4. Adhering

Materials and Equipment

- dry-mount press and tacking iron; *or* household iron
- print or picture to be mounted, untrimmed
- paper cutter or scissors
- card stock, such as railroad board
- large sheet of clean paper (butcher paper will do)
- books, magazines, or photographic weights
- mounting tissue, larger than final dimensions (Kodak tissue, Seal MT-5 and Seal Fotoflat with press; Seal Fotoflat with hand iron)

Procedure (Figure 4.2)

Arrange the materials to be used on a table. Set the iron to *wool* or turn on the dry-mount press. If you use a press with MT-5 or Kodak tissue, set the press to 225 degrees Fahrenheit. If you use Fotoflat with the press, set the press to 180 degrees Fahrenheit. To prevent the print from bubbling, remove any excess moisture by placing it in the dry-mount press for a few seconds, or by pressing it with a hand iron before mounting. Then follow these steps:

1. Attach the mounting tissue near the center of the back of the print with a tacking iron or the tip of a household iron. Use a sheet of mounting tissue slightly larger than the print. If you use a household iron for mounting, Seal's Fotoflat tissue gives best results. Use Seal MT-5 or Kodak tissue with a press.
2. Trim the picture and the mounting tissue simultaneously to ensure that the mounting tissue and print are the same size. You may use a piece of heavy cardboard or a large ruler held next to the edge of the paper cutter (as illustrated) to keep the picture and tissue flat. Otherwise, a crooked cut may result if the paper buckles during cutting.
3. Place the print on the mounting board, allowing approximately the same margin around the print at the sides and top, with a slightly

Figure 4.2
Dry-Mounting With Photographic
Mounting Tissue

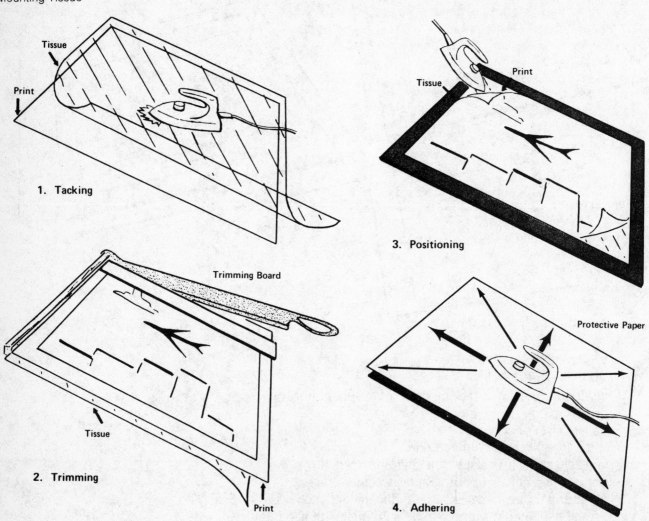

Tissue

Print

1. Tacking

Tissue

Print

3. Positioning

Trimming Board

Tissue

Print

2. Trimming

Protective Paper

4. Adhering

Mounting and Preserving

wider margin at the bottom. Attach two opposite corners of the tissue to the board with the tip of an iron.

4. If you use a household iron to mount the print, be sure it is clean, so foreign matter will not come off the iron onto the face of the print. Cover the print with a sheet of clean paper before applying heat to the print. Work the iron from the *center* of the picture to the *outer edges*. Move the iron slowly in a circular motion.

If you use a dry-mount press, place the print and board between the folds of a sheet of protective paper, and insert the pack into the preheated press for at least five seconds. Remove the mounted print from the press.

Place books or photographic weights on top of the print as it cools to prevent buckling.

To protect the mounted print from damage, laminate it with transparent adhesive shelf paper or heat-lamination film, or coat it with plastic spray or shellac. If you use shellac, apply it with smooth, even strokes in one direction.

Adhesive Paper Mounting

Adhesive mounting involves using a mounting paper that has an adhesive coating on both sides. This paper is placed between the item to be mounted and the mounting board to hold the materials together. When used as directed, adhesive paper such as Dri-Mount will give a smooth, permanent bond. Adhesive paper mounting may be accomplished easily and without expensive equipment.

Materials and Equipment
- sheet of adhesive paper, the size of the print to be mounted
- suitable print
- protective sheet (smooth white paper)
- mounting board
- scissors
- 6" ruler or comb
- clear varnish, plastic spray, or laminating plastic

Procedure (Figure 4.3)
1. Cut the adhesive paper to the size of the print to be mounted. Remove the protective backing sheet from one side of the adhesive mounting paper.
2. Press the print to be mounted on the exposed adhesive-coated surface. If wrinkles form, remove them by slowly lifting a corner of the print until the wrinkle is reached and pulled out. When the print is smooth and in the position desired, cover it with the protective sheet of white paper and rub firmly with a 6" ruler or the back of a comb.
3. Remove the remaining protective backing sheet, and place the print lightly on the mounting board. Position as desired and press into place. Again cover it with the protective sheet and rub firmly with the back of a comb or 6" ruler to create a firm bond. Protect the surface of the print with clear varnish, plastic spray, or laminating plastic.

Figure 4.3
Adhesive-Paper Mounting

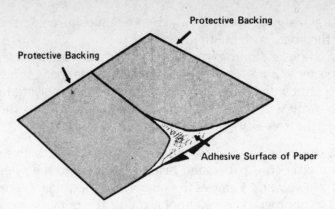

1. **Removing Backing**

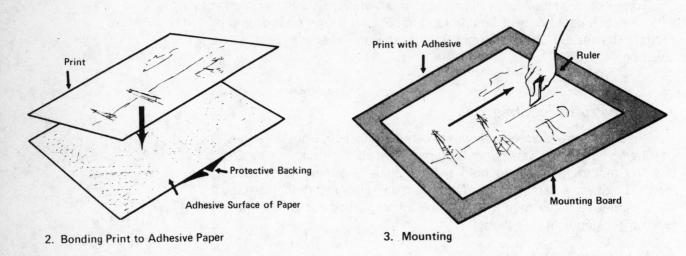

2. **Bonding Print to Adhesive Paper**

3. **Mounting**

Wet-Mounting on Cloth

Wet-mounting materials on cloth requires no special equipment or expensive materials. It also helps prolong the life of instructional materials by making them more durable.

Materials and Equipment

- map, chart, or print to be mounted
- muslin or flour-sack material
- wheat paste, such as wallpaper paste
- basin or pan of water
- pan or bowl
- brush or roller
- thumbtacks
- rolling pin
- paper strips (newspaper or butcher paper)
- smooth waterproof surface that will take thumbtacks (painted pressboard is a very good surface for this process; frame the edges of the pressboard mounting surface with soft wood strips)
- soft lead pencil
- clear plastic spray or shellac

Procedure (Figure 4.4)

1. Coat the surface of the map or print with a thin coat of plastic spray or shellac, and allow it to dry. Prepare paste by pouring a cup of water into the mixing bowl and adding paste *slowly*; mix continuously to avoid lumps. Continue to stir the mixture, adding paste or water as necessary until the paste has a creamy consistency. Soak the cloth in water until it is thoroughly wet. Gently squeeze out any excess water, lay the material on the waterproof surface, and smooth out the wrinkles and pockets of air. The threads of the cloth should run parallel with the edges of the waterproof surface. Tack the cloth down at three corners on the edge of the board as illustrated.
2. Proceed with the tacking process, working from two corners toward the third tack as illustrated. Alternate from one side to the other while tacking.
3. Tack down the fourth corner. Fill in the remaining two sides with evenly spaced tacks, working toward the fourth corner from the two sides previously secured. Be sure to eliminate any slack that may occur during the tacking process.
4. Place the material to be mounted face up on the muslin, and draw register marks on the cloth on all four corners with a soft lead pencil.
5. Place the pictorial material *face down* on a clean surface, and apply water to the back of the material until it lies flat and limp on the table.
6. Apply paste to the secured cloth with a brush (or roller), using uniform strokes to obtain a smooth, thin coat of paste. Extend the coated area slightly beyond the reference marks.
7. Place the map into position on the cloth, using the pencil reference marks as a guide. With a rolling pin, roll across the surface of the pictorial material from the *center* to each *side*, and then from *center* to each *corner*, as illustrated. Take care *not* to roll over the edges of the pictorial material, for this will deposit paste on the surface of the print. Lift corners of the print as necessary to relieve any tension built up during the rolling process.
8. Carefully arrange paper strips as shown, overlapping the edges of the pictorial material and the cloth surface. Lightly roll from the center of the map onto the paper strips. Repeat this process until all four edges of the pictorial material have been secured to the surface of the cloth. Remove and discard the paper strips.
9. Allow the mounted pictorial material to dry completely. Then, trim off the excess cloth and finish the project by applying grommets or hangers, or by using one of the suspension devices shown in Figure 4.6 (page 55).

Dry-Mounting on Cloth

Dry-mounting materials on cloth may be quickly and easily accomplished with Chartex, an inexpensive adhesive cloth specially prepared for cloth backing of charts, maps, and other pictorial or graphic materials. Chartex is available in sheet or roll form, in widths up to 42", and lengths of several yards.

Figure 4.4
Wet-Mounting on Cloth

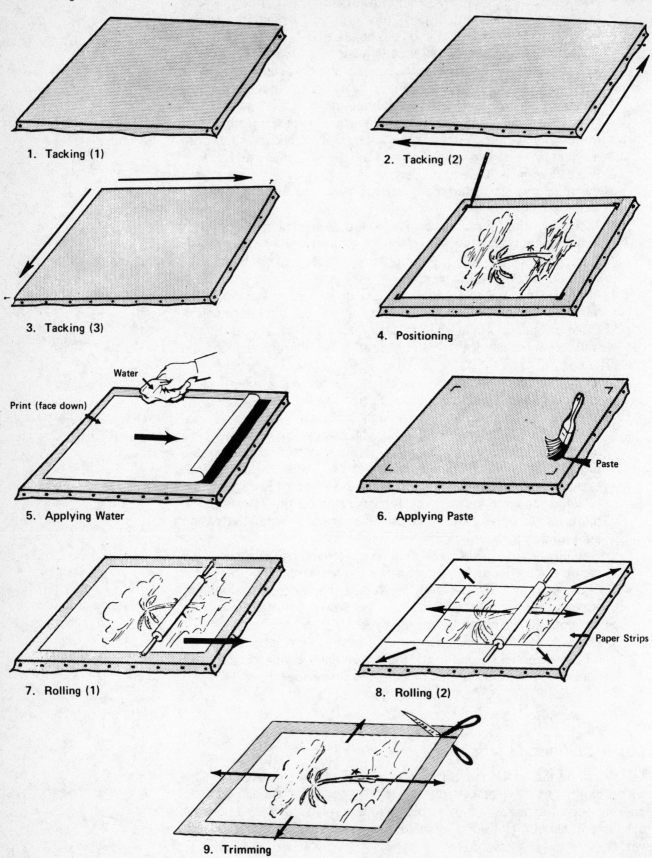

1. Tacking (1)

2. Tacking (2)

3. Tacking (3)

4. Positioning

Water

Print (face down)

5. Applying Water

Paste

6. Applying Paste

7. Rolling (1)

Paper Strips

8. Rolling (2)

9. Trimming

Mounting and Preserving

Materials and Equipment

- dry-mount press and tacking iron; *or* household iron
- Chartex of the desired dimensions (slightly larger than the object to be mounted)
- chart or map to be mounted
- several clean sheets of paper
- scissors
- paper cutter
- plastic spray, or shellac and brush
- several heavy books

Procedure (Figure 4.5)

1. Place all materials on a clean flat surface, and set the dry-mount press to 225 degrees Fahrenheit if the press has a temperature control device. Dry the map by placing it in the press for a few seconds. Or, set a hand iron to the *wool* setting and iron the map.

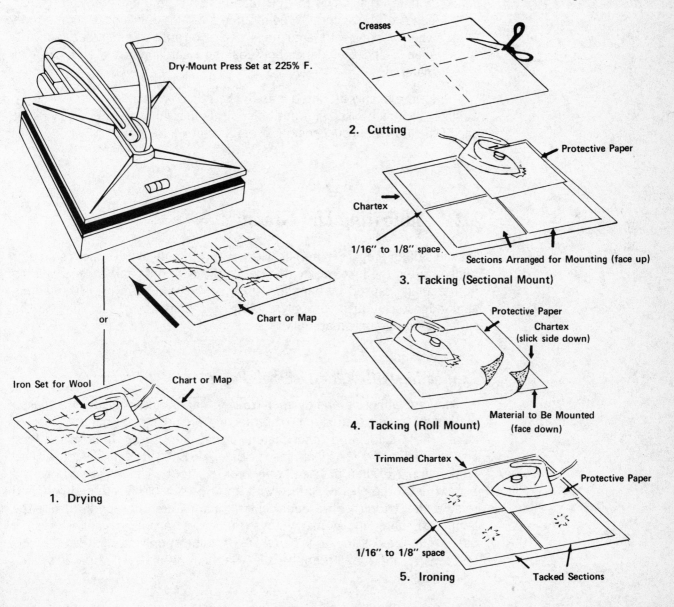

Figure 4.5
Dry-Mounting on Cloth

Dry-Mount Press Set at 225% F.

Chart or Map

or

Iron Set for Wool — Chart or Map

1. Drying

Creases

2. Cutting

Protective Paper

Chartex

1/16″ to 1/8″ space

Sections Arranged for Mounting (face up)

3. Tacking (Sectional Mount)

Protective Paper

Chartex (slick side down)

Material to Be Mounted (face down)

4. Tacking (Roll Mount)

Trimmed Chartex

Protective Paper

1/16″ to 1/8″ space

Tacked Sections

5. Ironing

2. If the chart or map is large and will be folded for storage, consider *sectional mounting*. To prepare a map or chart for sectional mounting, fold it to the desired storage size. Next, open it, lay it on a table, and cut it carefully into sections, using the folds as guides.

3. For *sectional mounting*, lay the sections of the map or chart *face up* on the slick side of a sheet of Chartex, leaving a space of approximately ⅟₁₆″ between sections. Tack each section individually to the dry mount cloth with an iron, as illustrated. Be sure to use a protective sheet of paper between the iron and map or chart.

4. If the map or chart will be *rolled* for storage, place it face down on a flat surface, and tack a sheet of Chartex, slick side down, to the back of the map or chart. Use a protective sheet of paper between the iron and pictorial material. Next, simultaneously trim the map and the cloth to size.

5. Place the bonded material on a table with the map or chart *face up*, and cover with a clean sheet of paper. Iron with a household iron or place in the dry-mount press for about five seconds. If you use a hand iron, move slowly with a circular motion from the center to the outer edges of the section to be mounted. Mount only a section at a time when working with large maps, charts, or prints. Remember to always keep a sheet of paper between the heat applicator and pictorial material.

Place the freshly mounted map or chart on a flat surface, and put heavy weights, such as books, on it until it cools. Finish the map or chart by using one of the illustrated suspension techniques in Figure 4.6.

4.2 Laminating Flat Graphics

Teachers often prepare materials with great care only to have them soiled or ruined during the first classroom use. To protect prints and other materials from damage caused by handling, dust, or moisture, you may use various laminating techniques to apply a piece of transparent plastic film to the surface of flat graphic materials.

Laminating with Adhesive Shelf Paper

Transparent adhesive shelf paper (called "paper" although it is a plastic film) is an excellent medium for protecting pictures, small charts, posters, games, flash cards, and other materials that need to be durable and long lasting. Shelf paper is a clear plastic, coated on one side with an adhesive to hold it in place when pressed firmly onto a smooth, clean, dry surface. You may write on the plastic surface with a water-soluable felt-tipped pen, and remove the writing with a damp cloth. This feature allows you to use the laminated materials in many ways. Purchase transparent adhesive shelf paper from almost any large hardware or home supply store. It is relatively inexpensive and may be applied as a laminating material without special equipment.

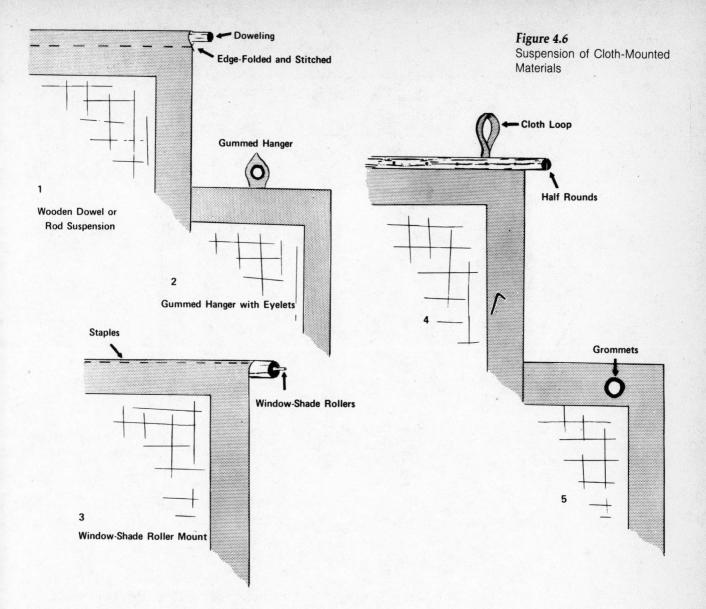

Figure 4.6
Suspension of Cloth-Mounted
Materials

Doweling

Edge-Folded and Stitched

Gummed Hanger

1

Wooden Dowel or
Rod Suspension

2

Gummed Hanger with Eyelets

Staples

3

Window-Shade Roller Mount

Window-Shade Rollers

Cloth Loop

Half Rounds

4

Grommets

5

Materials and Equipment
- material to be laminated
- clean table
- scissors
- adhesive transparent shelf paper (such as Con-Tact)
- small comb
- large ruler

Procedure (Figure 4.7)

1. Place the material to be laminated face up on a clean, flat surface, such as a table top. Before removing its protective backing, cut the shelf paper so that it is approximately ½" wider on all sides than the material to be protected. Remove the protective backing from one corner only by peeling the backing away from the plastic (which should be facing you). Adhere the exposed corner of the shelf paper to the table and to a corner of illustrative material.

Figure 4.7
Lamination with Adhesive
Shelf Paper

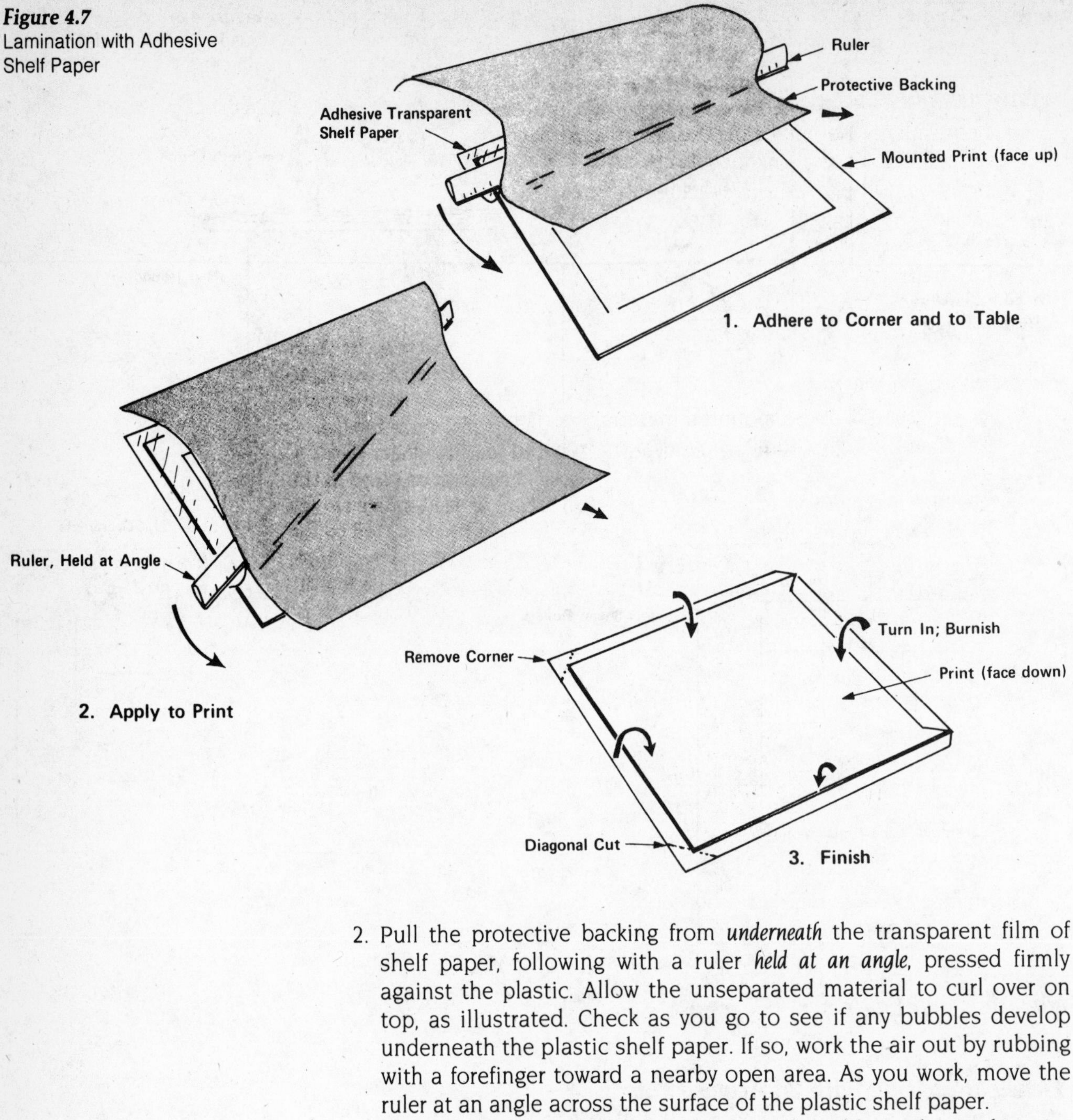

Ruler

Protective Backing

Adhesive Transparent
Shelf Paper

Mounted Print (face up)

1. Adhere to Corner and to Table

Ruler, Held at Angle

2. Apply to Print

Remove Corner

Turn In; Burnish

Print (face down)

Diagonal Cut

3. Finish

2. Pull the protective backing from *underneath* the transparent film of shelf paper, following with a ruler *held at an angle*, pressed firmly against the plastic. Allow the unseparated material to curl over on top, as illustrated. Check as you go to see if any bubbles develop underneath the plastic shelf paper. If so, work the air out by rubbing with a forefinger toward a nearby open area. As you work, move the ruler at an angle across the surface of the plastic shelf paper.

3. Pull the plastic shelf paper loose from the table, and turn the print over so that it is *face down* on the table. With a pair of scissors or a knife, cut diagonally across the edges and onto the back of the laminated print. After all four edges have been sealed, turn the print over, and rub down firmly with the back of a comb or short ruler to ensure a good bond. The lamination is now complete.

Heat Laminating with a Dry-Mount Press

Heat-sensitive laminating plastic applied with a dry-mount press provides a tough, durable protective covering for flat graphics such as drawings or pictures. One brand, Seal-Lamin, may be purchased in rolls of various widths, at prices similar to those of adhesive shelf paper. Seal-Lamin gives a harder finish after lamination than transparent shelf paper.

Materials and Equipment

- heat-sensitive laminating plastic (Seal-Lamin)
- mounted print, drawing, or picture
- dry-mount press, set to 270 degrees Fahrenheit
- tacking iron or household iron
- scissors
- old magazine
- large books to be used as weights, or photographic weight
- sheet of butcher paper or wrapping paper

Procedure (Figure 4.8)

1. If only *one side* of the mounted material needs protection, cut a piece of plastic long enough to overlap onto the back about 1½" at *both ends*. Lay the print *face down* on the *dull* side of the laminating plastic. Set the tacking iron to *high* or the household iron to *cotton*, and tack both ends of the plastic to the mounting stock by touching the iron to the plastic at the corners, as illustrated. If the material is to be protected on *both* sides, cut a sheet of plastic twice the size of the material to be mounted, and lay the print on the *dull* side of the film. Fold over and seal the *two ends* of the plastic together with a tacking iron or household iron.
2. After tacking or sealing the plastic, trim off the excess plastic on both sides up to the edge of the mounted print.
3. Cut a large piece of paper (butcher paper or brown wrapping paper), place a magazine on top, and place the film-covered print on top of the magazine *face up*. Fold the protective paper over as shown.
4. Insert the assembled materials into a press preheated to 270 degrees Fahrenheit. Leave them in for 15 to 30 seconds.
5. Remove the laminated material from the press and place *quickly* under a photographic weight or a few books. Allow the material to cool for a few seconds before removing the weights. The material is now laminated and ready for years of classroom use. If the bond is *not* complete, reheat the material in the press.

Heat Laminating with an Acetate Pouch

A lamination acetate pouch is used to laminate flat graphics on one or two sides. The pouch is available with clear plastic on one side and cardboard on the other side, or with clear plastic on both sides. You can use the pouch in a dry-mount press or run it through a special pouch laminator. In both cases, a *carrier* (two pieces of cardboard larger than the pouch) is used to hold and protect the pouch while it is being heated.

Materials and Equipment

- lamination acetate pouch
- carrier
- flat graphic to be laminated
- pouch lamination machine or dry-mount press

Figure 4.8
Heat Lamination Using a Dry-
Mount Press

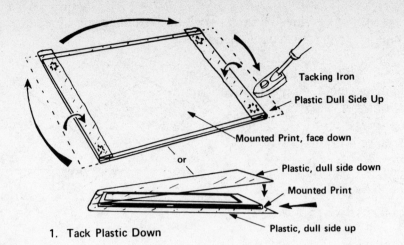

Tacking Iron

Plastic Dull Side Up

Mounted Print, face down

or

Plastic, dull side down

Mounted Print

Plastic, dull side up

1. Tack Plastic Down

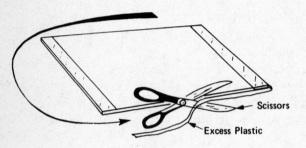

Scissors

Excess Plastic

2. Trim off Excess Plastic

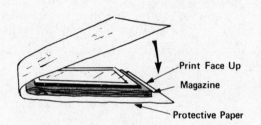

Print Face Up

Magazine

Protective Paper

3. Assemble for Press

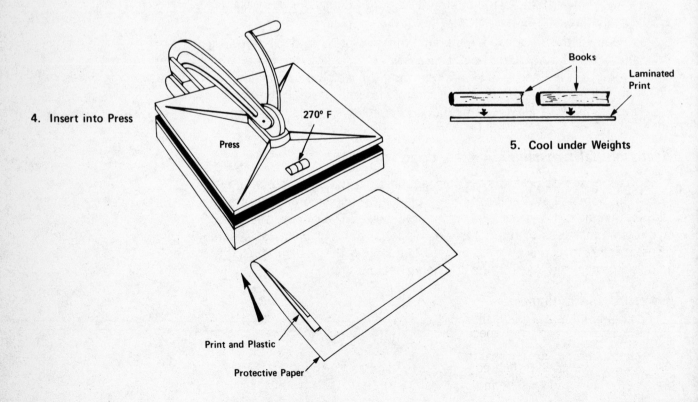

4. Insert into Press

Press

270° F

Print and Plastic

Protective Paper

Books

Laminated
Print

5. Cool under Weights

Mounting and Preserving

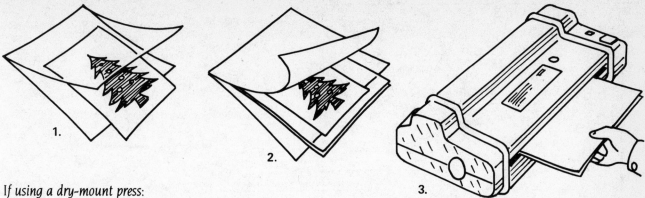

1.

2.

3.

Figure 4.9
Acetate Pouch Lamination

If using a dry-mount press:

- old magazine
- large books or photographic weights
- sheet of butcher paper

Procedure (Figure 4.9)

1. Place the items to be laminated in the pouch.
2. Place the pouch in the carrier.
3. Place the carrier into the dry-mount press and follow the directions for using a dry-mount press (steps four and five above), or feed the carrier into the pouch laminator.

4.3   Mounting and Protecting Specimens

Teachers and students sometimes collect fragile, valuable materials to share in the classroom. This section presents several useful techniques for preserving such specimens, including lamination mounting, gelatin mounting, plastic mounting, and cellophane mounting.

Cellophane Mounting

Preserve specimens for study and display by mounting them on a study card, as illustrated. For more durable protection, use transparent adhesive shelf paper or heat-lamination plastic (see pp. 54–59).

Materials and Equipment

- scissors
- specimen to be mounted
- study card
- clear tape
- masking tape
- cellophane and polyethylene film

Procedure (Figure 4.10)

1. Tape the specimen to the top of the study card with clear tape.
2. Cover the card and specimen with cellophane or polyethylene film, cut to overlap the card edges by ½″ or more.
3. Fold the overlapping edges of the cellophane around the edges of the card and tape them to the back of the card with masking tape.

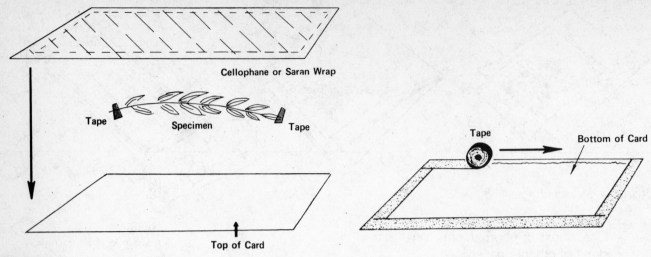

Figure 4.10
Cellophane Mounting

Mounting Specimens with Adhesive Shelf Paper

Use transparent adhesive shelf paper to laminate and preserve previously dried and pressed plant specimens. The lamination will protect them from damages and retard deterioration. Although the results of this process are not as durable as those of heat lamination (pp. 57–59), the process is far superior to using cellophane or nonadhesive plastic to cover specimens. Before mounting specimens, read the section in this book on laminating flat graphics with adhesive transparent shelf paper (pp. 54–59).

Materials and Equipment

- card stock
- dried specimen
- scissors
- adhesive transparent shelf paper (Con-Tact or other)
- small comb or short ruler
- large ruler
- clean flat surface (such as a table)

Procedure (Figure 4.11)

1. Be sure the specimen is pressed flat and is relatively dry. Do *not* try to mount plants until at least a week after they have been collected. Place the plant between pages of a magazine or newspaper and put several books on top to hold it flat. Let the plant dry.
2. Cut the card stock to the desired size and place it on the table. Position the specimen on the card stock. Be certain it is no closer than 1" from any edge of the card. Cut the adhesive shelf paper so that it is 2" longer and 2" wider than the card. Peel the protective covering back at one corner. Stick the exposed plastic to the table top and card, allowing a 1" overlap on the top and side as illustrated. Carefully pull the protective covering *out* from *under* the plastic.
3. Apply the plastic shelf paper to the specimen, taking particular care that the specimen is caught in place *before* continuing with the

Mounting and Preserving

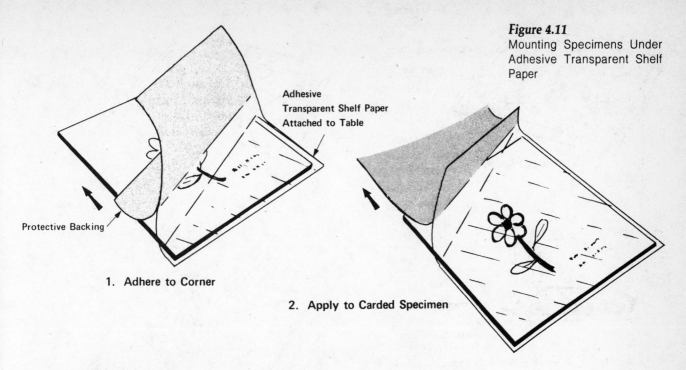

Figure 4.11
Mounting Specimens Under
Adhesive Transparent Shelf
Paper

Adhesive
Transparent Shelf Paper
Attached to Table

Protective Backing

1. Adhere to Corner

2. Apply to Carded Specimen

lamination process. You may find a ruler helpful to ensure even placement of the plastic. When all edges are sealed, turn the specimen over and press the adhesive shelf paper down firmly with the back of a ruler.

Mounting Specimens with Plastic

Heat-sensitive laminating plastic, such as the plastic manufactured under the trade name Seal-Lamin, is very useful for mounting specimens that require flat mounting. Flowers or insects protected by Seal-Lamin will not deteriorate as easily as specimens covered with cellophane, and will last for years of normal classroom use. Seal-Lamin is available in sheets and in rolls.

Materials and Equipment
- heat-sensitive laminating plastic (Seal-Lamin)
- mounting board (cardboard)
- dry-mount press
- paper cutter
- large, heavy books
- old magazines
- flat, dried specimen
- tacking iron or household iron

Procedure (Figure 4.12)
Preheat the press to 270 degrees Fahrenheit. Close the press and turn it on. When the desired temperature is reached, open the press.

Be sure the plant specimen is dry. If you suspect that moisture is still present, place the specimen between folds of paper towel and press it between the pages of a magazine. Place the magazine in the preheated press for a few seconds to remove the moisture. Open the press and remove the specimen. Then follow these steps:

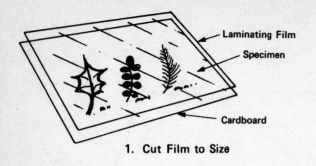

1. **Cut Film to Size**

Laminating Film
Specimen
Cardboard

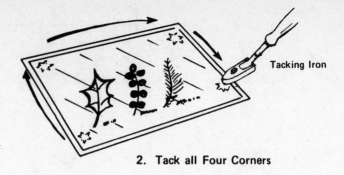

Tacking Iron

2. **Tack all Four Corners**

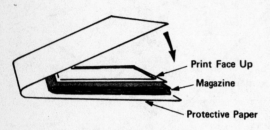

Print Face Up
Magazine
Protective Paper

3. **Prepare to Place in Press**

Figure 4.12
Mounting Specimens with
Heat-Lamination Plastic

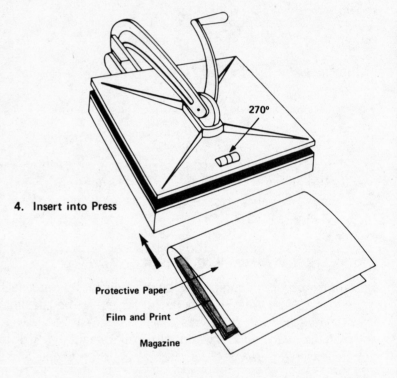

270°

4. **Insert into Press**

Protective Paper
Film and Print
Magazine

1. Cut cardboard to size. Cut a piece of laminating plastic so it is *slightly smaller* than the cardboard mount. Position the specimen on top of the board and lay the heat-sensitive plastic *dull* side *down* on *top* of the specimen. If two or more specimens are mounted, be sure the specimens are separated from each other. No specimen should come closer than ½" from the outer edges of the plastic.
2. Preheat the tacking iron (set at *high*) or the household iron (set at *cotton*). Tack the plastic at all four corners, as illustrated, by touching the tip of the iron to the plastic for only an instant. Do *not* push the plastic toward the center of the board while tacking, as this will cause wrinkles in the finished lamination.
3. Place the mounting board on top of a magazine, and then place both between the folds of a sheet of clean white paper.
4. Insert the assembled materials into the press. Leave them in the press for 15 to 30 seconds. Remove the materials from the press and quickly place books on top of them to prevent warping.
5. After the materials have cooled, trim the cardboard border off with a paper cutter or scissors. Note: If bubbles appear under the plastic,

puncture them with a straight pin or needle. Reinsert the board into the heated press to force the steam and air out. After 15 to 30 seconds, remove the board from the press and quickly place weights on top. Allow it to cool before removing the weights. A tacking iron or household iron may be used to press the plastic down close to the edge of the specimen. Be sure to use a piece of paper on *top* of the plastic and *under* the iron so the plastic will not stick to the iron.

Riker Mounting

Riker mounting has long been a favorite technique for arranging specimens for display and study. Any teacher can successfully employ this method to mount coins, insect collections, Indian artifacts, geological specimens, and other objects used as instructional materials.

Materials and Equipment
- shallow box
- cellophane, clear plastic wrap, or clear acetate
- cotton (preferably in roll form)
- pins or thumbtacks
- scissors
- specimen to be mounted
- tape (plastic or cellophane)

Procedure (Figure 4.13)
1. Cut the cotton to the desired size, usually slightly larger than the dimensions of the box. Place the cotton in the box, and pat into place. Cut a hole in the lid of the box 1" from each edge. Turn the lid over, cut a piece of cellophane or clear plastic large enough to cover the opening, and tape it into place inside the lid with plastic or cellophane tape.
2. Place the specimen in the box, lower the lid into place, and fasten with pins or thumbtacks on two or four sides. (Note: If desired, coat the specimen with plastic spray and allow it to dry before placing it

Figure 4.13
Riker Mounting

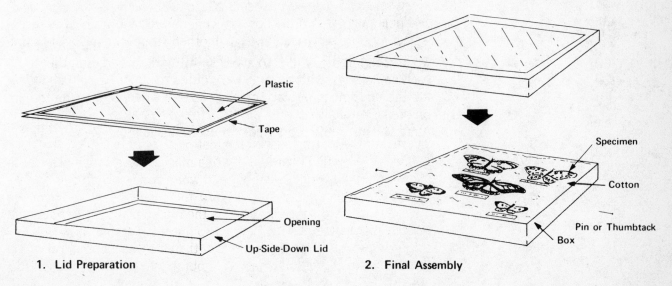

1. **Lid Preparation**

2. **Final Assembly**

Figure 4.14
Matchbox Mounting

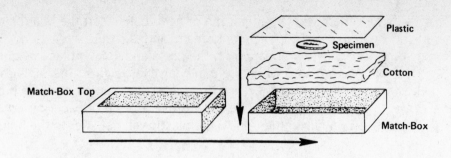

into the box. This will make the specimen more resistant to damage. If you are mounting insects, place a mothball under the cotton to prevent moth damage.)

Many types of small boxes may be used for Riker mounting. For small specimens, a matchbox works well (Figure 4.14). Cut the lid holes of small boxes closer to the edge than the 1" mentioned above. It may be difficult to tape plastic inside a matchbox cover; if so, tape the plastic over the opening on the outside.

Insect Display Jar

An insect display jar allows you to view specimens from all sides. The jar provides durable protection for specimens, shielding them from damage caused by atmospheric conditions or by active hands.

Figure 4.15
Insect Display Jar

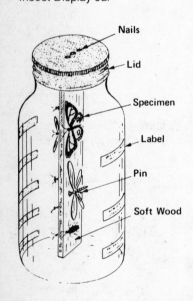

Materials and Equipment
- glass jar of appropriate size
- jar lid
- piece of balsa wood or soft pine
- dried specimens
- insect pins
- labels (adhesive, if possible)
- transparent tape (if adhesive labels are not available)
- nails
- hammer

Procedure (Figure 4.15)
1. Fasten the wood slab to the jar lid by nailing into the end of the wood through the jar lid. To avoid splitting the wood, dull the tip of each nail slightly with a gentle blow of the hammer before nailing.
2. Pin the specimens in place on the piece of wood, and fasten the lid on the jar carefully.
3. Attach labels in the proper positions on the jar.

Lettering Instructional Materials

V

To be most effective, displays, charts, graphs, bulletin boards, and other visual materials often must be accompanied by written explanations. The legibility and lettering quality of labels and captions can add to or detract from the effectiveness of any display, and thus facilitate or limit learning.

This chapter presents suggestions for lettering, as well as information on using lettering pens; lettering systems and guides; dry transfer and acetate letters; three-dimensional letters; flat opaque letters; and lettering for special effects.

5.1 General Suggestions

Some suggestions that you should consider when lettering instructional materials:

1. Keep labels and captions short and simple. Don't use unnecessary words; captions should be concise.
2. Keep the lettering style simple. Don't use fancy letters; use a style that is easy to read.
3. Use a uniform height when lettering materials. Horizontal guide lines, drawn lightly with a pencil, will help keep lettering straight and uniform.
4. Use optical spacing for clarity. Optical spacing allows for equal *area* between letters (Figure 5.1). Mechanical lettering has equal *distance* between letters (Figure 5.2). Optical lettering is more pleasing to the eye. Estimate the space needed for lettering by counting spaces, leaving two to four spaces between words. Next, adjust the estimate by allowing 1¼ spaces for the letters *M* and *W*, and ¼ space for the letter *I*.

Figure 5.1
Optical Lettering

Figure 5.2
Mechanical Lettering

5. Generally, it is best to allow about 1¼ to 1½ times the height of the caption line for spacing measurement between successive lines of lettering.
6. Be sure that display captions can be read from a distance. People with normal vision should be able to read letters 1″ high from a distance of 32′.
7. In lettering projection materials, such as overhead transparencies, be sure that the letters are large enough to be read easily when projected on the screen. For transparencies, the minimum lettering height should be ¼″.

5.2 Lettering Pens

Various types of lettering pens are available to help you do a more effective, professional job of lettering instructional materials. Easy-to-use, inexpensive lettering pens include felt-tipped and nylon-tipped pens, Speedball pens, and duck-bill (metal brush) pens.

Felt-tipped and Nylon-tipped Pens

Felt-tipped pens are available with a variety of points suitable for fine-line or wide-line drawing and lettering purposes. Instant-drying inks in many colors are available for drawing on glass, plastic, metal, or paper surfaces. Felt-tipped pens are especially useful for quick and easy lettering on display materials of all types, as well as for adding color to transparencies.

Nylon-tipped pens typically have much finer and more durable points than felt-tipped pens. Thus, for detail work and fine lettering in preparing transparencies, nylon-tipped pens are excellent. For transparency work, be sure you use pens suitable for writing on glass or plastic. Before making a purchase, *try out* the pen by drawing or writing on a piece of glass or plastic. If the ink beads up, it is not suitable. If the pen produces a continuous smooth line, it will probably work on transparency plastics.

Inks for felt-tipped and nylon-tipped pens may *not* project true color tones. Only when you project the color onto a screen will it be possible to tell whether the colors are correct.

Materials and Equipment
- nylon-tipped or felt-tipped pens
- drawing surface
- scratch paper

Procedure (Figure 5.3)
Before doing a final lettering job, sketch a layout of the proposed material and practice your lettering on scratch paper. If you accidently run a light-colored pen over dark-colored ink, clean the pen's tip by making a few lines on scratch paper. Be sure to cover the felt tips of the pens before putting them away.

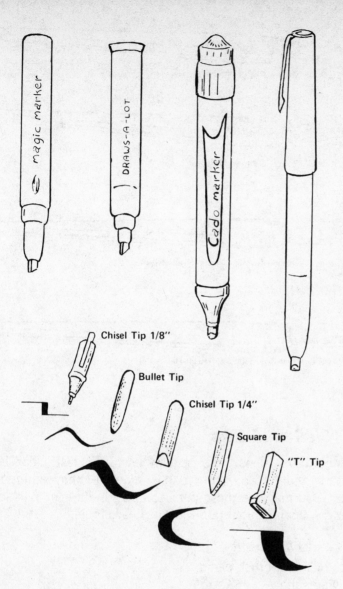

Figure 5.3
Felt-Tipped Pens

Chisel Tip 1/8"

Bullet Tip

Chisel Tip 1/4"

Square Tip

"T" Tip

Speedball Pens

When small or medium-sized letters are needed, consider using a Speedball pen. Pen points are available from ¼" wide (size 0) to the finest line (size 6). Four styles of points may be purchased for doing various lettering jobs. Pen size and style are imprinted on top of each pen point.

Materials and Equipment

- Speedball pen(s)
- drawing surface
- scratch paper
- drawing ink

Procedure (Figure 5.4)

Practice lettering with various Speedball points before attempting to finish the lettering on a display. After you have developed satisfactory skill in lettering, choose a pen nib and make a practice layout. Check the spacing and letter placement. Be sure to touch the point of the pen to a piece of scratch paper to remove excess ink before drawing letters.

Figure 5.4
Speedball Pens

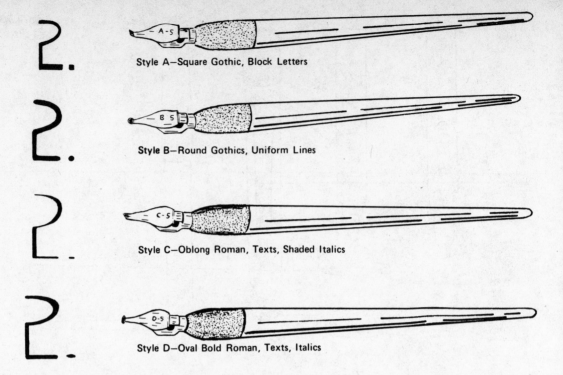

Style A—Square Gothic, Block Letters

Style B—Round Gothics, Uniform Lines

Style C—Oblong Roman, Texts, Shaded Italics

Style D—Oval Bold Roman, Texts, Italics

Duck-Bill Steel-Brush Pens

Duck-bill steel-brush pens are especially useful for fast, clean lettering on posters, charts, graphs, and other display materials that require medium or large letters. You may use these pens to apply India inks, plastic inks, oils, watercolors, and paints. Four pen widths are available: ⅜", ½", ¾", and ¼".

Materials and Equipment

- duck-bill steel-brush pen(s)
- drawing surface
- scratch paper
- straight edge (T-square or ruler)
- drawing ink

Procedure (Figure 5.5)

When you use steel-brush pens, plan to use a T-square or ruler with a raised edge to help make the lettering straight and neat. Block lettering is especially easy to do with steel-brush pens.

5.3 Stencils

Stencils are inexpensive, durable, and easy-to-use for making attractive letters for charts, posters, and other materials (see Figure 5.6). You may outline letters lightly in pencil, using a stencil, and later fill in the letters with a brush, felt-tipped pen, or other coloring device.

Stenso lettering stencils are easy to use and available in letter sizes from ½" to 8", in both upper and lower case Gothic, Roman, and Old

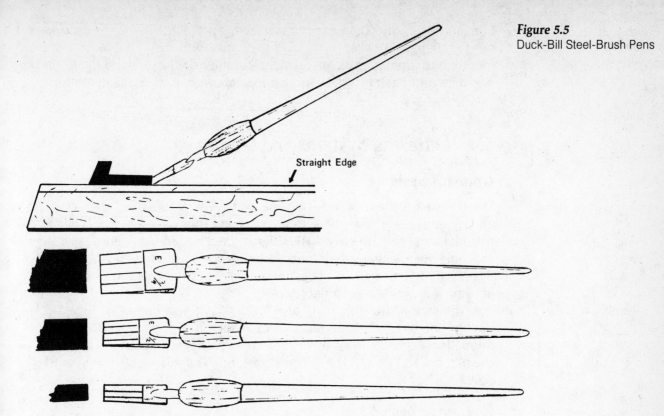

Figure 5.5
Duck-Bill Steel-Brush Pens

Straight Edge

English. These stencils have special guide holes which make the spacing and alignment of letters very easy.

Metal interlocking stencils are especially useful when words are used repeatedly in a chart or in several charts. You can construct words, use them

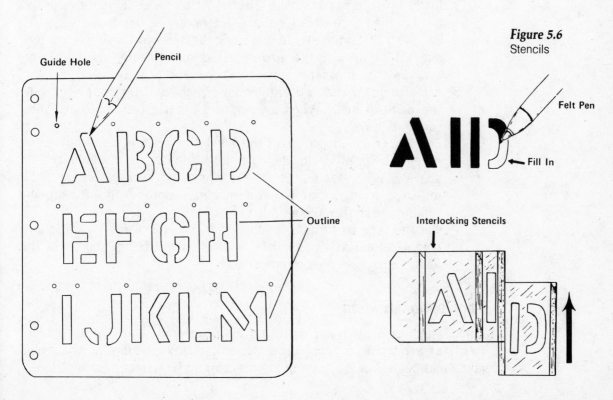

Figure 5.6
Stencils

Guide Hole

Pencil

Outline

Felt Pen

Fill In

Interlocking Stencils

over and over, and then easily take them apart when they are no longer needed. Be careful when using paints or inks with metal guides, for some inks tend to run under the metal stencils. Quick-drying inks and thick paints work best with metal guides. Apply the paints with quick dabbing motions.

5.4   Lettering Systems and Guides

Unimark System

The Unimark System provides an inexpensive way to make labels on tape quickly and easily. Use the letters on charts, maps, or any other smooth materials that require easy-to-read large lettering. Transparent tape is also available for making labels and lettering for transparencies. A Unimark System kit is an excellent investment if you wish to prepare professional-appearing letters at a reasonable cost.

The tape is available in 1" or ½" widths. A single line of ⅝" letters or a double line of ⅜" or ¼" letters can be made on 1" wide tape. The ½" tape allows for a single row of ⅜" or ¼" lettering. The ⅝" lettering is made with the pen marked LARGE. The ⅜" or ¼" lettering is made with the pen marked SMALL.

Procedure   (Figure 5.7)

1. Clip the tape cartridge onto the right-hand end of the lettering device, as in the illustration.
2. Load the tape, feeding the end of the tape into the slot until it meets resistance. Turn the knob at the rear of the machine to feed the tape forward until the end of the tape lines up with the arrow marked *tape*.
3. Insert the appropriate scale. The ⅝" letter scale slides into the full track or the inside track for single-line or double-line lettering.
4. The black line on the scale preceding the letter you wish to print first should line up with the arrow marked *print*. Keeping the pen in an *upright position*, press it firmly against the tape.
5. If the pen does not write immediately, shake it up and down until the ink flows freely. When the pen is not in use, be sure to place the cap on tightly.
6. For proper spacing, line up the black line on the scale before the letter to be printed with the *right edge* of the letter already printed. To space between words, use the space of an average letter. If the message is longer than the printing bed, simply advance the tape by turning the knob and continue printing.
7. Cut the tape by turning the cutter at the end of the machine in a complete *counterclockwise* circle. Peel off the backing, and press the letters into place on a clean surface.

Rapidograph System

Rapidograph pens and Rapidoguides are relatively easy to use, and not nearly as expensive as most other systems. Many teachers purchase two guide and pen sets, one appropriate for drawing ⅝" letters, and another for

Figure 5.7
Unimark Lettering System

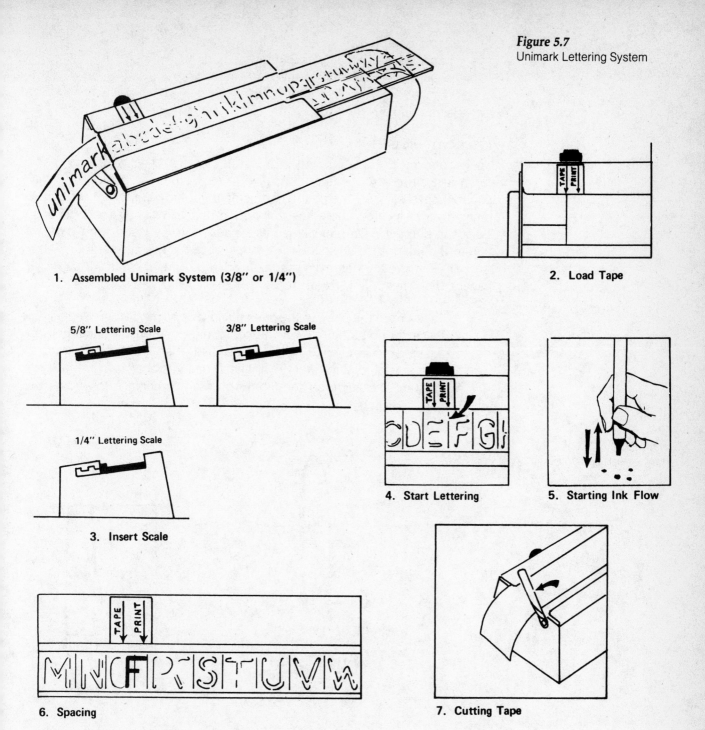

1. Assembled Unimark System (3/8" or 1/4")

2. Load Tape

5/8" Lettering Scale

3/8" Lettering Scale

1/4" Lettering Scale

3. Insert Scale

4. Start Lettering

5. Starting Ink Flow

6. Spacing

7. Cutting Tape

¾₆″ letters. These guides will suffice for most lettering on transparencies, picture captions, study maps, and learning center displays. For larger letters, consider using another system.

Materials and Equipment

- Rapidoguides
- straightedge (a T-square or ruler)
- masking or drafting tape and pins
- drawing ink suitable for paper or plastic (Pelikan or Koh-i-noor inks are excellent)

- Rapidiograph pens or equivalent
- paper, cardboard, or plastic drawing surface
- paper towel, one end moistened
- flat working surface
- scrap paper

Procedure (Figure 5.8)

Check to see if the pen is filled with ink and ready to use. Shake it up and down a few times to get the ink to flow. Test for flow on a piece of scrap paper. If necessary, fill the pen. When using a Rapidograph pen, take off the plunger cover located above the color-code ring by twisting *counterclockwise*. Twist the plunger counterclockwise as far as it will go. Insert the tip of the pen in the ink bottle, and twist the plunger *clockwise*. Ink will be sucked into the pen. Remove the pen from the ink bottle and wipe it clean with a moist paper towel. Then follow these steps:

1. Tape or pin the copy to the working surface at the corners.
2. Place the Rapidoguide on the copy, and position the straight edge against the *lower* edge of the guide. Use a loop of tape or strips of tape at each end to hold the straight edge in place.
3. Position the guide so the letter you wish to begin with is over the copy.

Figure 5.8
Rapidograph Pen and Guide

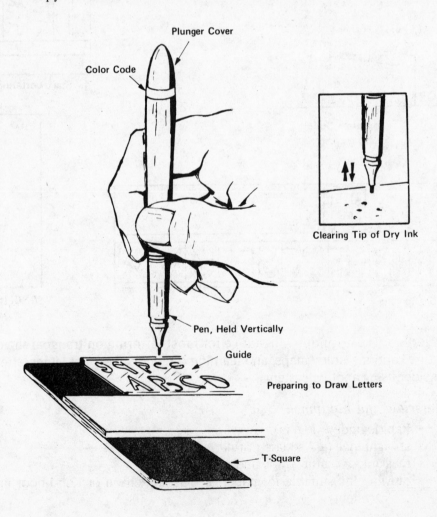

Plunger Cover

Color Code

Clearing Tip of Dry Ink

Pen, Held Vertically

Guide

Preparing to Draw Letters

T-Square

Lettering Instructional Materials

4. Hold the pen *perpendicular to the copy*, insert the point into the guide, and begin lettering. When a letter is complete, lift the pen out, move the guide over to the next letter, and proceed. The guide should be raised off the copy surface to prevent smearing. Determine the spacing by considering *area* between letters rather than *distance*. (Two curved lines opposite each other are spaced closer together than two vertical lines, for example.)

See Figure 5.9 for examples of Rapidoguide numbers and letters.

Figure 5.9
Rapidoguides: Guide Numbers and Pen Numbers

3030/A	**Rapidoguide** 5/64″ FOR USE WITH **RAPIDOGRAPH** No. 00	for swift sure lettering, use KOH-I-NOOR RAPIDOGUIDES ABCDEGHIJKLMNOPQRSTUVW abcdefghijklmnopqrstuvwxyz
3030/B	**Rapidoguide** 1/8″ FOR USE WITH **RAPIDOGRAPH** No. 00	for swift sure lettering, use KOH-I-NOOR RAPIDOGUIDES ABCDEGHIJKLMNOPQRSTUVW
3030	**Rapidoguide** 5/32″ FOR USE WITH **RAPIDOGRAPH** No. 0	for swift sure lettering, use KOH-I-NOOR RAPIDOGUIDES
3031	**Rapidoguide** 3/16″ FOR USE WITH **RAPIDOGRAPH** No. 1	for swift, sure lettering KOH-I-NOOR RAPIDOG
3032	**Rapidoguide** 1/4″ FOR USE WITH **RAPIDOGRAPH** No. 2	for swift, sure lett KOH-I-NOOR RAPI
3032/A	**Rapidoguide** 9/32″ FOR USE WITH **RAPIDOGRAPH** No. 2½	for swift, sure let KOH-I-NOOR RAP
3033	**Rapidoguide** 5/16″ FOR USE WITH **RAPIDOGRAPH** No. 3	for swift, KOH-I
3034	**Rapidoguide** 3/8″ FOR USE WITH **RAPIDOGRAPH** No. 4	for swift, KOH

Additional Information

Ink-filled pens should *always* be tightly capped when not in use. A special humidor may be purchased for pen storage to help prevent pens from drying out and clogging.

Clogged pens may be soaked in warm water to which detergent has been added. Let them soak *overnight*, and then clean the pens.

Several other brands of technical drawing pens may be used with Rapidoguides (Mars technical pens, for example). Be sure pen-point widths and Rapidoguides are compatible before you purchase them.

Wrico Signmaker Pens and Guides

Use Wrico Signmaker guides and pens to make large letters for charts, posters, and bulletin boards. The guides produce letters from ½" to 4" in height.

To use this system, you will need a stencil guide, a special brush pen or felt-tipped pen, and a guide holder.

Materials and Equipment

- stencil guide
- brush pen or felt-tipped pen
- guide holder
- hard-finished paper or cardboard
- clean, firm working surface
- paper towels or tissues
- drawing ink

Procedure (Figure 5.10)

1. Select the stencil guide by reading the code printed below the stencil openings. The code will indicate whether the letter is upper or lower case; the letter style and height; and the pen needed to complete the lettering. For example, for lettering 1½" in height, the following code might be printed on the guide: GUIDE NO. AVC 150. AV refers to the letter style; C indicates a capital letter (upper case); 150 indicates the letter height (1.50"). For other letter heights the code reads as follows: 100 = 1", 75 = ¾", etc. You will also find an instruction printed on the guide such as: USE WITH BRUSH PEN C OR FELT PEN NCF. This means that you should use a C-width pen. Be *sure* you use the specified pen, for the pen you use is important.
2. Select the pen needed. The brush pens will have an engraved letter near the tip—A through E, narrow through wide—indicating the width of line.
3. Adjust the brush pen so the brush is *slightly recessed*. Hold the collar while twisting the barrel of the pen to make the desired adjustment.
4. Turn the guide holder over and read the instructions on the back. Return the guide to the upright position, and place it on the copy to be lettered. Insert the guide into the holder, using the appropriate side.
5. Fill the pen by depressing the plunger and inserting the brush into the ink bottle. Wipe off the excess ink with a paper towel, after allowing the brush to retract into the barrel. Touch the tip of the pen

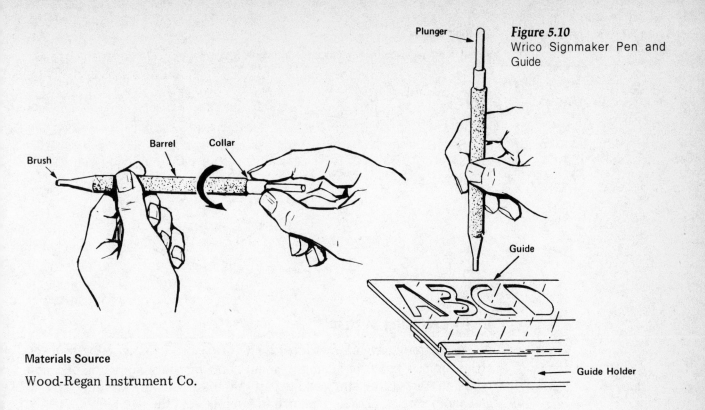

Figure 5.10
Wrico Signmaker Pen and Guide

Plunger

Brush

Barrel   Collar

Guide

Guide Holder

Materials Source

Wood-Regan Instrument Co.

to scrap paper to start the flow. If the line produced is not solid, readjust the brush until the line satisfies you.

6. Insert the pen into the guide, holding it perpendicular to the copy. Use a firm grip on the pen, but do *not* exert much pressure on the paper as this will damage the paper and stop the flow of ink. You may go over a letter more than once. It is best to start near the middle of the opening and work toward either end of the letter.

Determine the spacing optically by considering the area between letters rather than the distance. A little practice will help you decide how to do this on the final work. Be sure to clean the brush after each use. Simply depress the brush and rinse it under running water.

If you use felt-tipped pens, follow the guide openings, holding the pen perpendicular to the copy. Do *not* rinse these pens. Keep them tightly capped when they are not in use. Since felt-tipped pens are more expensive to use than brush pens, the brush pens may be more appropriate for general use.

Wrico Standard Pens and Guides

For *small* letters suitable for picture labels, transparency masters, and other similar jobs, Wrico Standard pens and guides are very useful and can yield professional results (Figure 5.11).

Use the Wrico Standard pen with the Wrico Standard or Wrico-Print guide. Interchangeable points are available for different lettering purposes. Be sure to hold the pen in a vertical position to avoid spilling ink and to ensure even, neat lettering.

Figure 5.11
Wrico Standard Pen and Guide

Materials Source

Wood-Regan Instrument Co.

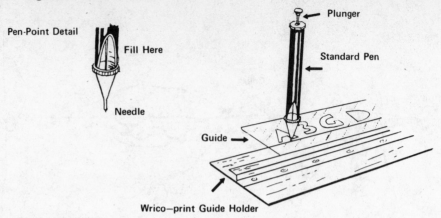

Leroy Lettering System

A Leroy lettering system produces high-quality precision lettering in many styles, from ⅟₁₆″ to 2″ in height. Its main parts are the scriber arm, pen, and template. The scriber arm has one part that traces the letter in the template and another part that holds the pen that reproduces the letter.

A Leroy system enables you to draw vertical or slanted letters of various heights, widths, and styles with consistent accuracy. Letters produced by this system often are mistaken for printed material due to the perfection of the lettering job. The lettering is done with the pen point free of the template, leaving the printing in view at all times, and reducing the possibility of smearing or smudging. If you need relatively small, accurate lettering for transparency masters, maps, charts, or other instructional materials, consider using the Leroy system.

Materials and Equipment
- Leroy lettering system
- masking tape
- straight edge
- drawing surface
- lettering ink

Procedure (Figure 5.12)
1. Select the pen with the desired line width. Insert the pen in the pen socket at the end of the scriber arm and tighten the set screw. Fill the reservoir with lettering ink.
2. Fasten a straight edge on the working surface with loops of masking tape (adhesive side out) under each end, as illustrated. Slide the material to be lettered under the straightedge at this time. Place a template with the desired size of letters along the straightedge, and place the tail pin of the scriber arm in the long straight groove of the template. Select the letter to be drawn. Place the tracer pin on the template in the lowest part of the letter. Move the template and scriber until the pen point is directly over the copy where the first letter is to be drawn, and draw the first letter.

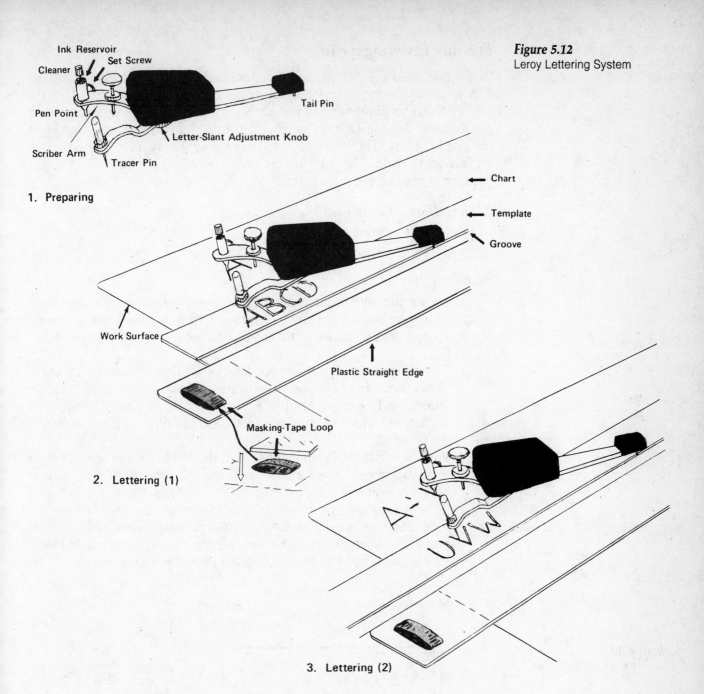

Figure 5.12
Leroy Lettering System

Ink Reservoir

Set Screw

Cleaner

Tail Pin

Pen Point

Letter-Slant Adjustment Knob

Scriber Arm

Tracer Pin

1. Preparing

Chart

Template

Groove

Work Surface

Plastic Straight Edge

Masking-Tape Loop

2. Lettering (1)

3. Lettering (2)

3. With the pen clear of the drawing, move the scriber arm to the next letter and slide the template along the straightedge until the pen is in position for the next letter. Draw the next letter, holding the template in place as the pen point moves over the drawing surface. Continue until the first line of lettering is completed.

When the pen is filled with ink, be sure to keep it in a vertical position to avoid spilling. When the scriber arm is not in use, move it aside to keep the pen point clear of the working surface. Lift the cleaner slightly to start the flow of ink if the scriber arm has been standing idle for some time. Be sure to blot the point of the pen tip before beginning to letter. After each use, clean the pen with running water to prevent the tip from clogging.

Pressure Lettering System

One widely used pressure lettering system is the Kroy 80 lettering machine. This machine produces an image by pressing a template against a carbon ribbon. A carbon impression of the image on the template is transferred to a plastic tape. The plastic tape is removed from the machine and placed on the graphic piece. This method of lettering is very easy, fast, and produces professional results. The type comes on prepared discs available in thirty-five type styles and eight type sizes.

Materials and Equipment
- Kroy 80 lettering machine
- typedisc

Procedure (Figure 5.13)

1. Locate the hole in the center of the underside of the type disc; then, locate the spindle (A) on the Kroy machine and place the disc on the spindle. You will have to tilt the disc to get it under the pressure bar (B).
2. Set the spacing adjustment (C). On the adjustment wheel, the white dot is the normal setting, +8 indicates the maximum space between letters, and –8 indicates the minimum space between letters. The adjustment wheel permits you to expand or reduce the line length of the lettering.
3. Print by rotating the type disc so that the character you want to print is across from the red arrow (D). Press the print button (E). Space between words is achieved by rotating the type disc to WORD SPACE (F) and pressing the print button. To cut off the tape, rotate the type disc to ADVANCE BEFORE CUT (G), press the print button; then press the cut button (H). The Kern button (I) reduces space between letters and is used for optical spacing with upper case letters.

Figure 5.13
Kroy Lettering System

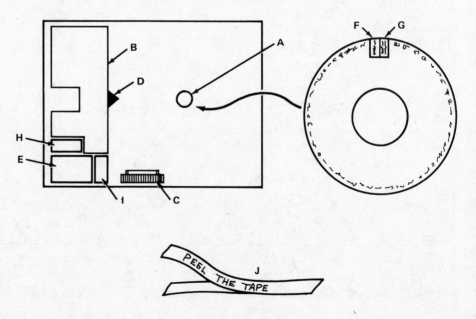

Lettering Instructional Materials

4. Apply the lettering by peeling the tape from the backing (J) and positioning it into place. For a more secure adhesion, burnish the tape by placing a piece of paper over the tape and rubbing the paper with your finger or a ruler.

5.5 *Letters, Symbols, Tapes, and Prepared Art*

A number of effective, commerically prepared letters, symbols, and tapes are available to help in preparing educational materials: printed-acetate (plastic) lettering sheets, dry-transfer lettering, adhesive pictorial charting symbols, and printed-acetate (plastic) charting tapes. All these materials can be applied directly to your artwork.

Dry-Transfer Lettering

One method for quick lettering, available under trade names such as Letraset Instant Lettering and Prestype is extensively used by commercial artists, draftsmen, and teachers (Figure 5.14).

Materials and Equipment
- instant lettering
- lettering surface
- dull pencil, ballpoint pen, or tool for transferring letters

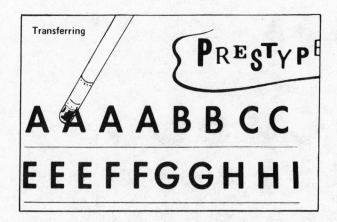

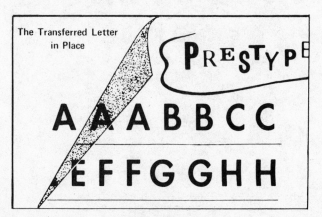

Figure 5.14
Dry-Transfer Lettering

Procedure

1. Place each letter on the spot where it is needed.
2. Pressure will transfer the letter quickly and easily to the artwork. Apply pressure by rubbing the letter with the point of a dull pencil, ballpoint pen, or a special tool designed for this purpose.

A variety of symbols for dry transfer are also available. Follow the same procedure to apply the symbols. Examples of dry-transfer symbols are given in Figure 5.15.

Printed-Acetate (Plastic) Lettering Sheets

Several companies produce self-adhering, printed-acetate sheets of letters, numbers, symbols, borders, screens, and shading mediums. One of these, Formatt, is a superior product useful for lettering materials of all types. The dry, nonsticky pressure-sensitive adhesive on the back of Artype sheets makes the application of letters a clean and simple task.

Figure 5.15
Examples of Dry-Transfer Symbols

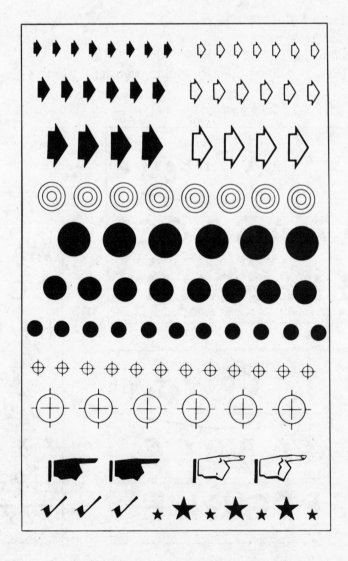

Lettering Instructional Materials

Materials and Equipment

- Formatt (printed acetate) sheets
- pencil
- paper clips or tape
- stylus

Procedure (Figure 5.16)

1. Loosen the backing sheet from the Formatt sheet as illustrated. Drop the backing sheet back onto the Formatt sheet.
2. With pencil, draw a lettering guideline lightly on the artwork. (Note: In the case of transparencies, draw a guideline on a sheet of paper, position the paper under the transparent sheet, and temporarily fasten the paper and transparency together with a paper clip or tape.) With a stylus, cut around the letter to be used, being sure to include the guideline printed below it. Do *not* cut through the backing sheet.
3. Lift the letter from the backing sheet with the point of the stylus.
4. Position the letter on the chart or transparency, placing the Formatt guideline in register with the pencil guideline. Burnish *lightly* with the beveled end of the stylus.
5. When all lettering is laid out on the artwork, make any changes needed in spacing or alignment, and burnish all letters *firmly* into

1. Loosen Backing

Figure 5.16
Printed-Acetate Lettering and Charting Sheets

2. Cut out Letter

3. Pick up Letter

4. Placement

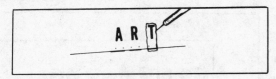

5. Burnishing

Letter and Pattern Samples

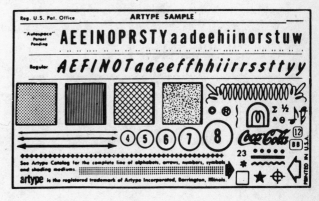

place until all edges disappear (be careful *not* to burnish the Formatt guidelines). Remove the Formatt guidelines with the point of the stylus, and erase the pencil guidelines.

Adhesive Pictorial Charting Symbols

Symbols backed with adhesive and printed on white opaque paper stock are available to illustrate comparative numerical quantities on charts. These symbols come in many sizes and represent people, ships, farms, buildings, animals, industrial concerns, mining properties, and gas and oil production. One kind of symbol sheet, Pictograph, is especially easy to use.

Suggestions for Using Pictorial Symbols

1. Numerical differences are best indicated by different numbers of symbols, rather than by symbols of different size (larger symbols with smaller symbols).
2. Use pictorial symbols to present an overall picture, not to show minute details. Use fractions of symbols sparingly.
3. Pictorial symbols are most effective when they represent quantitative comparisons, rather than isolated facts.
4. Symbols should usually look like the objects they represent.

Figure 5.17
Adhesive Pictorial Charting Symbols

Pictograph Symbols

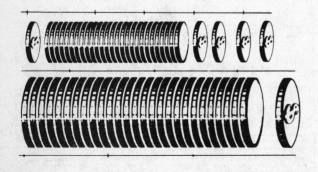

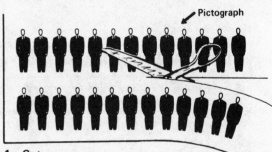
1. Cut

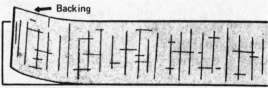
2. Remove Backing

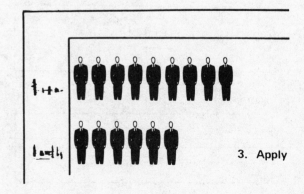
3. Apply

Lettering Instructional Materials

Materials and Equipment
- adhesive pictorial charting symbols
- scissors

Procedure (Figure 5.17)
1. Cut the desired number of symbols from the symbol line of the sheet.
2. Strip off the protective backing sheet and position the symbol line on the chart.
3. Rub the line firmly into place.

Printed-Acetate (Plastic) Charting Tapes

Several companies now produce printed-acetate tapes that are useful for all types of graphic work. One brand of tape, Chart-Pak, is an excellent product for applying symbols, borders, and graph lines to instructional materials of all kinds. Chart-Pak is available on an opaque or transparent plastic base.

Materials and Equipment
- printed-acetate charting tape
- stylus or knife

Procedure (Figure 5.18)
1. Unroll a short length of the pattern or color to be applied. Allow the end of the tape to overlap the starting point (see illustration) about one inch. Lay the tape on the desired area and press carefully into place.
2. Cut the tape where desired with a stylus or knife and pull away excess tape, holding the tape at a 45-degree angle. Trim away the excess tape at the starting point. Burnish the tape firmly into place.
3. If you revise a chart, peel off the tape at a 45-degree angle to avoid tearing the chart. Apply a new strip of tape to the chart to complete the revision.

Prepared Art

Professionally drawn, copyright-free art in a wide variety of styles is available for purchase (Figure 5.19). This art, sometimes called *clip art*, is black line on white paper. Clip art is available in booklet form, arranged by subject. Some clip art is adhesive-backed, and some clip art must be pasted down. The procedure is simple; select the art, cut it out, and paste it down.

5.6 Flat Opaque Letters

Teachers often have a need for opaque letters to use on charts, graphs, and displays of all kinds. Gummed-paper letters, construction-paper letters, and flexible-plastic letters are especially helpful.

Figure 5.18
Printed-Acetate Charting
Tapes

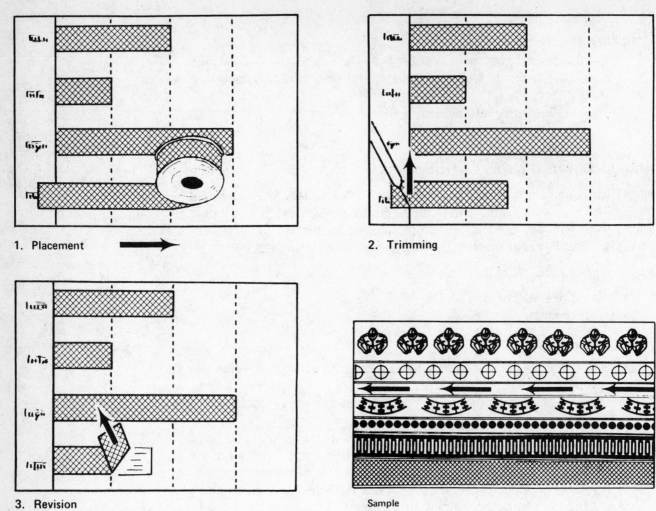

1. Placement

2. Trimming

3. Revision

Sample

Figure 5.19
Prepared Art *(From Formost clip art manufacturer's literature)*

Lettering Instructional Materials

Figure 5.20
Gummed-Paper Letters

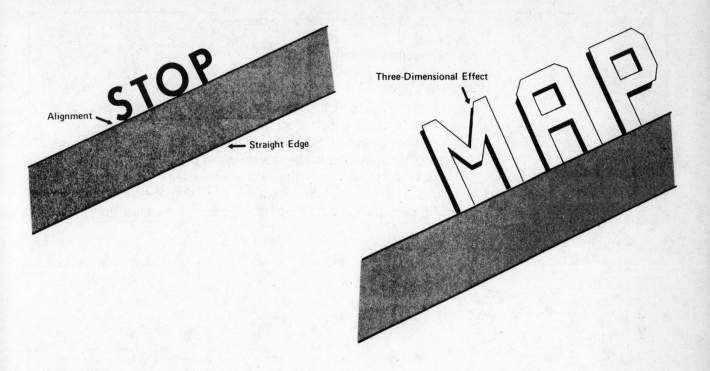

Gummed-Paper Letters

Gummed-paper letters, figures, and symbols are available in an assortment of styles and sizes; ranging from ⅛" to 4" in height (Figure 5.20).

Materials and Equipment
- gummed-paper letters
- straightedge (T-square or ruler)
- soft lead pencil

Procedure
1. Select the letters to be used, and lay them out on the display. Use a straightedge as a guide for even placement.
2. With a soft lead pencil, make marks on the display where letters are to be placed.
3. Moisten the gummed back of each letter and press it into place. A pleasing three-dimensional or shadow effect may be achieved by choosing two contrasting letter colors and superimposing one color on top of the other, as shown.

Construction-Paper Letters

Paper letters cut from construction paper make suitable flat opaque letters for charts and graphs.

Materials and Equipment

- colored construction paper
- scissors
- stencil or die-cut cardboard letters
- pencil
- paper clip or spring clip

Procedure (Figure 5.21)

1. Use a stencil, die-cut cardboard, or commercial letters as a pattern, if possible. Outline the letters on construction paper in pencil.
2. Cut two sheets of paper at once (contrasting colors) if a shadow effect is desired. Hold the two sheets of paper together with a clip or a spring clip while cutting. For a three-dimensional effect with a single letter, cut out the letters in contrasting colors and mount them with pins, pulling out the bottom letter as shown in Figure 5.21.

Figure 5.21
Construction-Paper Letters

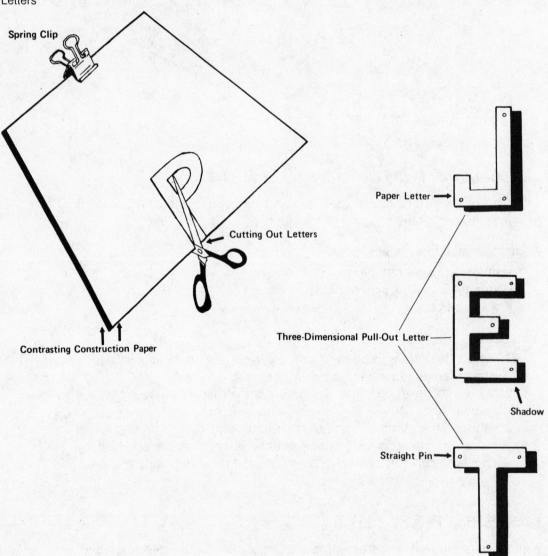

Spring Clip

Cutting Out Letters

Contrasting Construction Paper

Paper Letter

Three-Dimensional Pull-Out Letter

Shadow

Straight Pin

5.7 Lettering for Special Effects

In addition to the more usual lettering techniques, certain readily available materials greatly enhance the effectiveness of a display. Materials such as rope, cotton, sand, yarn, string, paper strips, colored tapes, and paper straws can be used creatively for special effects (see Figure 5.22).

You may also use colored chalk, broken to widths of the letters to be made, to draw soft-looking letters on construction paper or textured papers. Colored paper, cut into free-form shapes, makes a pleasing background for chalk lettering. To form the letters, hold the chalk between your index finger and thumb and press down firmly with the side of the chalk on the paper, moving with a smooth motion as you draw each letter. If you use letters repeatedly, fix them with plastic spray. Be aware, however, that fixing or preserving materials with plastic spray will often cause color changes in construction paper.

Figure 5.22
Lettering for Special Effects

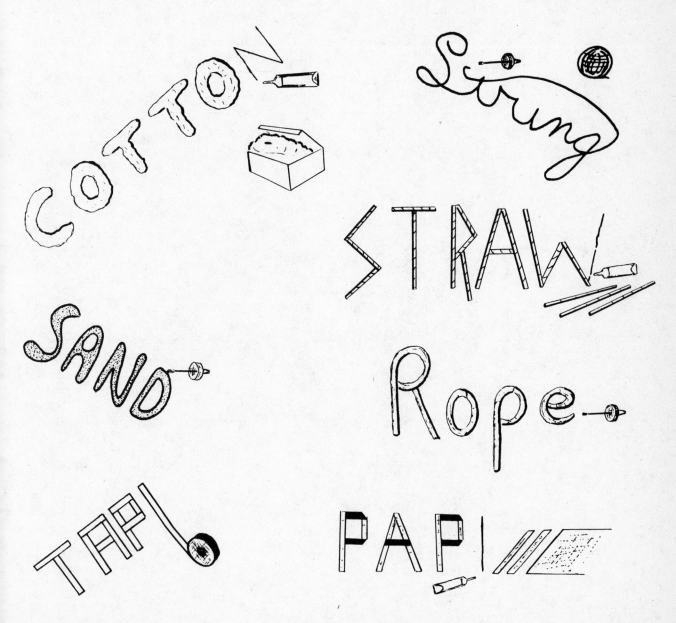

Display Devices and Study Boards

VI

This chapter includes directions for constructing several types of flannel boards, magnetic boards, combination boards, individual chalkboards, electric question-boards, display easels, visographs, accordion-fold displays, and diorama stages. These devices may be used by students and teachers for individual instruction, or for small or large group instruction.

6.1 Flannel Boards

Flannel boards or felt boards have long been favorite tools of elementary-school teachers, and are becoming more popular with teachers at the secondary and college levels as well. By using a flannel board, teachers can develop complex concepts or tell stories through easily understood step-by-step presentations. Flannel boards are simple to construct and easy to use. Detailed directions are given below for constructing metal-hinged folding boards and other types of flannel boards. Instructions for making a combination flannel and magnetic board are also provided.

Metal-Hinged Folding Flannel Board

Materials and Equipment
- plywood, cut to size (usually 24" × 36"; ⅜" or ½" thick)
- saw
- piano hinge
- screwdriver
- screws

- flannel or felt, cut to the desired size (30″ × 42″ for a 24″ × 36″ board)
- stapler and staples
- hammer
- masking or plastic tape
- pencil

Procedure (Figure 6.1)

1. Cut the plywood into two halves. Place the boards face up on a table and mark the placement of the hinge on each half of the mounting board. Use the hinge as a guide for marking. Remove the hinge and cut a groove in the plywood deep enough to allow for flush mounting the hinge. Fit the halves of the board snugly together and mount the hinge flush with the surface of the board as illustrated.
2. Lay the flannel or felt *nap side down* on a smooth surface. Place the plywood on top of the cloth with the hinged side against the material. Fold an edge of the flannel over onto the back of the board and staple it. Next, turn the board over and smooth the flannel tightly across the face of the board.
3. Holding the flannel snug, press the board, flannel side down, onto the work surface and staple the other three edges of the flannel into place.
4. Cover the stapled edges on the back of the flannel board with strips of masking or plastic tape. Carefully cut the flannel and the tape at the top and bottom along the joint so the board will fold with the flannel-covered sides inside. Straps or handles may be added at the ends of the board. The board is now ready to use. (Note: When using the board, be sure to slant it slightly, so materials used will adhere more readily to the surface.)

Slip-Cover Flannel Board

Materials and Equipment

- cardboard or plywood
- saw to cut plywood
- knife or paper cutter to cut cardboard
- needle and thread

Procedure (Figure 6.2)

Cut the board to the desired size. Cut the flannel so that two pieces are 1″ wider on all sides than the dimensions of the cardboard (or plywood). Sew three sides, slip the flannel over the cardboard, and stitch it closed.

Folding Cardboard Flannel Board

Materials and Equipment

- heavyweight cardboard
- scissors and paper cutter
- tape
- flocked adhesive shelf paper

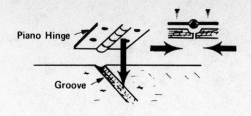

Piano Hinge

Groove

1. Hinging

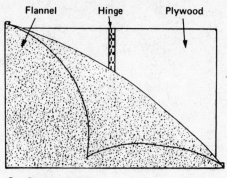

Flannel Hinge Plywood

2. Covering

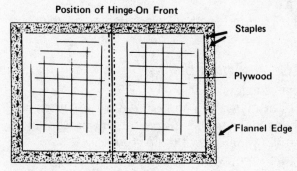

Position of Hinge-On Front

Staples

Plywood

Flannel Edge

3. Flannel Stapled to Board

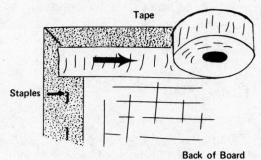

Tape

Staples

Back of Board

4. Taping to Cover Staples

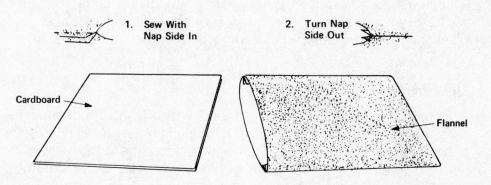

1. Sew With Nap Side In

2. Turn Nap Side Out

Cardboard

Flannel

Figure 6.1
Metal-Hinged Folding Flannel Board

Figure 6.2
Slip-Cover Flannel Board

Display Devices and Study Boards

91

Figure 6.3
Folding Cardboard Flannel
Board

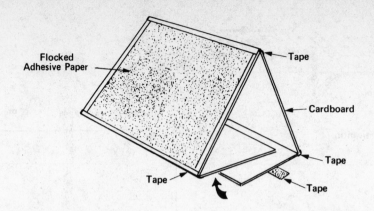

Flocked
Adhesive Paper

Tape

Cardboard

Tape

Tape

Tape

Procedure (Figure 6.3)

1. Cut four pieces of heavyweight cardboard to equal dimensions.
2. Tape as illustrated in Figure 6.3, and cover the two center pieces with flocked adhesive shelf paper.
3. Assemble and tape the boards together, overlapping the two end pieces as shown.

Instructional Materials to Use on Flannel Boards

1. Figures or letters cut out of flannel or felt.
2. Pictures cut from books or magazines and backed with flannel, felt, corduroy, or lightweight sandpaper. Use rubber cement or fast-drying glue to fasten the material to the back of the picture.
3. Small, lightweight pictures printed on textured paper. These often need no backing to keep them on the flannel board.
4. Pictures backed with flocked adhesive shelf paper.
5. String or yarn will adhere to the board without backing.

Flannel Map

If you teach social studies, you may wish to construct a flannel board and draw a map outline directly on the flannel board's surface with India ink, quick-drying paint, or a felt-tipped pen (Figure 6.4). Or, make a satisfactory folding flannel map by drawing a map outline on a piece of unmounted flannel. To use a flannel map of this type, drape the cloth over a chalkboard or bulletin board and fasten it at the top with a strip of pressure-sensitive tape; or, place the map over a flannel board and smooth it into place. Symbols may be added to the outline map to give detail during a presentation. Once you complete a presentation, pull the map loose and store it in a folder or an envelope along with the symbols used.

Flip Chart

A flip chart is a prepared set of paper visuals, usually in a fixed sequential order, placed on a stand for display. The flip chart user usually faces the audience and gives the presentation, flipping the charts at the appropriate time. Notes for each chart may be written on the back of the previously

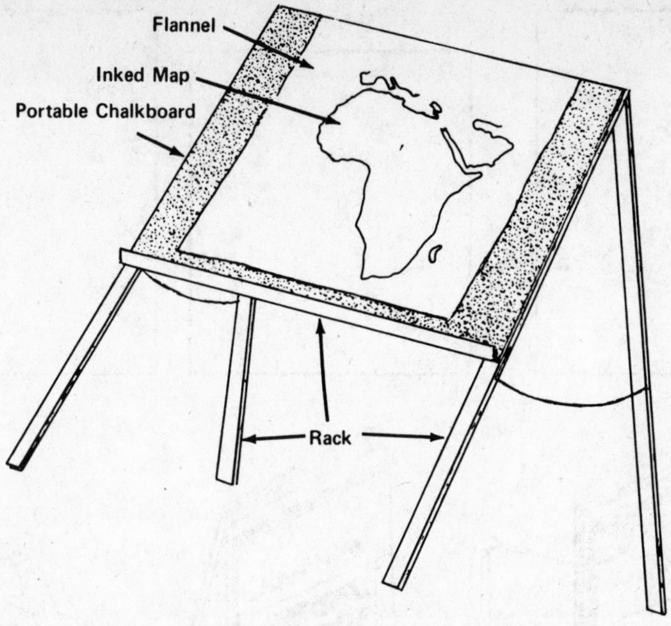

Figure 6.4
Flannel Map

Flannel

Inked Map

Portable Chalkboard

Rack

flipped chart. Small self-adhesive notesheets containing user notes or indexing material may be affixed to the charts as well.

You may also use a flip chart for small group instruction or individualized instruction. Flip charts are portable, inexpensive to produce, and excellent for pacing a presentation.

Materials and Equipment
- chart paper
- heavy cardboard
- two large paper fasteners
- paper punch
- matte knife
- 1" wide tape
- yarn

Procedure (Figure 6.5)
1. Cut the chart paper into the desired size.
2. Cut two pieces of heavy cardboard the same width but 3" longer than the chart paper.
3. Punch two holes in the top edge of the chart paper. Punch two holes in the same position, but 1" lower, on one piece of heavy cardboard.
4. Align the edges of the chart paper, and fasten the chart paper to the cardboard with the paper fasteners. With the chart paper attached, the flip chart should have 1" of cardboard on the top and 2" of cardboard on the bottom.
5. Hinge the two pieces of cardboard across the top with a piece of tape.
6. Punch holes 1" up from the bottom and 1" in on each piece of heavy cardboard, on both sides, and attach the yarn. The yarn will prevent the easel from spreading.

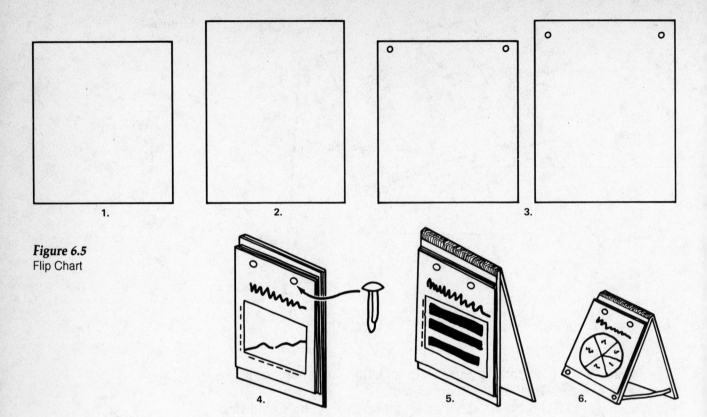

Figure 6.5
Flip Chart

6.2 Magnetic Chalkboards

A magnetic chalkboard is an extremely versatile device that works especially well with presentations requiring repeated use of accurate symbolic representation, or accuracy in scale and form. The magnetic chalkboard is also useful for storytelling, coaching, and presenting lessons that require movement and progression. Cardboard cutouts glued to small magnets will readily adhere to the steel surface of the board. Lightweight pictures may be held in place on the board by magnets placed at the corners. You may supplement magnetic materials with materials drawn on the chalkboard. Many teachers have found the magnetic chalkboard an invaluable addition to their collection of teaching tools.

Framed Magnetic Chalkboard

Materials and Equipment
- ¼" plywood (usually 24" × 36")
- sheet iron, sheet steel, or sheet tin 2" less in length and width than the plywood
- glue or adhesive that will hold metal to wood
- 1" molding, enough to frame the steel
- small brads or nails
- small magnets
- paint brush
- chalkboard paint

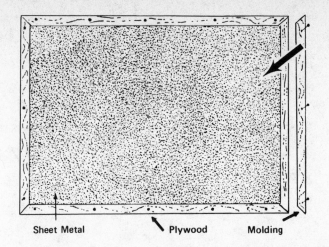

Figure 6.6
Framed Magnetic Chalkboard

Sheet Metal   Plywood   Molding

Procedure (Figure 6.6)

1. Paint the sheet iron or steel with chalkboard paint. If you use galvanized metal, the surface of the metal must first be chemically treated, or cleaned. Coat the surface of the galvanized sheet with common household vinegar and allow to stand for 15 minutes; then wash the sheet with tap water. As soon as the metal dries, it is ready for the application of chalkboard paint or automobile enamel. Apply a minimum of *two coats* of paint, carefully following the manufacturer's directions.

2. When the paint dries, glue the metal to the plywood base, chalkboard (painted) side up, and leave a 1″ border on all sides.

3. Cut the 1″ molding to frame the metal on all sides, and glue or nail the molding to the plywood backing. Finish the molding with paint or varnish if desired.

Combination Magnetic Board and Flannel Board

A combination board is easy to construct, and gives teachers and students many options. The board may be quickly and easily constructed with readily available, inexpensive materials.

Materials and Equipment

- galvanized steel oil-drip pan
- flocked adhesive shelf paper (or flannel and white glue)
- vinegar
- chalkboard paint
- scissors
- chalkdust-filled eraser

Procedure (Figure 6.7)

1. Clean the inside of the drip pan with vinegar and water. Allow it to dry thoroughly, and then apply chalkboard paint according to the directions on the can. When the chalkboard surface is dry, pat it and rub it with a chalkdust-filled eraser. The chalkboard will be easier to erase if you have already rubbed chalk into the surface of the board.

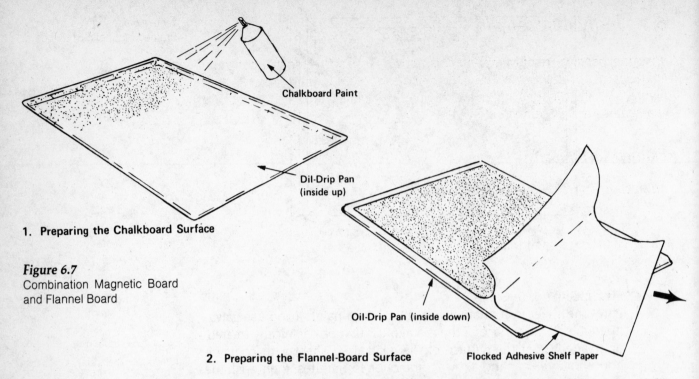

Chalkboard Paint

Dil-Drip Pan (inside up)

1. **Preparing the Chalkboard Surface**

Figure 6.7
Combination Magnetic Board
and Flannel Board

Oil-Drip Pan (inside down)

2. **Preparing the Flannel-Board Surface**

Flocked Adhesive Shelf Paper

2. Turn the pan over and attach one end of the adhesive paper to the board, pulling off the protective sheet as you apply the adhesive paper. If you use flannel instead of the flocked paper, cut the flannel to size, mark the pan area to be covered, and spread glue on it. Roll the flannel onto the glue as soon as it becomes tacky, using a ruler to prevent wrinkles. The combination board is now ready to use.

Preparing Materials to Use with Magnetic Boards

Construction paper, tagboard, and cardboard may be used to prepare magnetic board symbols (see Figure 6.8). Draw the symbols, cut them out, and tape or glue magnets to their backs. Small, real objects may be prepared and displayed in the same way. Taped magnets may be removed easily for use on other symbols. Plastic magnetic strips are self-adhesive, easy to use, and may be cut to size with a pair of scissors. Display pictures and other graphics on the surface of the board by placing magnets on the picture's corners, as illustrated.

Figure 6.8
Materials for Use with
Magnetic Boards

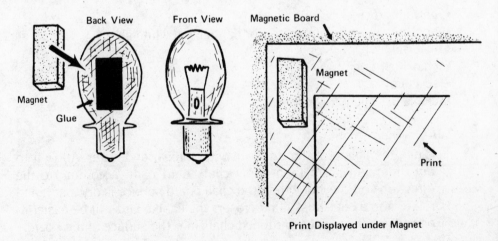

Back View   Front View   Magnetic Board

Magnet

Glue

Magnet

Print

Print Displayed under Magnet

Display Devices and Study Boards

6.3 Individual Chalkboards

With inexpensive, readily available materials, you may prepare individual chalkboards for students to use at their desks or in learning centers (see Figure 6.9). Instructions for preparing painted chalkboards and cardboard chalkboards are presented below.

Painted Chalkboard

Materials and Equipment
- masonite or plywood
- saw
- chalkboard paint (brush or aerosol type)
- shellac or varnish
- brush
- brush cleaner or turpentine

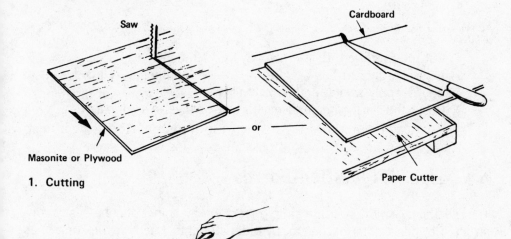

Figure 6.9
Individual Chalkboards

1. Cutting

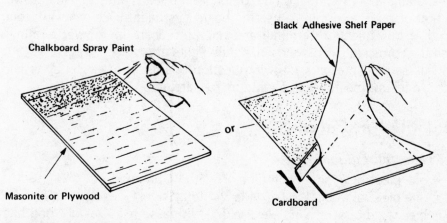

2. Applying Shellac

3. Painting or Covering

Procedure

1. Cut wood or masonite to size (usually 8″ × 10″ or 11″ × 14″).
2. Prepare the surface for paint by coating it with shellac. Allow the shellac to dry completely before proceeding.
3. Paint the surface with chalkboard paint. Chalkboard paint is available in cans for brush application, and in aerosol spray cans. Two coats of paint are needed. Follow the manufacturer's directions. When the paint is thoroughly dry, prepare the surface to take chalk by rubbing it with a chalk-filled eraser. The board is now ready to use.

Cardboard Chalkboard

Materials and Equipment

- heavyweight, pressed cardboard
- black adhesive shelf paper (Con-Tact or other)
- ruler
- scissors
- paper cutter

Procedure

1. Cut the cardboard to size (usually 8″ × 10″ or 11″ × 14″).
2. If the cardboard has a smooth surface, no shellac is needed. If in doubt, apply shellac and allow it to dry.
3. Cover the cardboard surface with black adhesive shelf paper.

6.4   Electric Question-Boards

The electric question-board, a simple teaching machine, may be easily constructed by classroom teachers or by older students. Use it as a testing or as a learning device. In addition to motivating students, the electric question-board helps to promote cooperative and peer group learning. This device provides many hours of useful and interesting instruction, and it may be used in any subject area.

An electric question-board is designed with a question terminal on one side and an answer terminal on the other. Next to each question and answer is a bolt or a piece of foil. To use the board, a student uses two wires, one placed on the question terminal and one placed on the answer terminal. When the correct answer is chosen, a bulb lights up.

This section presents electric question-boards with wire circuits and electric question-boards with aluminum foil circuits.

Board with Wire Circuits

Materials and Equipment

- one piece of wood: 1″ soft pine or ¼″ to ½″ plywood, 18″ × 24″ (top)
- one piece of wood 4″ to 6″ wide, 24″ long (sides)
- brace and bits, or hand electric drill with assorted sizes of wood bits

- small low-voltage bulb
- battery
- battery bracket
- socket
- saw
- several feet of insulated wire (bell wire or other single-conductor wire)
- 16 stove bolts with nuts and washers
- household cement or other permanent waterproof glue
- tagboard or other pliable, lightweight cardboard
- scissors
- finishing nails
- hammer
- pencil
- yardstick or ruler
- staples

Procedure (Figure 6.10)

1. Cut the wooden top to 18″ × 24″. Draw a diagonal line from one lower corner of the 4″ × 24″ board to the opposite upper corner and saw along this line. The two triangular-shaped halves will be the sides of the electric question-board.

2. Nail the top to the sides. Draw vertical lines from the top to the bottom of the board face, approximately 4″ from each side. Draw eight short *horizontal* lines spaced every 2⅝″ along both *vertical* lines to serve as drill references. Drill eight holes on each side for stove bolts; then, drill a hole in the *center* of the board for the low-voltage bulb.

3. Fasten the stove bolts in place, with the washers and nuts together on the *underside* of the board. Make question and answer holders from tagboard or light cardboard by folding the edges of the cardboard to form a card holder. Glue these into place beside the stove bolts. Fasten the lamp socket into the hole provided, and screw the low-voltage bulb into place.

4. Wire the underside of the box, connecting an *answer*-terminal bolt to a *question*-terminal bolt for each pair of questions and answers (eight pairs in all). Fasten the battery bracket to one side of the box on the inside, and connect a wire from one end of the battery bracket to the bulb socket. A connecting *answer line* should go from the bulb socket to the outside of the box. Be sure to allow enough line to reach all the answers provided on the face of the board. The *question line* should extend to the outside of the box from the battery and be long enough to reach all the questions.

The electric question-board is now ready for operation. Whenever a correct answer is matched to a question (the answer line to an answer-terminal bolt and the question line to the proper question-terminal bolt) the bulb lights up, confirming the correct response.

To keep students from memorizing the location of matching terminals, occasionally rewire the connections from answer terminals to question terminals and change the placement of questions and answers accordingly.

Figure 6.10
Electric Question-Board with
Wire Circuits

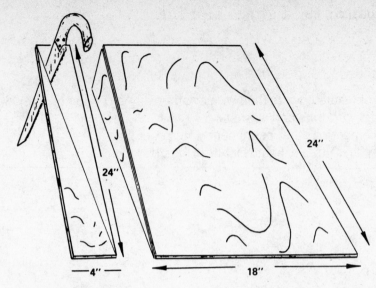

1. Assembling Board

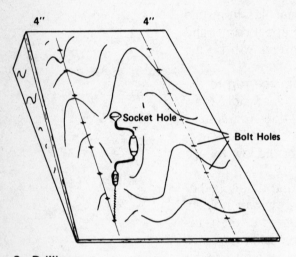

2. Drilling

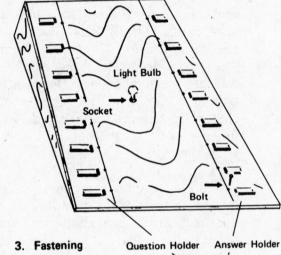

3. Fastening

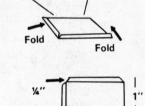

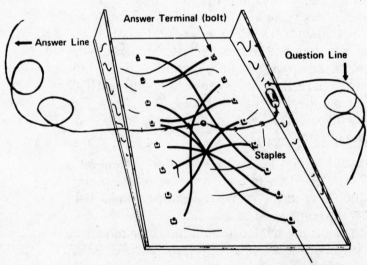

4. Wiring

Display Devices and Study Boards

Board with Aluminum Foil Circuits: Type One

Constructing an electric question-board with cardboard and aluminum foil is easy and inexpensive. Pupils as young as ten can make these boards and use them for presenting interesting information to their classmates.

Materials and Equipment

- paper
- aluminum foil
- rubber cement
- paper cutter or scissors
- cardboard or manila folder
- tape
- hole punch
- transparent plastic sheet or plastic bag
- battery and matching lamp bulb
- No. 22 stranded, rubber-coated copper wire
- one brad
- pencil
- ruler

Procedure (Figure 6.11)

1. Cement the foil to the paper with rubber cement.
2. Cut the paper-backed foil into strips. Cut the cardboard to the desired size; two pieces the *same size* will be needed.
3. Punch holes one inch in from the edge, or as far in as your hole punch will reach on both sides of one piece of cardboard. The number of holes and the space between the holes depends on the length of the programs you intend to design. Usually eight holes spaced one inch apart will do. Tape the cardboard pieces together at *one edge only*. Draw lines from *question holes* to *answer holes* using a pencil and ruler. Tape the foil strips to the board, *foil side down*, with each end of a strip covering a hole as shown, until all the circuit lines have been covered.
4. Fold the cardboard pieces together and close the open edge with tape. Attach a transparent plastic bag or sheet of plastic to the board with tape, as shown. The bag or plastic is the program holder; it should fit between the question and answer holes.
5. Construct an answer indicator. Cut two pieces of cardboard the same size, both larger than the battery and bulb when the bulb is placed against the tip of the battery. Cut two pieces of wire, eighteen inches in length each. Strip off two inches of insulation from each end of both wires. Tightly tape one end of one probe to the bottom of the battery. Tightly tape one end of the other probe to the screw base of the bulb. Push the bulb tightly against the tip of the battery, and tape the battery and bulb in place. A bracket, if available, is better than tape for holding the battery and bulb in place; hardware and radio stores often sell such brackets at little cost. Tape the answer indicator to a piece of cardboard, as shown. An additional piece of cardboard is used as a cover.

Figure 6.11
Electric Question-Board with
Aluminum Foil Circuits

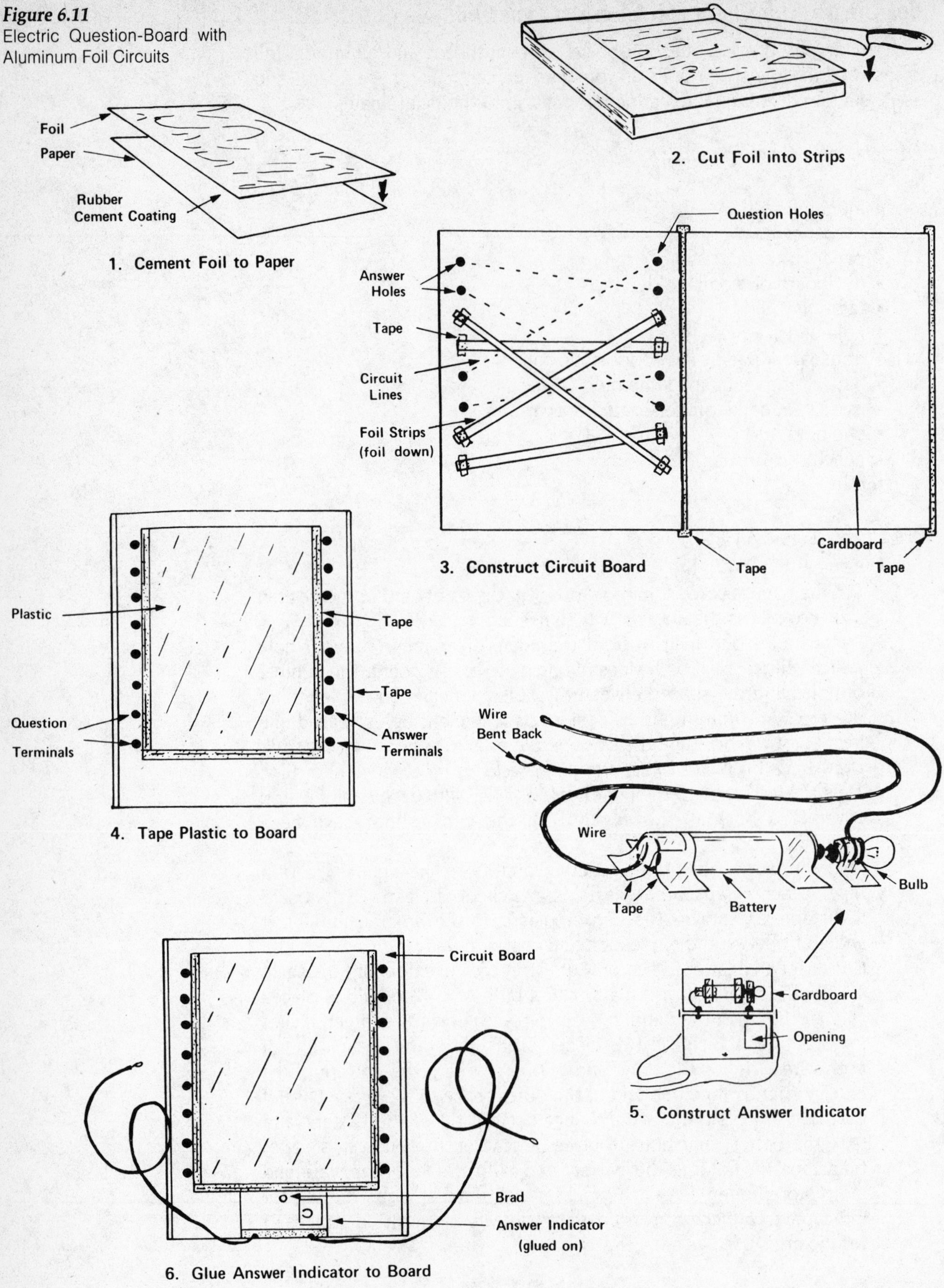

Foil

Paper

Rubber
Cement Coating

1. **Cement Foil to Paper**

2. **Cut Foil into Strips**

Question Holes

Answer
Holes

Tape

Circuit
Lines

Foil Strips
(foil down)

3. **Construct Circuit Board**

Tape

Cardboard

Tape

Plastic

Tape

Tape

Question
Terminals

Answer
Terminals

4. **Tape Plastic to Board**

Wire
Bent Back

Wire

Tape

Battery

Bulb

Cardboard

Opening

5. **Construct Answer Indicator**

Circuit Board

Brad

Answer Indicator
(glued on)

6. **Glue Answer Indicator to Board**

6. Glue the answer indicator to the circuit board with rubber cement. Fold the cover of the indicator closed so only the bulb shows; fasten it down with a brad. The board is ready to use as soon as questions and answers, matching the circuitry, are printed or typed on a piece of paper and put behind the plastic sheet or into the plastic bag.

When you touch the foil to the left of a question with the question wire and, at the same time, touch the foil to the right of the correct answer with the answer wire, the bulb should light up, confirming the correct choice.

Board with Aluminum Foil Circuits: Type Two

The electric question-board shown in Figure 6.12 is made with a circuit tester.

Materials and Equipment
- household aluminum foil
- cardboard (tag or file folders work well)
- power-off circuit tester (available from auto supply, hardware, and electronic stores)
- cellophane tape
- pencil
- rubber cement or glue
- hole punch or matte knife

The circuit tester (Figure 6.13) contains a battery or batteries and a lamp. One end of the circuit tester has a wire with a clip, and the other end has a probe.

The lamp in the circuit tester lights up when an electrical circuit is complete. Because aluminum conducts electricity, when you touch both the probe and the clip to a piece of aluminum foil (Figure 6.14), an electrical circuit is created between them, and the lamp lights up.

Figure 6.12
Electric Question-Board Made with Cardboard and Aluminum Foil

Figure 6.13
Circuit Tester

Probe—**Be sure** the point is dull; bend or file it.

Clip   Wire   Batteries   Lamp

Figure 6.14
Electrical Circuit

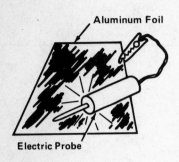

Aluminum Foil

Electric Probe

The circuit boards are made of a piece of aluminum foil sandwiched between two pieces of cardboard (Figure 6.15).

The questions have holes next to them that expose the aluminum foil. The *correct* answer has a hole next to it that also exposes the aluminum foil. The *wrong* answer has a hole next to it that exposes aluminum foil *insulated* from the circuit foil by cellophane tape. When the probe is placed in a question hole and the clip in an answer hole, *only* the correct answer will light the lamp, for the wrong answer is insulated from the electrical circuit by the cellophane tape.

Procedure (Figure 6.16)

1. Cut both pieces of cardboard and the aluminum foil to the same size.
2. Prepare the top piece of cardboard by making the holes with a hole punch or matte knife.
3. Use rubber cement or glue to bond the aluminum foil to the bottom piece of cardboard.
4. Place the top piece of cardboard over the aluminum foil. Using a pencil, outline the *wrong* answer holes on the foil. Place cellophane tape over the *wrong* answers outlined on the foil. Glue aluminum foil over the cellophane tape, taking care not to allow the *dummy* answer foil to touch the circuit foil.
5. Place the top piece of cardboard on top of the aluminum foil, and fasten the edges together with glue, tape, or staples.

Figure 6.15
Circuit Board

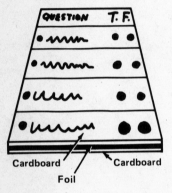

Cardboard   Cardboard
Foil

Figure 6.16
Circuit Board Construction

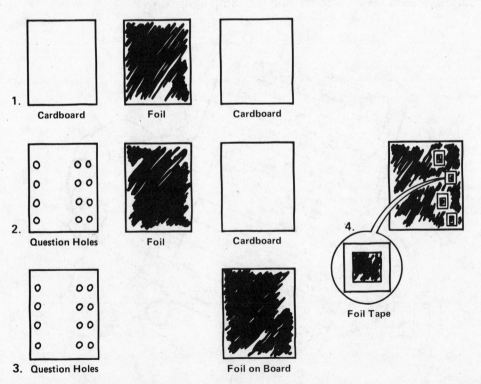

Display Devices and Study Boards

6.5 Display Easel

A display easel for mounted materials is easy to make and quite useful. Use the easel to attract attention, to motivate students, or to display materials in learning centers.

Materials and Equipment
- 24-ply cardboard
- pencil
- tape
- straightedge (ruler or T-square)
- knife or razor blade

Procedure (Figure 6.17)

1. Refer to the pattern layout in Figure 6.17 to determine the proportions for the display easel halves. Determine the size of the easel by finding the dimensions of the mounted materials to be displayed. Measure and draw one side of the easel on 24-ply cardboard as

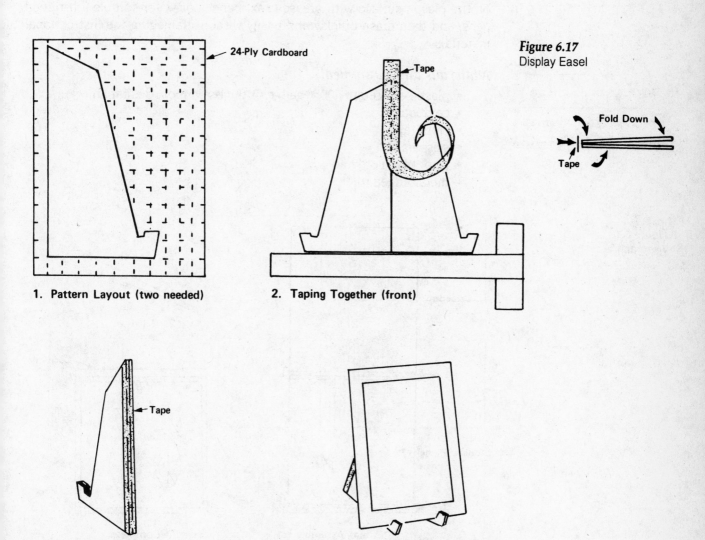

Figure 6.17
Display Easel

1. **Pattern Layout (two needed)**

2. **Taping Together (front)**

3. **Taping (back)**

4. **Finished Easel with Mounted Material**

illustrated. Cut this side out, lay it on a second piece of cardboard, and trace the outline with a pencil. Cut out the second half.

2. Join the two pieces together with tape as shown, using a straight-edge (T-square) to line up the bottom edges of the cardboard pieces.
3. Fold the two pieces with the *tape inside*, and apply tape to the *back* of the easel as shown. This double-taping adds rigidity and strength to the stand.
4. Display materials on the easel as shown.

You may also decorate easels with patterned shelf paper or spray them with acrylic paints.

6.6 *Visograph*

A visograph is a versatile, transparent-faced display pocket with one open edge. Use it to display unmounted pictures under a protective plastic covering and to hold work sheets, tests, and outline maps. You can write or draw on the plastic surface with grease (wax) pencils or water-soluble felt-tipped pens, and then erase quickly and easily without damaging the instructional materials.

Materials and Equipment
- plastic or acetate (.005" gauge or thicker is most desirable)
- cardboard
- cloth tape
- scissors
- razor blade or knife
- metal-edged ruler

Figure 6.18
Visograph

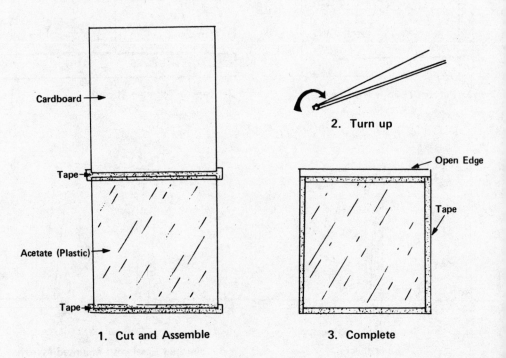

Cardboard

Tape

Acetate (Plastic)

Tape

1. Cut and Assemble

2. Turn up

Open Edge

Tape

3. Complete

Display Devices and Study Boards

Procedure (Figure 6.18)

1. Cut the cardboard base to the desired dimensions (according to the size of materials to be inserted into the visograph). A base of 11″ × 14″ will accommodate most pictures and work sheets. Cut the plastic to the same *width*, but slightly *shorter in length*. Cut three pieces of tape longer than the width of the cardboard. Apply one piece to the *back bottom edge* of the cardboard, allowing the tape to *overlap* by half its width. Turn the cardboard over, and place the plastic (acetate) sheet on the sticky tape as illustrated, leaving a separation between board and plastic of about ⅛″. Add a second piece of tape over *the top of the first piece* of tape; trim off the excess tape at the ends. Add a third piece of tape at the opposite edge of the plastic sheet and fold over. Trim off the excess tape.
2. Fold the plastic sheet up and onto the cardboard.
3. Tape along both sides. The visograph is now ready to use.

6.7 *Visograph Accordion Fold*

A visograph accordion fold is very useful for displaying pictures in sequence, or for giving directions for a particular assignment. This type of visograph is usually placed on a table.

Materials and Equipment
- several completed visographs
- tape
- scissors
- yardstick or T-square

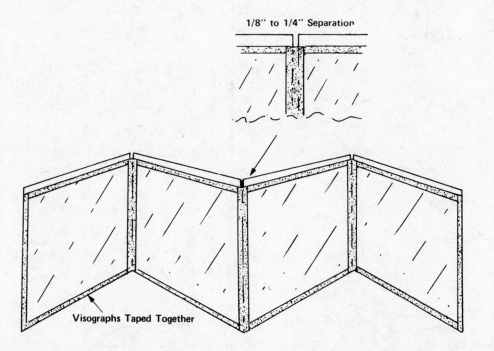

1/8″ to 1/4″ Separation

Visographs Taped Together

Figure 6.19
Visograph Accordion Fold

Procedure (Figure 6.19)

1. Place the visographs *face up* on the table. Separate them, leaving ⅛" to ¼" in between, as illustrated.
2. Use a yardstick or T-square to align the bottom edges of the visographs.
3. Apply tape to hold the sections together.
4. Turn the assembly over and apply strips of tape on the back side of each fold. The visograph accordion fold is now ready to use.

6.8 Diorama Stages

Dioramas are effective, easy-to-construct displays that are useful in a number of subject areas, including language arts, social studies, and science. Diorama stages allow teachers and students to communicate ideas by placing objects in realistic, three-dimensional surroundings. Objects that may be displayed include plastic models, plaster-of-Paris models, papier-mache figures, small specimens, and cardboard cutouts. Teachers and students can illustrate what the class is studying by constructing a scene on a diorama stage. Several types of diorama stages are illustrated in Figure 6.20. One stage, the semicircular stage, is discussed and illustrated below in a step-by-step presentation.

Figure 6.20
Diorama Stages

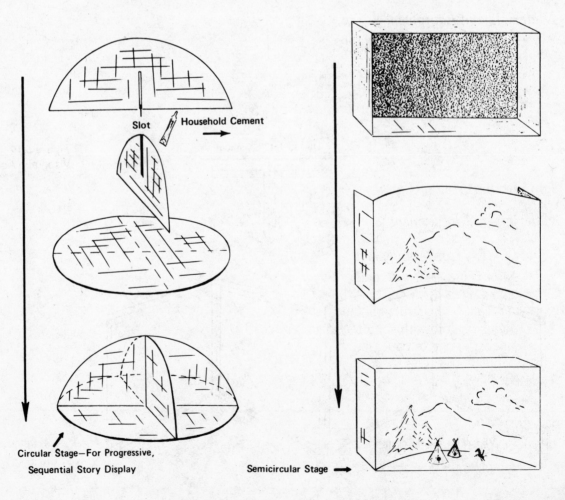

Slot   Household Cement

Circular Stage—For Progressive,
Sequential Story Display

Semicircular Stage ➡

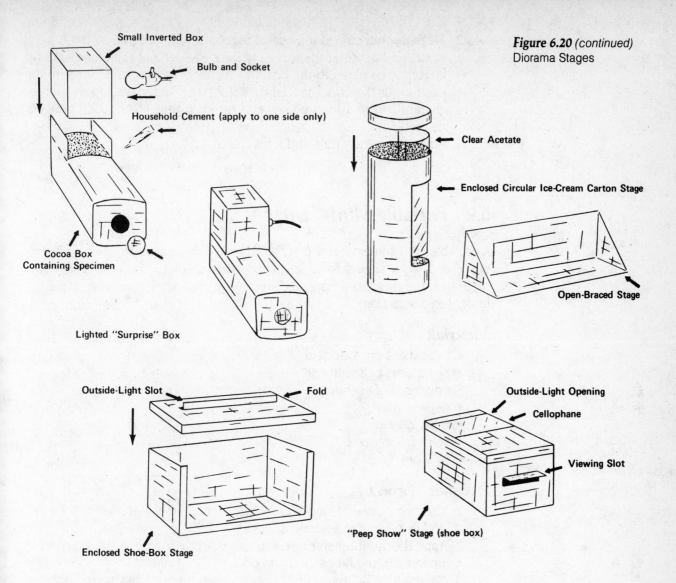

Figure 6.20 *(continued)*
Diorama Stages

Small Inverted Box

Bulb and Socket

Household Cement (apply to one side only)

Clear Acetate

Enclosed Circular Ice-Cream Carton Stage

Cocoa Box
Containing Specimen

Lighted "Surprise" Box

Open-Braced Stage

Outside-Light Slot

Fold

Outside-Light Opening

Cellophane

Viewing Slot

Enclosed Shoe-Box Stage

"Peep Show" Stage (shoe box)

Semicircular Stage

Materials and Equipment

- box
- paints or felt-tipped pens
- scissors or other cutting devices
- objects for display
- tagboard or construction paper
- extension cord with socket and lamp if the display is to be lit
- rubber cement or paper glue
- stapler and staples
- pencil
- sheet of paper

Procedure

1. Sketch the layout on a sheet of paper. Select an appropriate box and remove one side or the top.

2. Measure and cut off a piece of tagboard that is equal to the length, width, and depth of the box. Fold back each end of the tagboard strip so it may be glued to the box. Lay the tagboard flat and sketch in the desired background material. Refold the tagboard, apply rubber cement to the folded edges, and fasten it into place. Use staples if desired.
3. Add display materials and label the display.

6.9 Portable Mini-Center

A portable mini-center (Figure 6.21) holds materials such as directions, illustrations, and work sheets in a small, portable display. The unit also helps separate students from one another by acting as a partition, reducing unwanted distractions.

Materials
- two pieces of cardboard, 9″ × 11″
- two pieces of acetate, 9″ × 11″
- one piece of acetate, 8½″ × 10″
- paper cutter
- tape, ½″ wide
- spirit master box
- scissors

Procedure (Figure 6.22)
1. Cut two pieces of cardboard 9″ × 11″, two pieces of acetate 9″ × 11″, and one piece of acetate 8½″ × 10″.
2. Tape the spirit master box, top and bottom, together. Cut a 1½″ wide opening in the lid as in Figure 6.22.
3. Tape a 9″ × 11″ piece of acetate to each piece of cardboard, and the 8½″ × 10″ acetate to the box, taping on *three sides* as shown in Figures 6.22 and 6.23.
4. Place the cardboard wing on a book, with the wing separated at least ¼″ from the edge of the box. Apply tape as shown in Figure 6.24.

Figure 6.21
Portable Mini-Center

Display Devices and Study Boards

5. Lift up the wing, fold it over, and pull it tight. Apply a strip of tape along the edge of the wing and box, as shown in Figure 6.25.
6. The bottom view of the completed Mini-Center is shown in Figure 6.26.

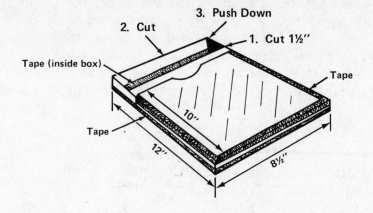

Figure 6.22
Side View

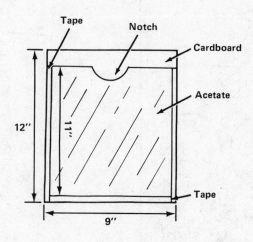

Figure 6.23
Front View

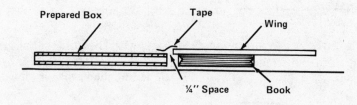

Figure 6.24
Tape the Wing

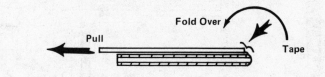

Figure 6.25
Fold Wing Over

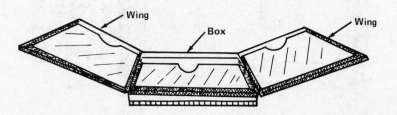

Figure 6.26
Bottom View

6.10 *Penny Teaching Machines*

Inexpensive drill or testing devices, called *penny teaching machines*, can be made from construction paper, tagboard, or other heavyweight paper. You may wish to laminate these simple devices and decorate them with creative graphics. If students have a chance to construct and program the devices, they will learn as they put them together. The *Mini-Computer* (Figure 6.27) illustrates a penny teaching machine; a simple linear program.

The teaching machine shown in Figure 6.28 is excellent for peer group learning. Make the device out of lightweight cardboard and place a pencil in

Figure 6.27
Mini-Computer

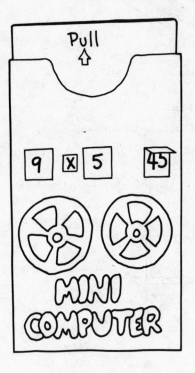

The Program:
Prepare on standard sized
paper or on cardboard.

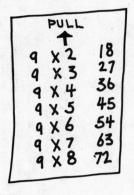

The Program Holder:
Use construction paper or cardboard.

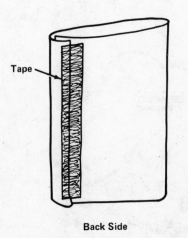

Back Side   **Front Side**

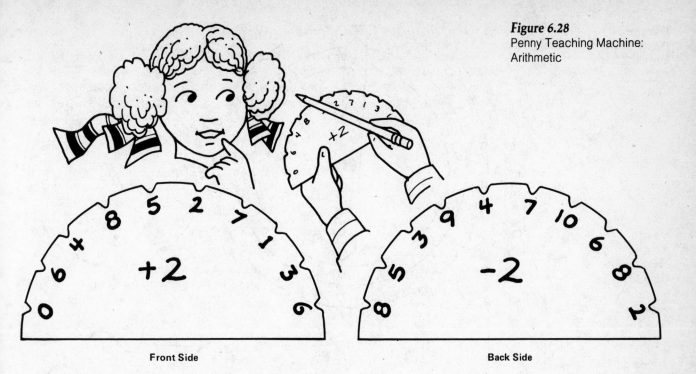

Figure 6.28
Penny Teaching Machine:
Arithmetic

Front Side

Back Side

the slot as shown. Have students work together to drill each other with the penny teaching machine.

Figures 6.29 through 6.32 illustrate various penny teaching machines students can make. Creative teachers and students can invent others.

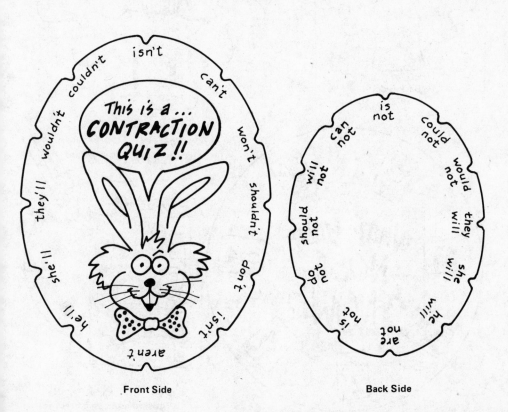

Figure 6.29
Penny Teaching Machine:
Word Contraction

Front Side

Back Side

Figure 6.30
Penny Teaching Machine:
Multiplication

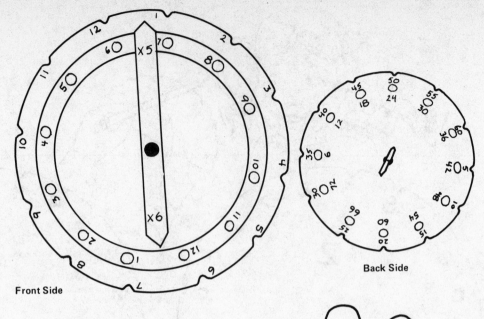

Front Side

Back Side

Figure 6.31
Penny Teaching Machine:
Arithmetic

Back Side

Front Side

Figure 6.32
Penny Teaching Machine:
Identifying Smells

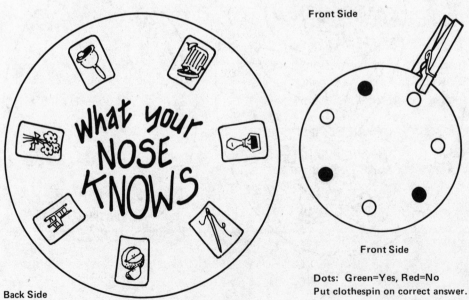

What your
NOSE
KNOWS

Back Side

Front Side

Dots: Green=Yes, Red=No
Put clothespin on correct answer.

Maps, Models, and Mock-Ups

VII

Teacher-made and student-made maps, models, and mock-ups are very helpful for motivating students and explaining specific concepts. This chapter includes materials useful in the social sciences, the natural sciences, aerospace study, and geometry.

7.1 Maps

Several types of maps can be constructed by teachers and students to facilitate learning and understanding in social studies. Plastic-surfaced maps and three-dimensional maps are useful for teachers at all grade levels.

Plastic-Surfaced Map

A plastic-surfaced map is most helpful when you need to add details to a map during a presentation or when you plan to check student understanding. Write on the map surface with a wax crayon or a china-marking pencil. These marks can be easily erased with a soft cloth.

Materials and Equipment
- map, mounted on poster board
- clear acetate sheet, large enough to cover the poster board
- tape
- scissors

Procedure (Figure 7.1)
1. Select the map to be used for instructional purposes, and mount it on poster board (or other mounting board). To mount the map,

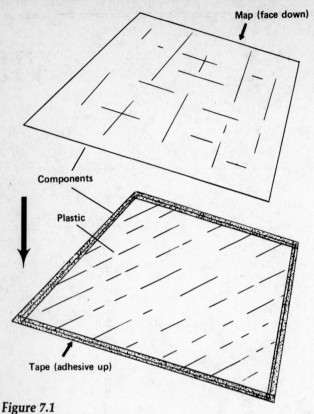

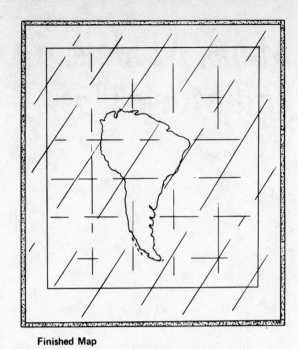

Finished Map

Figure 7.1
Plastic-Surfaced Map

consider the permanent rubber-cement method (page 45) or the dry-mount method (page 46). If a map outline is needed, consider tracing a map projected from a book or slide (page 174) directly onto poster board instead of using a mounted map.

2. Cut a sheet of clear acetate the size of the poster board with the map on it, and lay it on a flat surface.

3. Cut four strips of tape to the length of each edge of the acetate sheet. Attach the tape along each edge, allowing half of the width of each tape strip to protrude beyond the edge of the acetate on all sides.

4. Turn the acetate sheet over so the sticky side of the tape is up. Lay the poster board, with the map face down, on the acetate sheet.

5. Fold the tape over onto the back of the poster board, and press it into place. The plastic-surfaced map is now ready to use.

Three-Dimensional Map

Constructing and using three-dimensional maps may be a very worthwhile educational experience. Papier-mâché, salt and flour, and sawdust may be used to produce effective maps for teaching and learning situations.

Materials and Equipment

- heavy cardboard or light plywood
- pencil

- map
- molding material (prepared papier-mâché, salt and flour, or sawdust)
- paint and paintbrush
- weights
- plastic spray

Procedure (Figure 7.2)

1. Outline the map on heavy cardboard or light plywood.
2. Select one of the molding materials described below (papier-mâché, salt and flour, or sawdust), and prepare it as directed. Apply it to the map and shape it.
3. When the map is shaped and molded, place weights on its corners to prevent it from warping. Allow it to dry completely.
4. Paint the map as desired.
5. When the map has dried, protect the surface with a coating of plastic spray.

PAPIER-MÂCHÉ

Papier-mâché maps are made from paper strips (newspaper or toweling) soaked in smooth, creamy wheat paste. Apply the paper strips to the map and mold them into the desired formations. Use large, crumpled strips of paper for mountain formations.

SALT AND FLOUR

Salt-and-flour maps are made from a mixture of equal parts of salt and flour moistened with water. Mold the mixture into the shapes desired.

SAWDUST

Sawdust, available from lumber yards, is an excellent medium for making three-dimensional maps. (Note: Do *not* use redwood or cedar sawdust.) To prepare the mixture, add wheat paste to the sawdust, and moisten with water until easy to mold.

THREE-DIMENSIONAL MAP

Wood Surface

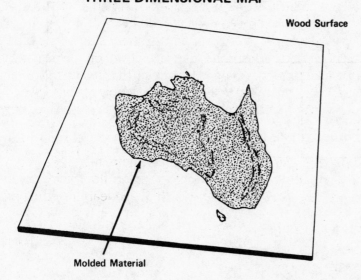

Molded Material

Figure 7.2
Three-Dimensional Map

7.2 Models of Geometric Solids

Cardboard and transparent models of geometric solids may be made easily by teachers or students (see Figure 7.3). These models are especially useful in mathematics study.

To make transparent models, cut out the pattern pages from this manual and copy the patterns onto thermal transparency film. A film producing a *black line* on *color background* is especially good. For printing directions, see "Thermal-Copy Transparencies" (pp. 25–26). Cut the patterns out, fold them, and tape them together with transparent tape.

A Ditto master may be made directly from the patterns using either a Thermo-Fax machine and master, or a Masterfax machine and thermal master. Ledger paper or construction paper may be cut to size and printed from the master, providing enough prints for all students to use if desired. Cut the patterns out, fold them, and paste them together.

For large models, project the patterns onto cardboard using an opaque projector. Then trace, cut out, fold, and glue the patterns together.

Figure 7.3
Patterns for Geometric Solids

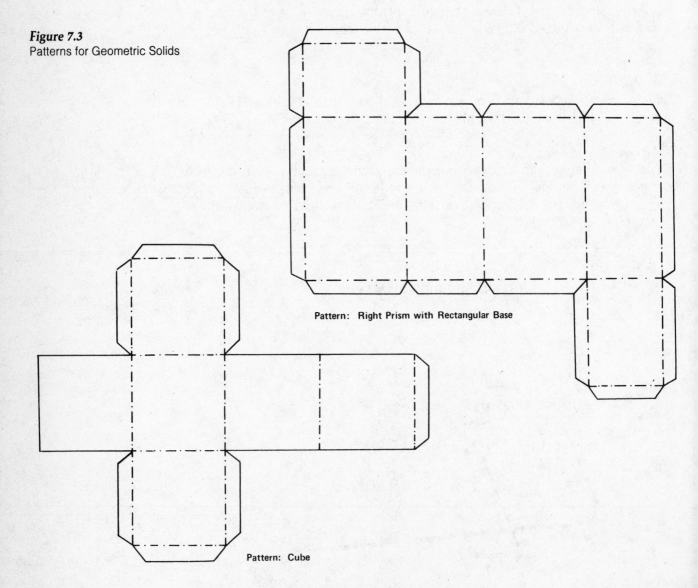

Pattern: Right Prism with Rectangular Base

Pattern: Cube

Maps, Models, and Mock-Ups

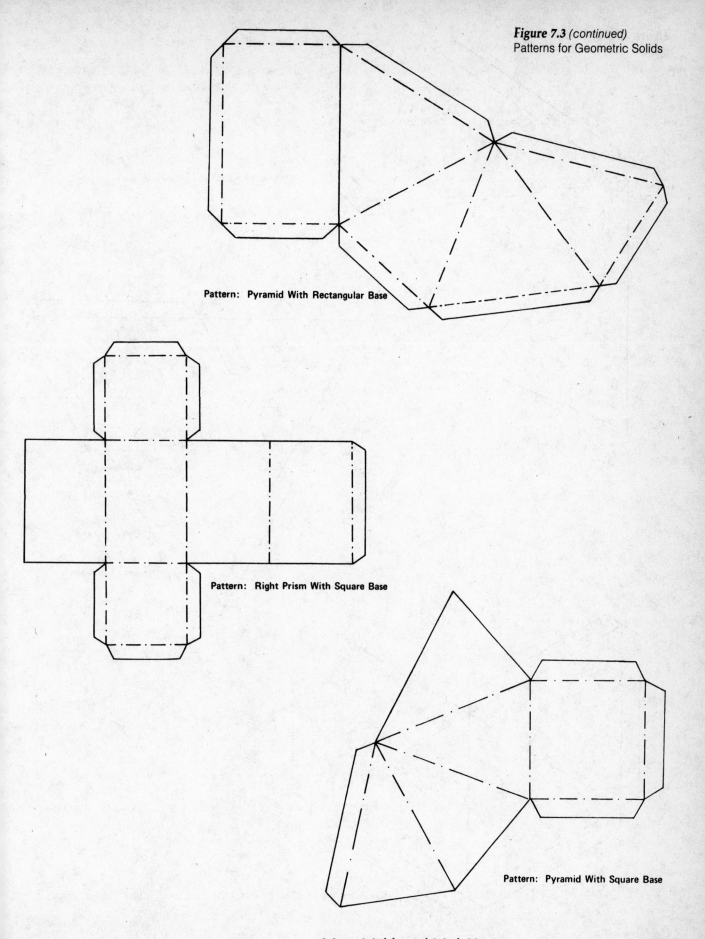

Figure 7.3 *(continued)*
Patterns for Geometric Solids

Pattern: Pyramid With Rectangular Base

Pattern: Right Prism With Square Base

Pattern: Pyramid With Square Base

Figure 7.3 *(continued)*
Patterns for Geometric Solids

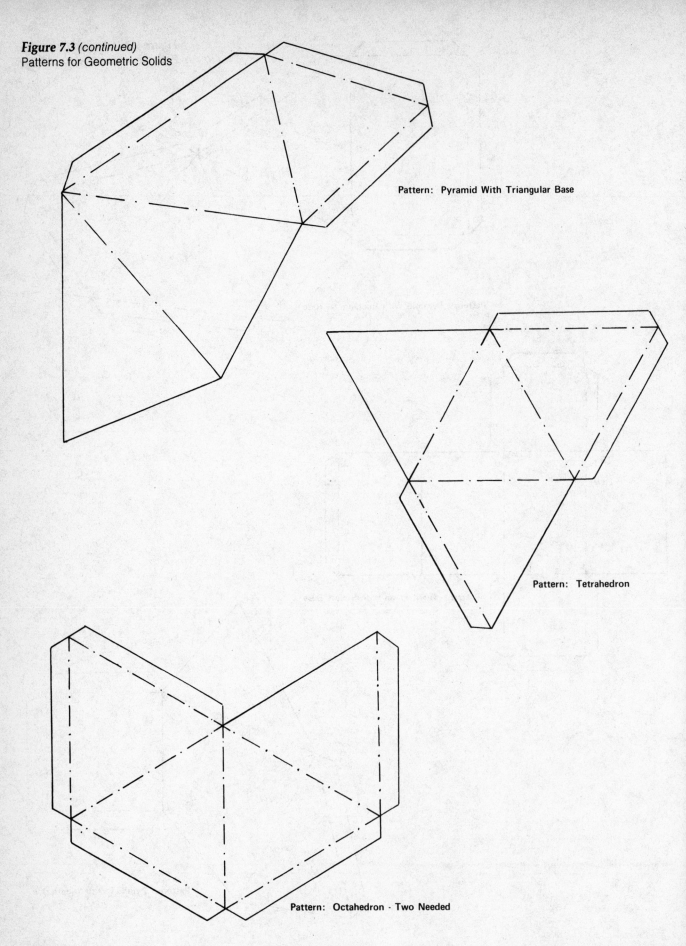

Pattern: Pyramid With Triangular Base

Pattern: Tetrahedron

Pattern: Octahedron - Two Needed

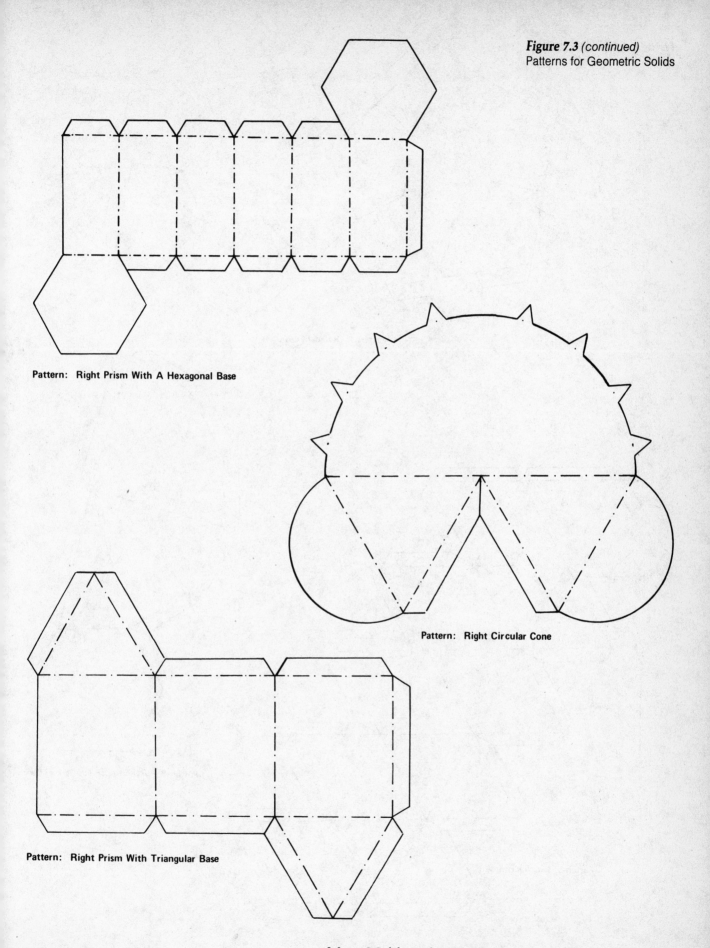

Pattern: Right Prism With A Hexagonal Base

Pattern: Right Circular Cone

Pattern: Right Prism With Triangular Base

Figure 7.3 *(continued)*
Patterns for Geometric Solids

Figure 7.3 (continued)
Patterns for Geometric Solids

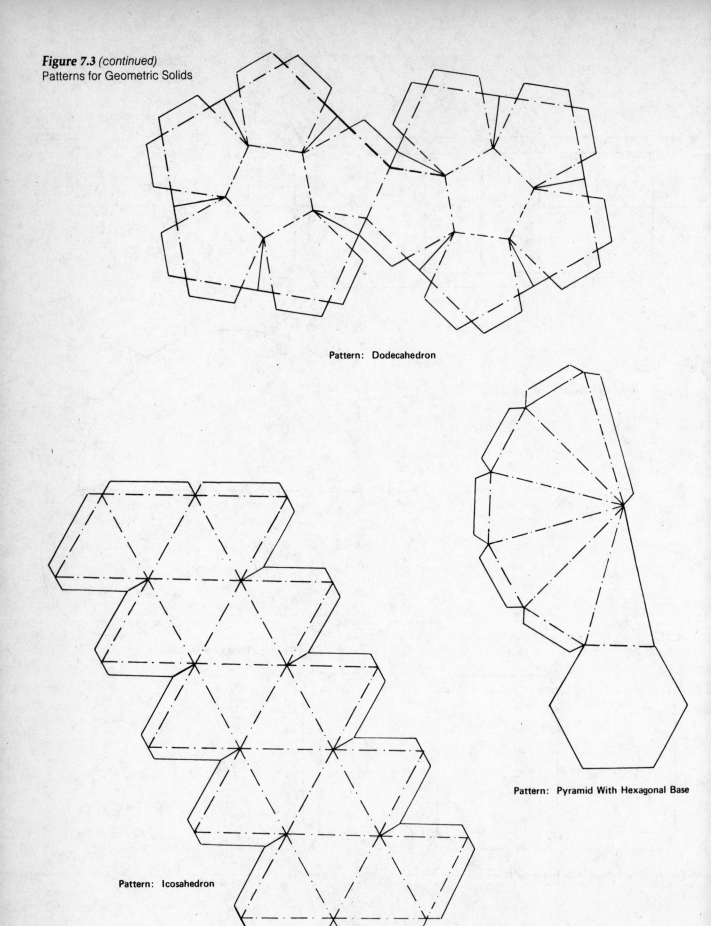

Pattern: Dodecahedron

Pattern: Pyramid With Hexagonal Base

Pattern: Icosahedron

7.3 Weather Instruments

Several simple weather instruments that will help stimulate interest in weather study can be constructed easily by students or teachers. Five kinds of weather instruments are described and illustrated in the following pages.

Anemometer

A model anemometer, used to estimate wind speed, can be easily made from readily available materials.

Materials and Equipment

- four conical paper cups; *or* the halves of two small hollow rubber balls or ping-pong balls (cut with a razor blade)
- two kite sticks or other small, light sticks, approximately 1' long
- one pencil with the eraser intact
- small finishing nail
- ball of clay or plaster of Paris for the base of the anemometer
- household cement
- hammer
- petroleum jelly or machine oil

Procedure (Figure 7.4)

1. Glue paper cups to the ends of two sticks, or cut two balls in half, and glue each cup or ball to the sticks as illustrated.

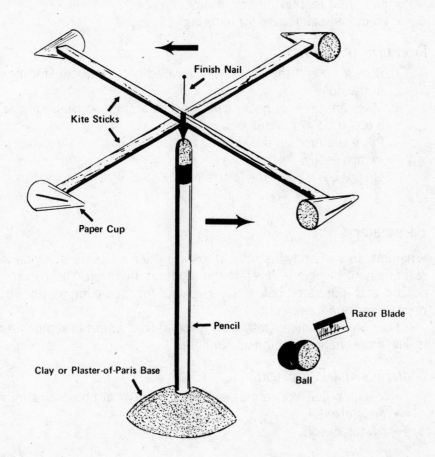

Figure 7.4
Anemometer

2. Cross the sticks and glue them together with household cement.
3. When the cement is dry, make a hole in the center of the cross with a finishing nail. Lubricate the hole with petroleum jelly or machine oil.
4. Nail the assembly to the end of the pencil, and secure the pencil in the clay or plaster of Paris. The anemometer is now ready to use.

If the anemometer becomes sluggish, enlarge the nail hole *slightly*. A very small washer or a bead on the nail between the eraser and the crossed sticks will also help, especially if it is lubricated with a drop of machine oil. A satisfactory washer can be made with a button-sized piece of aluminum foil or thin, smooth cardboard.

A small, light anemometer may be made from drinking straws and paper cups. Follow the same general procedure outlined above.

Wind Vane

Constructing and using a wind vane may be an interesting educational experience for students studying weather. A simple wind vane is illustrated here.

Materials and Equipment
- soft wood, 6″ × 6″ × ½″
- steel knitting needle
- test tube
- heavy cardboard or shingle wood
- rubber band
- nail or bit for making hole in wooden base
- paint and paintbrush for lettering

Procedure (Figure 7.5)
1. Bore a hole in the center of the wood base. Insert a knitting needle in the hole.
2. Make an arrow of heavy cardboard or shingle wood and attach it to a test tube with a rubber band.
3. Place the tube on the knitting needle and balance the vane so that it swings easily.
4. On the base, paint the letters *N, S, E*, and *W* to indicate directions.

Barometer

A barometer is a handy instrument to have when a class is studying weather, regardless of the grade level of the students involved. The barometer described and illustrated below is very useful for predicting weather from the pressure-system movements.

Note: This barometer may also respond to changes in temperature. Use it *only* in the shade, *not* in direct sunlight.

Materials and Equipment
- ½-gallon flat-topped milk carton, or a cardboard box of a similar size
- razor blade
- sewing needle

Maps, Models, and Mock-Ups

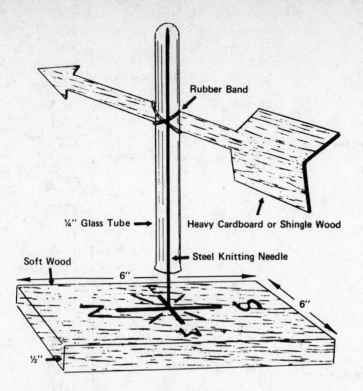

Figure 7.5
Wind Vane

Rubber Band

¼" Glass Tube →

Heavy Cardboard or Shingle Wood

Soft Wood

Steel Knitting Needle

6"

6"

½"

- broom straw
- two paper clips
- thread
- thin sheet of rubber or plastic
- small wide-mouthed jar
- household cement or glue
- penny
- cardboard

Procedure (Figure 7.6)

After acquiring the necessary materials and equipment, wait for a day when the barometric pressure is about average for the area in which the school is located.

1. Cut an opening in the side of the box or carton. Make the opening large enough for the jar to pass through. Cut an H-shaped opening in the top of the carton, making the parallel cuts shorter than the length of the needle. Prepare a cardboard gauge, as illustrated.

2. Tack or glue the cardboard gauge to the back of the carton. Insert the needle in the cardboard tabs as shown, and place the end of a broom straw in the eye of the needle.

3. Place the thin rubber or plastic sheet over the mouth of the jar and fasten it on tightly with a rubber band. Attach the thread to one end of a paper clip, and glue the paper clip to the center of the rubber covering.

4. Place the jar inside the carton, pull the thread up through the opening previously cut in the top of the carton, and wrap the thread twice around the needle. Lay the free end of the thread over the side of the carton and tie it to a paper clip. Place a penny in the clip. Rotate the needle so that the straw points up.

Figure 7.6
Barometer

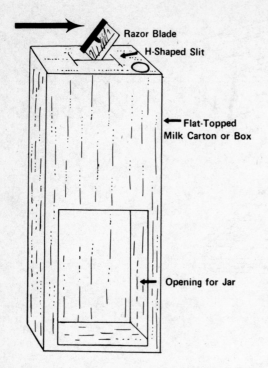

Razor Blade

H-Shaped Slit

Flat-Topped
Milk Carton or Box

Opening for Jar

1. Preparing Carton

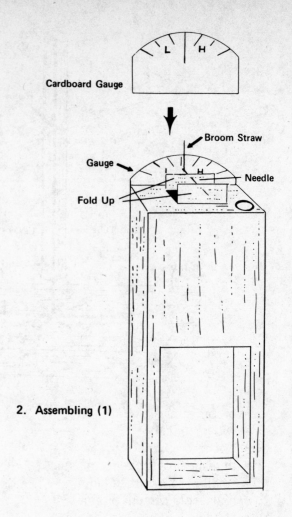

Cardboard Gauge

Broom Straw

Gauge

Needle

Fold Up

2. Assembling (1)

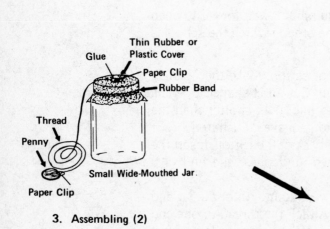

Thin Rubber or
Plastic Cover

Glue

Paper Clip

Rubber Band

Thread

Penny

Paper Clip

Small Wide-Mouthed Jar

3. Assembling (2)

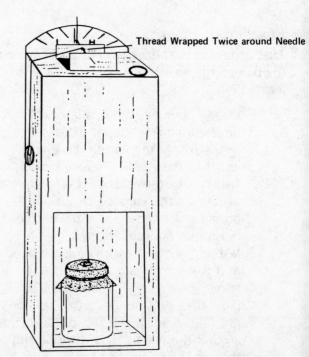

Thread Wrapped Twice around Needle

4. Finishing

Maps, Models, and Mock-Ups

Variations in barometric pressure will be registered by movements of the straw to the right for high pressure, and to the left for low pressure. (High pressure pushes down on the rubber, pulling the thread that is wrapped around the needle and causing the straw to turn to the right. Low pressure causes the opposite to occur.) If they are opposite in direction, rewind the thread around the needle in the opposite direction. If the needle does not turn easily, put a *small* drop of machine oil where it passes through each cardboard tab.

Mechanical Thermometer

A mechanical thermometer of the type described here is useful for indicating low and high temperature in weather study. In social studies, use the thermometer to illustrate the temperature range in various geographical locations at different times of the year. The thermometer must be manipulated; it does not respond to changes in atmospheric temperature.

Materials and Equipment
- piece of red ribbon or elastic, and a piece of white ribbon or elastic
- heavy cardboard or soft wood
- pen suitable for lettering on soft wood or cardboard
- needle and thread
- brads or small nails, if a base will be used
- knife or razor blade

Procedure (Figure 7.7)
1. Cut the front of the thermometer to size. Draw on it the outline of the bulb and the temperature scale.

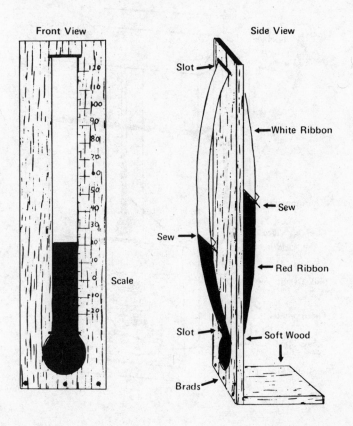

Figure 7.7
Mechanical Thermometer

2. Paint the bulb red to match the ribbon, or paste in some ribbon to fill the outline.
3. Cut one slot above the scale and another slot below the scale, wide enough to accommodate the ribbons. Attach the ribbons as illustrated.
4. Nail the thermometer to a base if desired.

Hygrometers

Relative humidity is an important indicator of potential precipitation and should be studied and measured by students engaged in weather study. Two simple, effective, easily constructed hygrometers are described and illustrated here.

Materials and Equipment for a Wet-Bulb Hygrometer

- one ½-gallon milk carton
- two thermometers
- rubber band
- razor blade
- small jar
- old tubular shoelace with ends removed

Procedure (Figure 7.8)

1. Cut an opening in the side of the carton large enough for the jar. Attach two thermometers to the carton with a rubber band as illustrated.

Figure 7.8
Wet-Bulb Hygrometer

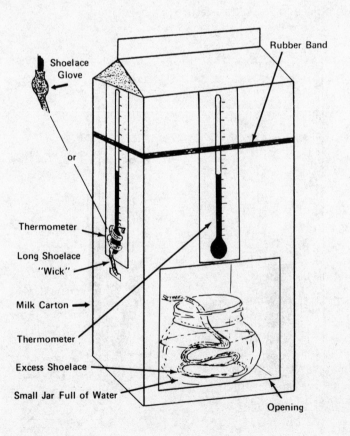

Shoelace
Glove

or

Rubber Band

Thermometer

Long Shoelace
"Wick"

Milk Carton

Thermometer

Excess Shoelace

Small Jar Full of Water

Opening

Maps, Models, and Mock-Ups

2. Cut a slot large enough for the shoelace to pass through immediately below the thermometer located on the side of the carton.
3. Place the small jar, full of water, inside the carton.
4. Take a shoelace, open one end of it, and slip it over the bulb of the thermometer on the side of the carton; or, wrap the end of the shoelace around the bulb of the thermometer, as illustrated.
5. Place the other end of the shoelace through the slot into the jar of water.

The shoelace will act as a wick and keep one thermometer bulb wet. When the humidity is very high, there will be little or no difference in the readings of the thermometers. During dry weather, the water will evaporate, cooling the bulb, and lowering the temperature registered on the wet-bulb thermometer. The temperature registered on the second thermometer will not be affected by humidity change, so there will be a difference in what the two thermometers register during dry weather. The lower the humidity, the greater the difference in the readings.

Materials and Equipment for a Hair Hygrometer
- quart milk carton, flat-top type, or a box of a similar size
- razor blade
- sewing needle
- broom straw
- two paper clips
- clean, *long* human hair
- two pennies
- cardboard

Procedure (Figure 7.9)
After acquiring the necessary materials and equipment, wait for a day when the relative humidity is average for the area in which the school is located.

1. Cut an H-shaped opening in the side near the center of the carton, making the parallel cuts shorter than the length of the needle. Prepare a cardboard gauge as illustrated.
2. Tack or glue the cardboard gauge to the back of the carton. Insert the needle in the cardboard tabs as shown, and place the end of a broom straw in the eye of the needle. Cut a slot at one end of the carton, and insert a paper clip as illustrated. Tie or glue a long, clean human hair to the paper clip. Wrap the hair twice around the needle, and attach the other end of the hair to another paper clip. Place two pennies in the paper clip, and suspend them over the end of the carton.

During damp weather, the hair will become saturated with moisture and expand, causing the needle to move to the right and indicating higher relative humidity. During dry weather, the hair will contract and cause the needle to move to the left, indicating lower relative humidity. If the needle moves in the contrary directions, rewind the hair in the opposite direction. If the needle moves with difficulty, put a *small* drop of machine oil where it goes through the cardboard tabs.

Figure 7.9
Hair Hygrometer

1. Preparing Components

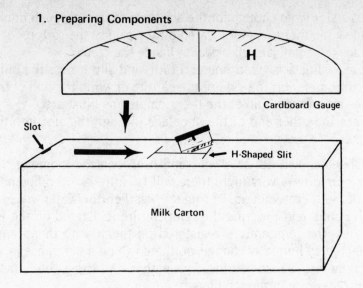

Cardboard Gauge

Slot

H-Shaped Slit

Milk Carton

2. Assembling and Finishing

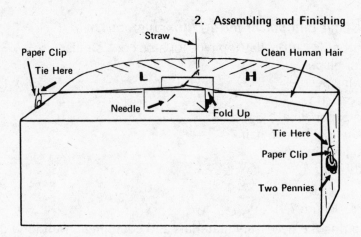

Straw

Paper Clip

Tie Here

Clean Human Hair

Needle

Fold Up

Tie Here

Paper Clip

Two Pennies

7.4 Compasses

Students will understand what magnetism is and how a compass works if they are given an opportunity to make a compass themselves. With little equipment and know-how, students can produce compasses that are acceptable for teaching the fundamentals of compass operation. Three types are discussed and illustrated in this section: a floating compass, a balanced compass, and a suspended compass.

Floating Compass

Materials and Equipment

- permanent magnet
- large sewing needle
- two corks
- sharp razor blade
- cup or bowl of water
- indelible-ink pen

Maps, Models, and Mock-Ups

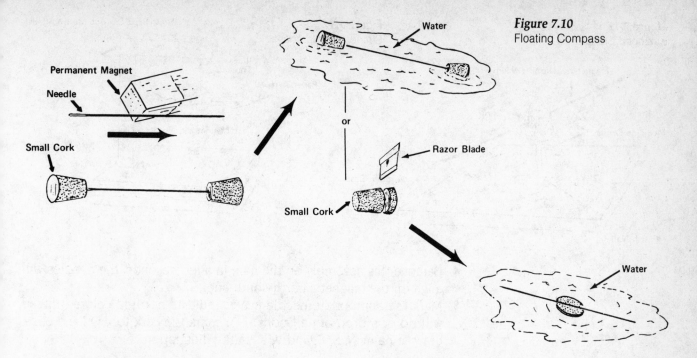

Figure 7.10
Floating Compass

Procedure (Figure 7.10)

1. Pick up the sewing needle and stroke it in *one* direction *only* with one pole (or end) of a permanent magnet.
2. Stick two small corks on the needle, one on each end, *or* slice off a thin piece of cork.
3. Place the needle with corks on both ends in the cup or bowl of water, *or* place the magnetized needle on the slice of cork, and float it in the cup or bowl of water. The magnetized needle will soon point along the magnetic north-south line. Mark the corks *N* and *S* to show which direction is north and which is south.

Balanced Compass

Materials and Equipment

- medicine dropper
- long finishing nail and hammer
- board to serve as a base
- cork or stopper with a hole in it
- two darning or knitting needles
- permanent magnet
- pen and ink, or paints

Procedure (Figure 7.11)

1. Saw the base to the size desired, and hammer the nail down through the center of the base. Insert the medicine dropper in the hole in the cork or rubber stopper.
2. Magnetize the two needles, stroking in *one* direction *only* with the permanent magnet. Stroke from the eye to the point of one needle and from the point to the eye of the other needle.
3. Use the needle points to insert the needles in the cork, as illustrated.

Figure 7.11
Balanced Compass

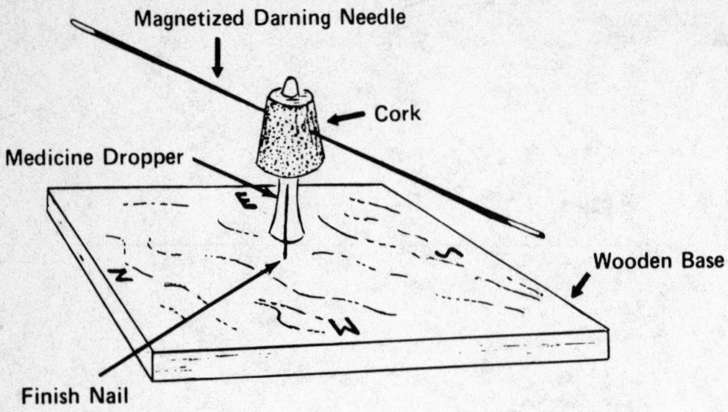

Magnetized Darning Needle

Cork

Medicine Dropper

Finish Nail

Wooden Base

Figure 7.12
Suspended Compass

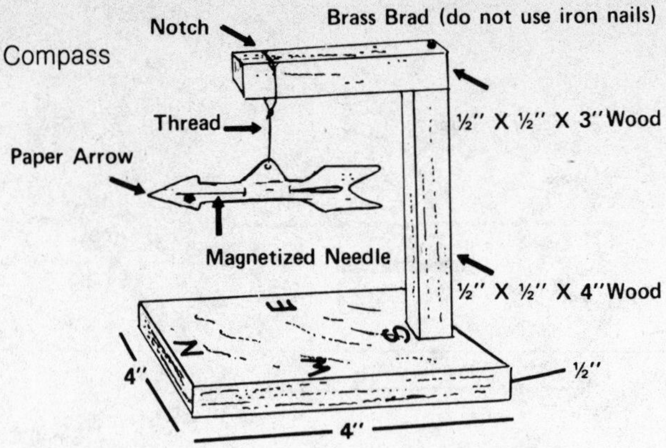

Notch

Brass Brad (do not use iron nails)

Thread

Paper Arrow

½" X ½" X 3" Wood

Magnetized Needle

½" X ½" X 4" Wood

4"

½"

4"

4. Balance this assembly on the nail; in a few seconds, the needles will align on the magnetic north-south line.
5. Mark the appropriate needle eye to indicate north (a colored thread will do or a drop of nail polish), or mark the cork top. On the base, draw or paint *N*, *S*, *E*, and *W* as in the illustration.

Suspended Compass

Materials and Equipment
- one ½" × ½" × 3" piece of wood
- one ½" × ½" × 4" piece of wood
- one 4" × 4" × ½" piece of wood
- several brass brads
- hammer
- piece of paper
- scissors
- sewing needle
- thread
- permanent magnet
- knife or razor blade
- pen and ink, or paints

Procedure (Figure 7.12)
1. Saw the base and suspension pieces to size, and assemble them with brass brads. Cut a notch in the wooden suspension arm as shown.
2. Magnetize the needle by stroking it in *one direction only* with the permanent magnet.
3. Cut an arrow from a piece of paper, and insert the magnetized needle through two slots cut in the arrow.
4. Hang the arrow with thread as illustrated. The needle may be moved toward or away from the point of the arrow so that the arrow will balance properly while suspended. The arrow will point to magnetic north or south in a few seconds; if it points south, insert the needle in the opposite direction.
5. Mark the base of the compass to indicate directions: *N*, *S*, *E*, and *W*.

Maps, Models, and Mock-Ups

Display Devices for Studying Live Specimens

VIII

The study of live specimens in the classroom can do much to promote interest in life science. Students may become directly involved in the care and feeding of insects, fish, and animals on display.

This chapter presents representative devices for displaying and studying live specimens, including insect cages; an insect-study case; a vivarium; an animal cage; a four-sided terrarium; two jar terrariums; a jar aquarium; an aquarium with funnel and fish trap; and a seed-germination case.

8.1   Insect Cages

Although insects captured, killed, and preserved are often very useful in science education, at times live specimens are more useful to an enterprising teacher. Four insect cages are presented below. All the cages allow students to see insects in action.

Shoe Box Insect Cage

A shoe box cage for insects is inexpensive to make and may be assembled by teachers or students.

Materials and Equipment
- shoe box
- glass pane or clear acetate (plastic)
- masking tape
- knife or razor blade
- scissors
- glass cutter (if glass is used)

- milk carton, ½ pint
- water
- small plant
- pins
- fine wire screening

Procedure (Figure 8.1)

1. Measure and draw the window area on the box lid; window glass or plastic should have a ½" margin of lid on all sides.
2. Cut out the window area.
3. Tape the glass pane or plastic to the inside of the box lid; use enough tape to provide rigidity.
4. Cut a trap door in the top end of the cage as illustrated. Secure this door with tape.
5. Cut a small hole in the back of the box and tape a piece of wire screen over this air hole.
6. Put a plant in the milk carton and place it in the box.
7. Put live insects in the cage.
8. Pin the lid to the box (see illustration).

Oatmeal Box Insect Cage

A cylindrical oatmeal box or ice-cream carton can be made easily and quickly into a cage for use in the study of various insects. This cage has a ready-made door—the box lid—through which you can place insects, food, and other materials.

Materials and Equipment

- cylindrical oatmeal box or ice-cream carton
- fine wire screening
- cloth tape

Figure 8.1
Shoe Box Cage

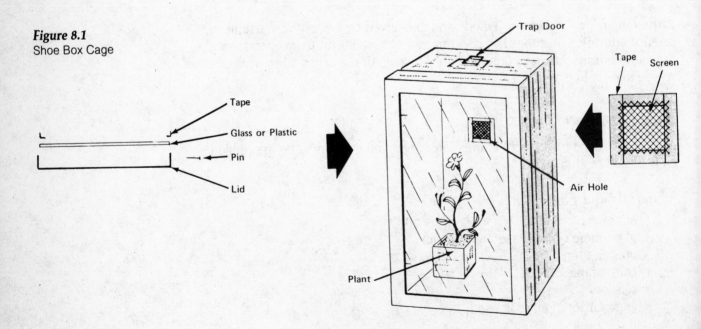

Display Devices for Studying Live Specimens

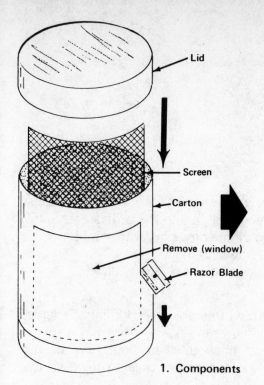

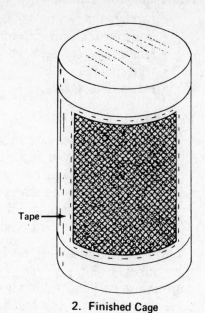

Figure 8.2
Oatmeal Box Insect Cage

1. Components

2. Finished Cage

- wire shears or old scissors
- razor blade or sharp knife

Procedure (Figure 8.2)

1. Cut the window in the side of the box. Leave the box lid in place to make the cutting easier.
2. Cut the wire screen somewhat larger than the window it will cover.
3. Tape the screen to the inside of the box. The cage is now ready to receive insects.

Jar Cage

A jar cage is probably the simplest cage to construct if the materials are available. A common type of canning jar cap consists of two pieces: a metal screw band and a metal lid. The jar cage uses a metal screw band to hold a wire screen to the jar.

Materials and Equipment

- glass jar with a wide mouth
- canning jar screw band that fits the glass jar
- galvanized wire, cut to the size of the lid
- wire shears

Procedure (Figure 8.3)

1. Insert the precut screen wire in the jar's screw band.
2. Put the insect into the jar and screw the band on tightly.

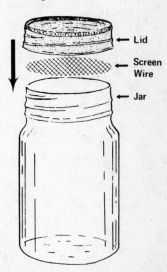

Figure 8.3
Jar Cage

Jar-Lid Screen-Wire Cage

Materials and Equipment

- two large mayonnaise-jar lids
- one piece of wire screening, 12" × 12"
- stapler (regular desk type)
- wire shears
- masking tape

Procedure (Figure 8.4)

1. Curve the screening to form a cylinder. Allow for a 1" overlap. Adjust the cylinder so that the open ends will fit into the jar lids. Fasten the overlapped edges of the screen cylinder together with staples.
2. Tape the exposed edges of the screen cylinder.
3. Fit a mayonnaise-jar lid on each end of the screen cylinder.
4. Stand the cylinder upright.

This same procedure can be followed to make cages for animals larger than insects. Simply use heavier materials. Cake tins may replace mayonnaise-jar lids, and hardware cloth of about ¼" mesh may replace the screening. Consider placing a brick on top of the cage to increase the stability of the upright cylinder.

Insect-Study Case

A glass study case is useful for studying burrowing insects and for observing a termite colony at work.

Figure 8.4
Jar-Lid Screen-Wire Cage

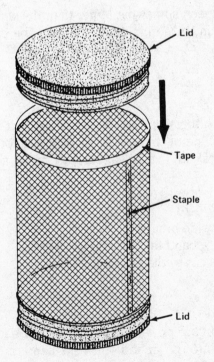

Lid

Tape

Staple

Lid

Materials and Equipment

- two equally sized pieces of window glass
- three wooden strips, slightly wider than the specimen to be placed in the case (if burrowing insects will be displayed)
- roll of wide adhesive plastic or masking tape
- wire screening
- scissors
- dirt containing specimens, or rotted wood with termites

Procedure (Figure 8.5)

1. Lay a piece of glass flat on a table. Place dirt containing the live specimen or a damp, rotted piece of wood containing the termites on the glass.
2. Lay wooden strips cut to size (slightly wider than the specimen to be displayed) around the edges of one piece of glass, as illustrated.
3. Place a second piece of glass on the top of the wooden strips, and tape the sides together.

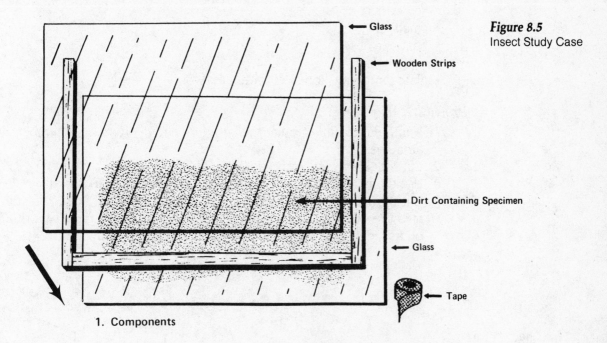

Glass

Wooden Strips

Dirt Containing Specimen

Glass

Tape

1. Components

Figure 8.5
Insect Study Case

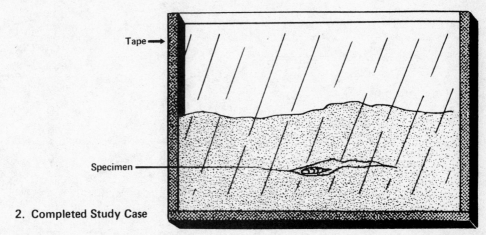

Tape →

Specimen

2. Completed Study Case

A display case for burrowing insects generally requires no cover. A termite display should be covered. Tape wire screening over the opening so that the insects will not escape. Keep the case enclosed in dark cloth or paper, except when you observe the insects.

8.2   Terrariums

Jar Terrarium: Type One

A jar terrarium makes a good display for small specimens, and is easier to construct than a larger four-sided terrarium.

Materials and Equipment

- galvanized wire screening
- small piece of wood, 1″ × 6″ × 6″
- two screws, 1¼″ or 1½″ in length
- screwdriver
- small nail
- hammer
- wire shears
- glass jar (one-gallon size), with metal lid

Procedure   (Figure 8.6)

1. Hammer the nail through the jar lid repeatedly to make a number of air holes.
2. Cut the screen wire to fit *inside* the lid.
3. Use the nail to make two holes in the piece of wood as shown.
4. Cut the wood so it will *not* cover the nail holes in the lid, and fasten it to the lid with screws. Screw the lid on the jar. Place the terrarium on its side. It is now ready for the soil and specimens.

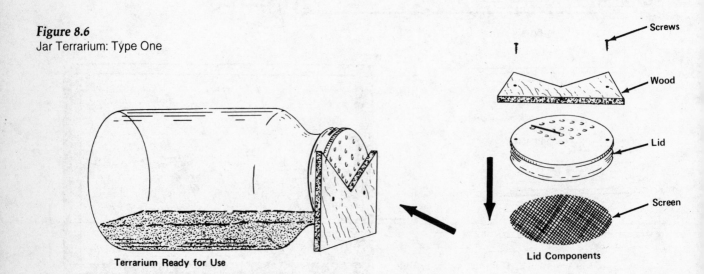

Figure 8.6
Jar Terrarium: Type One

Screws

Wood

Lid

Screen

Terrarium Ready for Use

Lid Components

Display Devices for Studying Live Specimens

To Stock and Care for the Terrarium

Cover the bottom with clean gravel, sand, and peat. Choose attractive rocks and small potted plants, or plants such as shield fern, creeping snowberry, or polytrichum moss, and place them in the bottom of the terrarium. The terrarium is then ready to receive animals. Clean the terrarium at least once a week. (Note: Vary the terrarium's contents when needed so that the animals' terrarium environment will conform as closely as possible to their natural environment.)

Jar Terrarium: Type Two

Materials and Equipment

- glass jar with metal lid (one-gallon size)
- galvanized wire screening, cut to interior size of lid
- piece of heavy cardboard, cut to interior size of lid
- one piece of wood, 1″ × 4″ × 8″
- two pieces of wood, each 1″ × 2″ × 8″
- nails and hammer
- household cement

Procedure (Figure 8.7)

1. Nail the wooden base and sides together as shown.

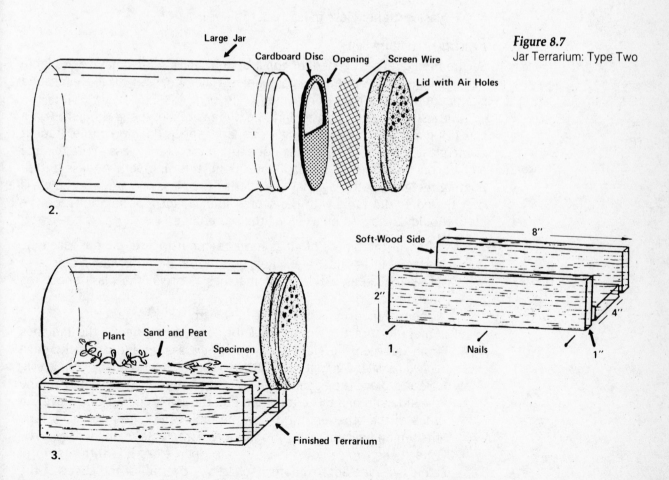

Figure 8.7
Jar Terrarium: Type Two

2. Prepare the lid by punching small holes in it from the top side. Cut a hole in the cardboard disc as illustrated and cement the screen wire to the cardboard.
3. Lay the jar on its side in the wooden frame. Arrange the jar's contents (soil, plant, specimen). Put the cardboard disc with the screen wire inside on the jar's mouth and screw the lid on.

Four-Sided Terrarium

A terrarium is a worthwhile addition to any elementary school classroom or secondary school biology room because it affords students an excellent opportunity to learn more about living plants and animals. Stimulate student interest in nature study by assigning student committees or individual students to stock and care for the terrarium. A simple terrarium can be constructed easily by older students or by the teacher.

Materials and Equipment
- four pieces of glass: 9″ × 12″ each for a large terrarium, or 6″ × 10″ each for a small terrarium
- two pieces of glass: 9″ × 9″ each for a large terrarium, or 6″ × 6″ each for a small terrarium
- two rolls of 2″ plastic, masking, or other adhesive tape
- eight safety matches with the heads removed
- lock hasp
- glass cutter (if glass must be cut to size)

Procedure (Figure 8.8)

Secure the materials needed for construction. Glass scraps may be available free of charge from some glass companies. Have the glass cut to the desired size or cut the glass to the proper size.

Suggestions for cutting glass: Mark the dimensions of the glass pieces on a sheet of paper. Place the glass over the paper sheet. Position a ruler (tape it to the glass if necessary—it must not slip) on top of the glass along the line marked on the sheet of paper. Score along this line with a glass cutter, holding the glass cutter against the ruler as the glass is cut. Place the glass over the edge of a table with the scored line *face up*. Pressing down on the glass should cause it to break along the scored line.

1. After all the pieces of glass have been cut to size, lay the assembly on a table as illustrated. Reserve one of the four larger pieces of glass to use as a lid. Insert matches between the glass sheets as illustrated.
2. Tape the ends and sides to the base with adhesive tape.
3. Carefully turn the entire assembly over, and remove the matches from between the glass sheets. Fold *one end* up and place the edge *flat on the table*, against the bottom or base sheet of glass. Pull up *one side* and place the edge flat *on top* of the edge of the glass base. Tape the side and end piece together. Pull the other end up, and place the edge of the other end firmly on the table, and tape into place. Tape the remaining side piece into place to complete the open glass box.
4. Attach the top or cover glass to the open glass box with a strip of adhesive tape approximately 10″ long. Cover all of the edges of the

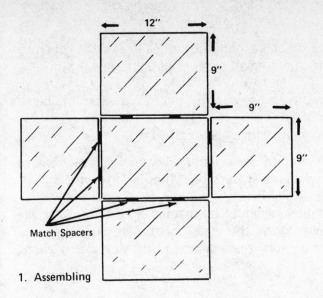

1. Assembling

Match Spacers

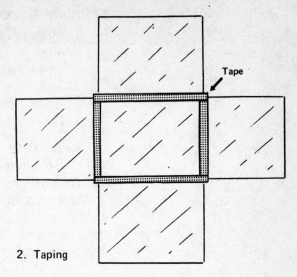

2. Taping

Tape

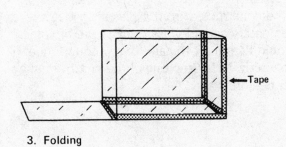

3. Folding

Tape

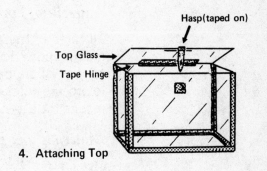

4. Attaching Top

Hasp(taped on)

Top Glass

Tape Hinge

Figure 8.8
Four-Sided Terrarium

terrarium with tape so that hands will not be cut. Attach a hasp with tape to hold the lid in place, if desired. *Always leave enough space between the cover glass and the glass box to allow air circulation for animals.*

Stock and care for the four-sided terrarium as you would for the jar terrarium (see page 138).

8.3 Aquariums

Gallon-Jar Aquarium

A gallon-jar aquarium allows students to observe simple animal life. This inexpensive aquarium requires few materials.

Materials and Equipment

- gallon jar with wide mouth
- pane of glass or saucer for cover
- pebbles or gravel
- elodea (aquatic herb)
- animal specimen(s)

Procedure (Figure 8.9)

1. Place pebbles in the jar, and anchor the elodea in place. A generous amount of plant life and a small number of animals will provide a balanced aquarium.
2. Add water to the jar (about two cups of water to one inch of animal length is a good ratio).
3. Cover the aquarium mouth with a glass pane.

Rather than crowd animals into one aquarium, set up several aquariums and house a different type of animal in each one. These will provide numerous observational activities for children.

Having a snail in an aquarium will offer students close-up views of the animal and the eggs it may lay on the inside of the jar. Snail eggs are translucent, and students can study the anatomy of the developing young with a magnifying glass.

Aquarium, Funnel, and Fish Trap

All three of these devices may be constructed from a glass jug. Use these multipurpose devices in the elementary school classroom or the biological science laboratory. Students should be taught to care for the aquarium and to procure animals for classroom study. *Note:* Step one of the procedure may require the assistance of another person.

Materials and Equipment

- glass cutter
- gallon jug
- desk drawer or sturdy box slightly wider than the diameter of the jug
- sharp knife
- device for breaking the top of the jug: a coat hanger and nut; *or* string, lighter fluid, and water; *or* an electric bottle cutter (see p. 145 for construction)

Figure 8.9
Gallon-Jar Aquarium

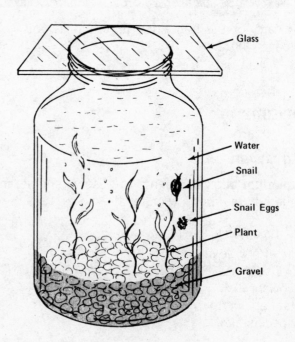

Glass

Water

Snail

Snail Eggs

Plant

Gravel

- sandpaper or file
- materials for stocking the aquarium

Procedure (Figure 8.10)

1. Place the gallon jug in the desk drawer (or box) with the bottom of the jug held firmly against the end of the drawer. Have a friend help you hold the jug in place if possible. Draw a line with a pencil on the side of the drawer approximately 2" below the base of the neck of the jug. Cut a notch in the drawer, place the glass cutter in the notch, and have your assistant rotate the jar against the glass cutter.

2. Separate the jug top (funnel) from the body of the jug (the aquarium). Take a coat hanger and attach the nut to the end of it as shown. Tap against the scored line inside the bottle until the glass begins to chip. Continue tapping all the way around until the bottle top breaks free. Another way to remove the jug top is to fill the jug to the scored

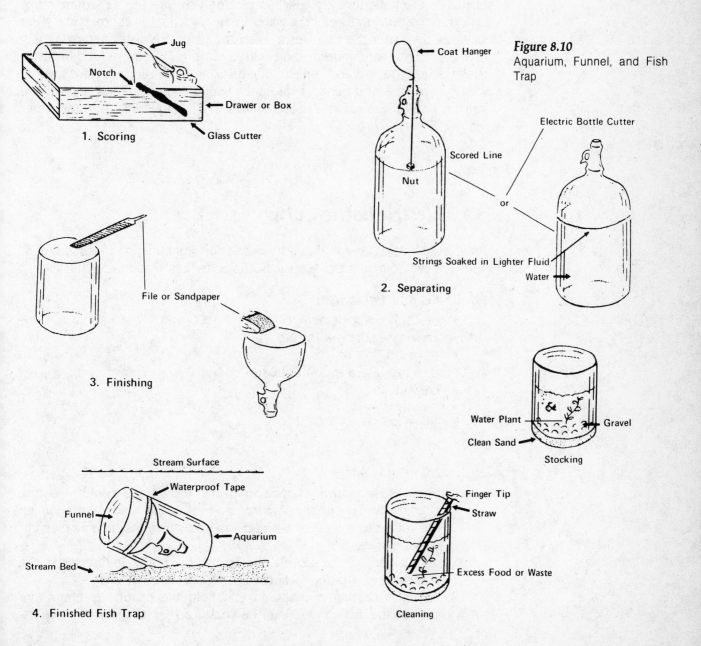

Figure 8.10
Aquarium, Funnel, and Fish Trap

1. Scoring

Jug
Notch
Drawer or Box
Glass Cutter

File or Sandpaper

3. Finishing

Coat Hanger
Scored Line
Nut
Electric Bottle Cutter
Strings Soaked in Lighter Fluid
Water

2. Separating

Water Plant
Clean Sand
Gravel
Stocking

Stream Surface
Waterproof Tape
Funnel
Aquarium
Stream Bed

4. Finished Fish Trap

Finger Tip
Straw
Excess Food or Waste

Cleaning

line with water, soak a string with lighter fluid or turpentine, wrap the string around the scored line, and set it on fire. The top should break loose. Still another method of breaking the top off the bottle is to use an electric bottle cutter.

3. Smooth off any rough or sharp edges on both the aquarium and funnel with a file or with sandpaper.

4. To make a fish trap, place the funnel inside the aquarium and tape the two components together. Take the fish trap to a stream. Face the trap toward the source of the stream, in shallow water. Small water animals will swim through the funnel and into the aquarium portion of the trap.

To Stock and Care for the Aquarium

Place a thin layer of clean sand in the bottom of the aquarium. Cover the layer of sand with a thin layer of gravel or rocks. Place water plants and a fish or two in the aquarium. (Note: When placing fish into the aquarium, make sure that the temperature of the water in the aquarium is approximately the same as the water the fish are in. Feed the fish once a day, removing any excess food not eaten after a short period of time. To remove food or waste from the aquarium, place one end of a drinking straw on the excess food or waste, cover the other end of the straw with a finger tip, and remove the straw from the water. Excess food or waste will be picked up in the water removed by the straw.

8.4   Electric Bottle Cutter

An electric bottle cutter makes bottle-aquarium construction much less difficult. You can construct this electric bottle cutter easily and inexpensively.

Materials and Equipment
- conical heating element (600-watt or 1000-watt)
- screw base socket with cord
- 18" board, 1" × 6"
- screws to fasten socket to board
- screwdriver
- hammer
- pliers
- two sticks

Procedure   (Figure 8.11)

1. Uncoil a few turns of wire from the top of the conical heating element, and shape the wire into an oval shape, using pliers. Fasten the socket to the board with screws, and screw the heating element into the socket.

2. With a glass cutter, score a line around the bottle as directed in the procedure for making an aquarium, funnel, and fish trap.

3. Turn the heating element on and hold the heating element wire against the scored line. Use the sticks to keep the wire in place. As

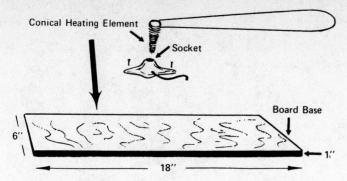

Conical Heating Element

Socket

Board Base

6"

1"

18"

1. Components

Figure 8.11
Electrical Bottle Cutter

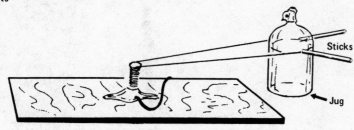

Sticks

Jug

2. Finished Cutter

the bottle cracks, rotate it slowly until the top breaks free. (Note: Have an assistant hold the bottle-cutter board so that it will not slip or slide. This bottle cutter should be used carefully, and only by the teacher. It is *unsafe for children*.)

8.5 *Seed-Germination Case*

A seed-germination case may interest and motivate children studying such botanical phenomena as the conditions necessary for seed germination; germination times; and growth rates and stages.

Materials and Equipment
- shallow pan (a baking pan works well)
- sand
- rubber bands
- blotter, cut to the size of the glass panes
- seeds
- water
- glass panes

Procedure (Figure 8.12)
1. Cut the glass to the desired size, or use small, precut panes. *Be sure to smooth the edges or tape around them* to avoid cutting the hands of curious children.
2. Wet the blotter, and place it on *top* of a pane of glass. Lay several seeds on the blotter.
3. Place the second pane of glass on top of the blotter and seeds. Use rubber bands to hold the assembly together.

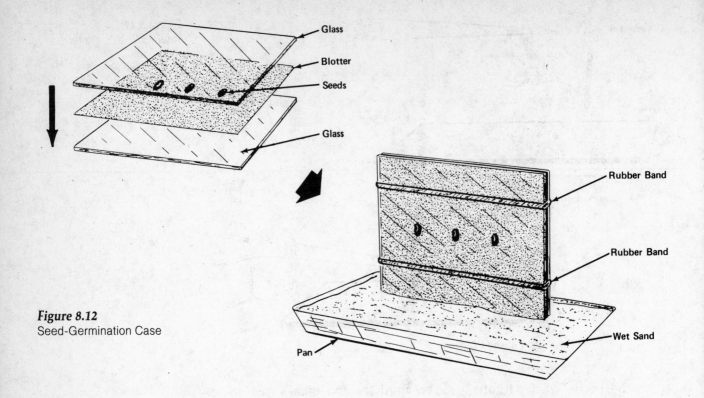

Figure 8.12
Seed-Germination Case

Labels in figure: Glass, Blotter, Seeds, Glass, Rubber Band, Rubber Band, Wet Sand, Pan

4. Partly fill the baking pan with wet sand.
5. Place the panes in the sand as shown in the illustration. Wait for the seeds to sprout. Have teams of children observe and record the stages of development.

8.6 Ant Vivarium

An ant vivarium, or ant farm, is easy to build and will provide many enjoyable and useful experiences for interested students. Since ants are easy to keep and study, both teachers and students will enjoy the vivarium.

Materials and Equipment
- two pieces of glass, 10" × 16" each
- one 1" × 4" piece of wood, 15½" long
- two 1" × 4" pieces of wood, each 11½" long
- one 1" × 4" piece of wood, 17½" long
- an assortment of wood screws or nails
- sandpaper or emery cloth
- hammer or screwdriver
- fine screen wire, 3" × 11"
- hasp
- hinge
- household cement
- stapler and staples
- keyhole saw

- glass cutter (if glass must be cut to size)
- device for cutting grooves in the wooden frame (wood carving tool, power saw, or rabbeting plane—a knife will do if no other tool is available)

Procedure (Figure 8.13)

1. Cut the glass to the desired size if necessary (see p. 140 glass-cutting procedure for the four-sided terrarium). Usually the glass will be cut to size for you free of charge when it is purchased from a glass shop or lumberyard. Smooth off any sharp edges carefully with sandpaper

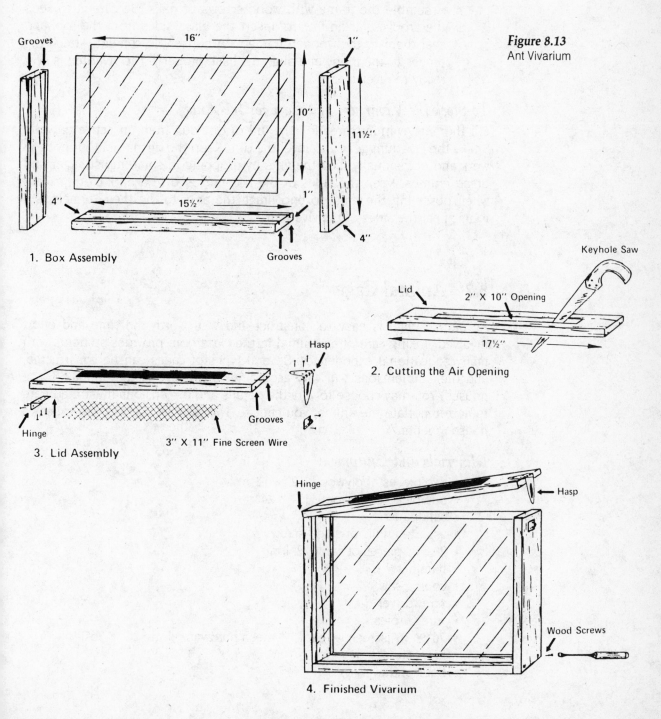

Figure 8.13
Ant Vivarium

1. Box Assembly

2. Cutting the Air Opening

3. Lid Assembly

4. Finished Vivarium

or emery cloth. Prepare the wooden ends and bottom by cutting two 1″ × 4″ pieces of wood to a length of 11½″, and one piece to a length of 15½″. Cut two parallel grooves lengthwise in each piece of wood, ¼″ deep and approximately ⅛″ wide, about 3″ apart.

2. Cut a 1″ × 4″ lid, 17½″ long. Cut grooves in the lid in the same manner as the frame. A 2″ × 10″ opening should be cut in the lid with a keyhole saw or similar cutting tool.

3. Attach the fine screen wire to the bottom of the lid, covering the opening in the board. Use a stapler to fasten the wire in place, and trim away any excess wire covering the grooves in the lid. Attach a hasp and a hinge as illustrated.

4. Assemble the frame with wood screws or nails. Be careful to keep the grooves facing inward. Insert the glass sides from the top, and seal them to the wooden frame with household cement. Attach the hinges to the frame and align the hasp properly. The vivarium is now ready to receive ants.

To Stock the Vivarium and Care for the Ants

Fill the ant vivarium three-fourths full of dirt dug from an active ant hill. Shake the vivarium gently to level the dirt. Keep the dirt moist (but not too wet), and occasionally feed the ants by dropping in some moist sugar and bread crumbs. Keep the sides of the box enclosed in a dark cloth, except when observing the ants, to encourage the ants to dig their tunnels and rooms near the sides of the vivarium.

8.7 Animal Cage

An animal cage is easy to construct and well worth the time and effort involved. Taking care of an animal in the classroom provides students with many educational experiences. Several types of cages can be constructed, and their dimensions will vary according to the size of the animals to be housed. You may choose to vary the details and dimensions illustrated here to accommodate the animal you choose. Note: Do not use wooden cages to house rodents.

Materials and Equipment
- two pieces of plywood, 12″ × 12″
- one piece of plywood, 12″ × 24″
- sandpaper
- assorted nails or wood screws
- 2″ × 2″ pieces of wood, 2′ long
- hammer
- coping saw
- screwdriver
- wire staples
- 26″ × 36″ screen wire (or ½″ mesh hardware cloth, 26″ × 36″)
- hinges
- hook and eye

Procedure (Figure 8.14)

1. Cut an opening in one piece of 12″ × 12″ plywood with the coping saw. The piece of wood that is cut out will serve as a door. Remove the door. Sandpaper the opening and the door so that no rough edges are exposed to injure the animals or the hands of children who handle the cage.

2. Attach one side of both hinges to the door, and then fasten the other side of both hinges to the door frame. With the door closed, attach the hook and eye as illustrated.

3. Nail the end pieces to the 12″ × 24″ bottom, and then nail the 2″ × 2″ frame pieces into place.

4. Use the hammer and wire staples to fasten the screen or hardware cloth to the frame. When you nail the screen wire covering to the frame, work from the *bottom* on one side to the *top* on the *same* side, across the top, and down the other side. Be sure to keep the screen wire or hardware cloth pulled tightly across the frame.

For information on the care and feeding of small animals, consult the nearest natural science museum, zoo, or library.

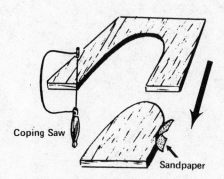

Coping Saw

Sandpaper

1. Cutting the Opening

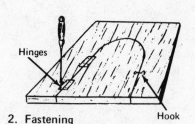

Hinges

Hook

2. Fastening

Figure 8.14
Animal Cage

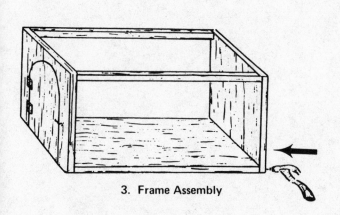

3. Frame Assembly

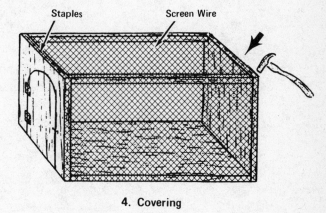

Staples   **Screen Wire**

4. Covering

Devices for Dramatization and Storytelling

IX

Numerous devices for dramatizing stories may be constructed easily by students and teachers. This chapter presents three such devices: hand puppets and puppet stages; scroll theaters; and shadow screens.

9.1 Hand Puppets and Puppet Stages

Constructing puppets and presenting dramatizations gives students the opportunity for creative expression. A few basic hand puppets, a finger puppet, and two simple puppet stages are illustrated in Figure 9.1. All the puppets are suitable for classroom construction and use. No written instructions are given in this section because the drawings for the puppets and puppet stages are detailed enough for teachers and students to understand how each item is constructed.

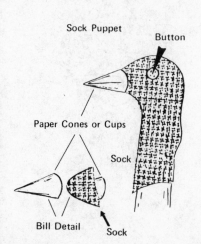

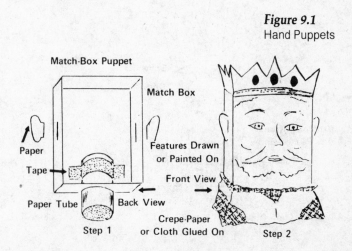

Figure 9.1
Hand Puppets

Figure 9.1 *(continued)*
Hand Puppets

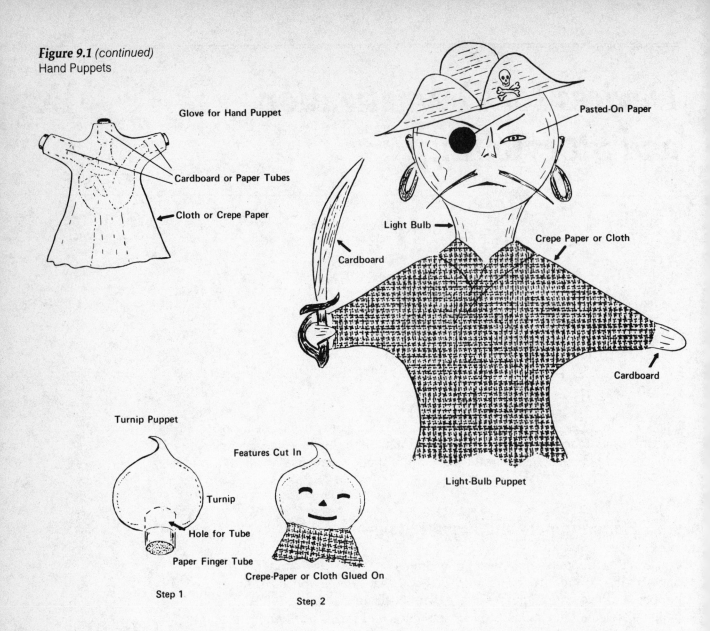

Glove for Hand Puppet

Cardboard or Paper Tubes

Cloth or Crepe Paper

Pasted-On Paper

Light Bulb

Crepe Paper or Cloth

Cardboard

Cardboard

Light-Bulb Puppet

Turnip Puppet

Turnip

Hole for Tube

Paper Finger Tube

Step 1

Features Cut In

Crepe-Paper or Cloth Glued On

Step 2

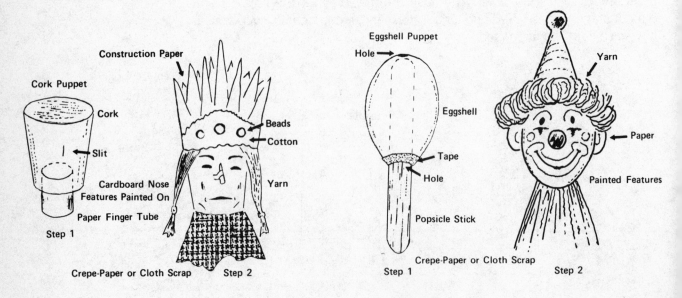

Cork Puppet

Cork

Slit

Cardboard Nose
Features Painted On

Paper Finger Tube

Step 1

Construction Paper

Beads

Cotton

Yarn

Crepe-Paper or Cloth Scrap

Step 2

Eggshell Puppet

Hole

Eggshell

Tape

Hole

Popsicle Stick

Crepe-Paper or Cloth Scrap

Step 1

Yarn

Paper

Painted Features

Step 2

Paper-Sack "Talking" Puppet

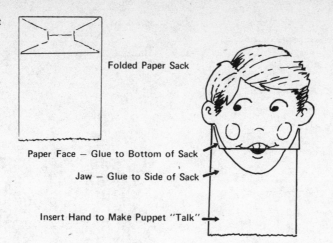

Folded Paper Sack

Paper Face — Glue to Bottom of Sack

Jaw — Glue to Side of Sack

Insert Hand to Make Puppet "Talk"

Figure 9.1 *(continued)*
Hand Puppets

Flip-Top Box "Talking" Puppet

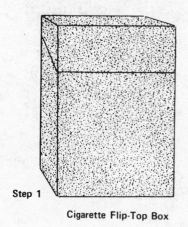

Step 1

Cigarette Flip-Top Box

Spoon Puppet

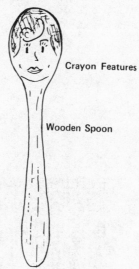

Crayon Features

Wooden Spoon

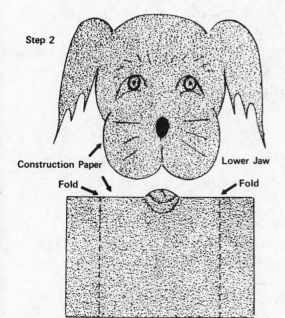

Step 2

Construction Paper

Lower Jaw

Fold

Fold

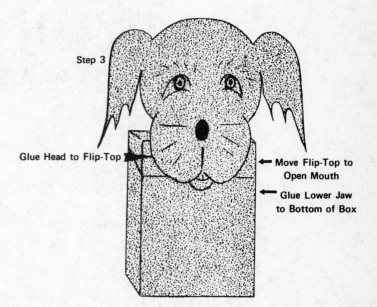

Step 3

Glue Head to Flip-Top

Move Flip-Top to Open Mouth

Glue Lower Jaw to Bottom of Box

Devices for Dramatization and Storytelling

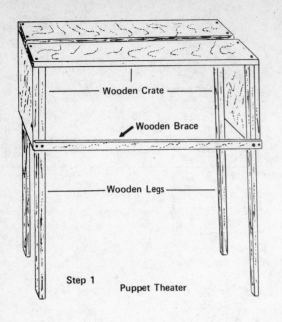

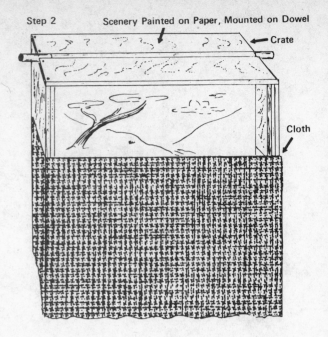

Step 1   Puppet Theater

Temporary Puppet Theater

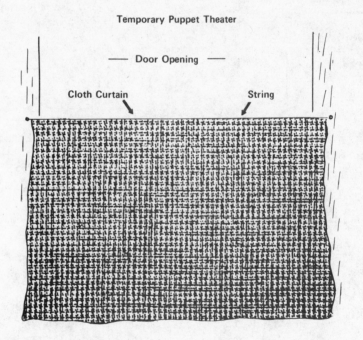

Figure 9.1 (continued)
Puppet Stages

9.2 *Scroll Theater*

A scroll theater can help illustrate and enliven any story. Simply draw the illustration on long strips of paper and roll them into view, one at a time, as you tell the story. You may use a scroll theater in language arts, social studies, and science classes. Use them whenever you have a story to illustrate. The device helps in pacing a story as well.

Horizontal-Roll Theater

The horizontal-roll theater is used to roll a series of pictures and drawings into view horizontally. No dimensions of the materials needed for this type of theater are given; select the dimensions that will meet your needs.

Materials and Equipment

- 1" pine, or ½" plywood, for the frame, top, bottom, and sides of the theater
- old broom handle, for scroll rods (or use ¾" dowel)
- assorted sizes of nails, including two very large ones for rod handles
- large finishing nails
- saw
- hammer
- strip of butcher paper for scroll
- drawing and coloring instruments
- small drill, or brace and bit
- ½" diameter doweling
- pressure-sensitive tape

Procedure (Figure 9.2)

1. Saw the top, bottom, and necessary side pieces to the desired size.
2. Before nailing the materials together, cut holes in the top piece where the broom-handle rods will fit. Be sure to cut a slot large

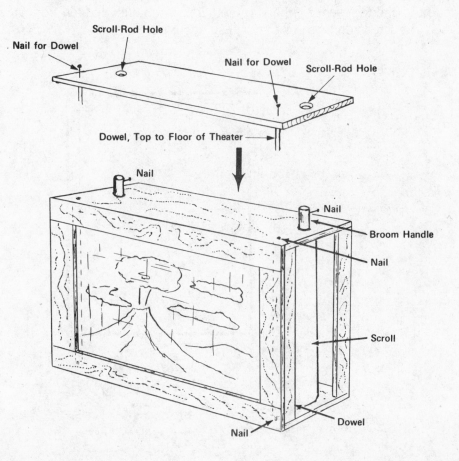

Figure 9.2
Horizontal-Roll Theater

enough to allow for insertion and removal of rod handles from the theater when changing scrolls.

3. Nail the doweling into place.
4. Hammer a large nail into the end of each broom handle as shown.
5. Hammer a finishing nail into the other end of each rod.
6. Bore two holes, opposite the top openings, in the bottom piece of wood large enough to accommodate the finishing nails in the end of each scroll rod.
7. Draw or paint pictures and scenes large enough to fill the theater opening. After finishing the scroll, fasten one end to a scroll rod with pressure-sensitive tape, and roll up on the rod.
8. Fasten the other end of the scroll to the other rod with pressure-sensitive tape.
9. Insert the rods through the opening in the back of the stage, in the appropriate holes, and present the show.

9.3 *Shadow Screen*

A shadow screen is most useful in language arts classes for developing students' clarity and ease of expression. This device allows even the most timid student to present a dramatization using cutout figures and illustrations pressed against a plastic screen. Due to the semitransparent nature of the plastic screen covering, the cutouts may be seen clearly by the class while the child presenting the story remains completely hidden from view. Select the screen dimensions that will suit your needs.

Figure 9.3
Vertical Shadow Screen

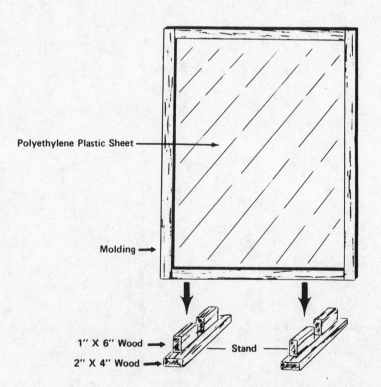

Polyethylene Plastic Sheet ⟶

Molding ⟶

1″ X 6″ Wood ⟶ ⟵ Stand
2″ X 4″ Wood ⟶

Devices for Dramatization and Storytelling

Materials and Equipment
- polyethylene plastic sheet
- wooden molding
- two pieces of wood, 2″ × 4″
- four pieces of wood, 1″ × 6″
- nails and hammer
- wood saw
- stapler

Procedure (Figure 9.3)
1. Assemble a frame out of molding as shown, and then staple the polyethylene sheet to its back.
2. Make the stand by nailing the 1″ × 6″ pieces of wood to the 2″ × 4″ pieces of wood.
3. Place the frame onto the stand as shown.

Bulletin Board
Display Techniques

X

Because many bulletin board displays are not well planned or carefully executed, they are not effective in communicating messages to students. By following some basic guidelines, you can make your bulletin board displays effective teaching devices.

This chapter contains guidelines for constructing good bulletin board displays and methods for displaying three-dimensional objects, pictures, and prints on bulletin boards. Disclosure techniques for involving students in active learning through bulletin board displays are also presented.

10.1 Guidelines for Using Bulletin Boards

1. Plan the display around a central theme.
2. Use thumbnail sketches to develop your idea (see page 10).
3. Change the bulletin board display frequently to keep student interest high.
4. Involve students in planning bulletin board arrangements. Have students bring magazines from home that contain useful pictures.
5. Use lettering that can be easily seen and that can be read at a distance.
6. Use pictures or prints that are well mounted.

Bulletin Board Design Principles

Simplicity
Keep the bulletin board display simple. Use a few well-chosen pictures rather than too many. The display in Figure 10.1 is formal in design and

Figure 10.1
Simplicity

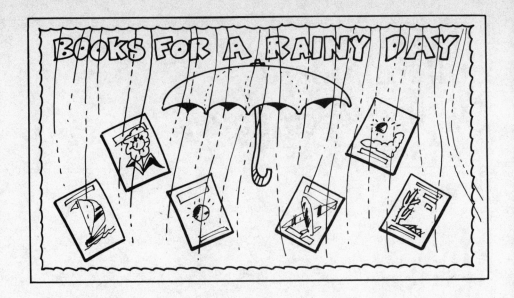

contains only a few, simple shapes. Clear cellophane strips, representing rain, hang in front of the display and move when a person passes the display, attracting attention to the display.

Balance

The display must have balance. To achieve balance, imagine a vertical line in the center of the bulletin board; both sides of the display must have equal weight. Two kinds of balance are possible: formal and informal. In formal balance, each side mirrors the other (Figure 10.2). Informal balance has equal weight on both sides, but the weight is made up of different arrangements of the elements (Figure 10.3).

Figure 10.2
Formal Balance

Figure 10.3
Informal Balance

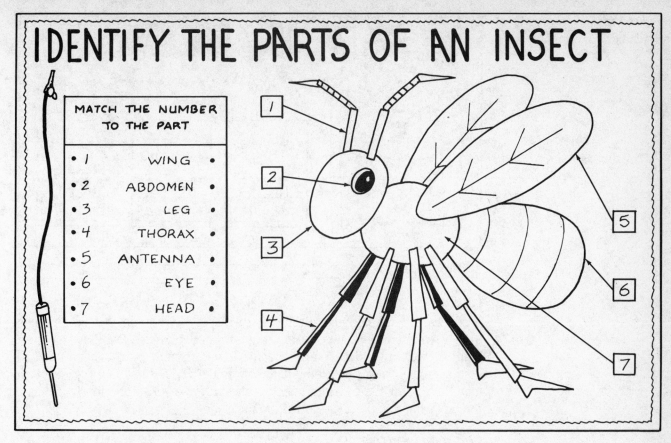

IDENTIFY THE PARTS OF AN INSECT

MATCH THE NUMBER TO THE PART

- 1   WING
- 2   ABDOMEN
- 3   LEG
- 4   THORAX
- 5   ANTENNA
- 6   EYE
- 7   HEAD

Figure 10.4
Proportion

Proportion

Proportion, the size of the elements in relation to each other, influences the overall visual effect of a bulletin board. In Figure 10.4, the large size of the insect attracts attention to the board, and the proportion of the elements is effective.

Contrast

Contrasting sizes, shapes, and colors will attract attention. In Figure 10.5, the large size of the bear attracts attention and contrasts with the small rectangles.

Figure 10.5
Contrast

Figure 10.6
Rhythm

Rhythm

A successfully designed bulletin board display will guide the viewer's eye from element to element in a predetermined course. Use lines, shapes, graphics, colors, and pointers to achieve this rhythm. Yarn can be used to guide the eye from one element to another. The physical shape of an item may also point the eye in a specific direction. For example, in Figure 10.6, the boy's hand and eyes point to the message.

Unity and Harmony

When a bulletin board display has unity and harmony, it conveys the intended message and pleases the eye. To produce a strong visual impact, each element of the display should complement the entire display. The paper should complement the lettering style, the lettering style should complement the graphics, and the colors should complement the intended message.

Figure 10.7
Unity and Harmony

Plan your lettering and colors to achieve a unified design. Color can be used to create a mood, attract attention, give emphasis, provide contrast, and guide the eye through the display. Usually, lettering size should be limited to three different heights. In general, 4″ letters should be used for the title, 2″ letters for the subtitles, and 1″ letters for the text. In Figure 10.7, the size of the lettering is appropriate, and the design is unified by the matching pattern of the letters and the clowns' clothing. If the letters and the clowns' clothing were made of matching, brightly colored cloth, the effect would be even more striking.

10.2 *Displaying Three-Dimensional Objects*

Three-dimensional objects such as leaves, cloth samples, building materials, and other objects may be attached directly to bulletin board displays with staples, pins or brads. Display small objects, such as geological specimens, cultural artifacts, and small models, by placing them on shelves attached to the bulletin board. Figure 10.8 presents three shelf designs that teachers have found useful and attractive. Figure 10.9 shows a container for handouts. You can make this container from a spirit master box or another box that

Figure 10.8
Bulletin-Board Shelves

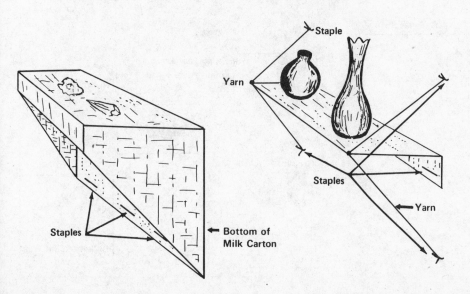

Figure 10.9
Bulletin-Board Container

will hold the appropriate paper size. Cut off one-third of the box's lid, and then tape the lid back on the box. Staple the container to the bulletin board.

10.3   *Attaching Prints to Bulletin Boards*

Attach prints to a bulletin board without damage by using clips, staples, tape, plastic envelopes, tacks, grommets, pins, and bulletin board wax. Figure 10.10 illustrates these methods.

10.4   *Disclosure Techniques*

A bulletin board display may motivate and challenge viewers by asking a question and then providing the answer to the question. The following five disclosure techniques have proven effective.

Folded Card

Place an index card on a flat surface and draw a horizontal line through the middle of the card (see Figure 10.11) Fold the card down along the line. On the outside of the folded card, write a question. Open the card flap and write the answer on the lower half of the inside of the card. Staple the card

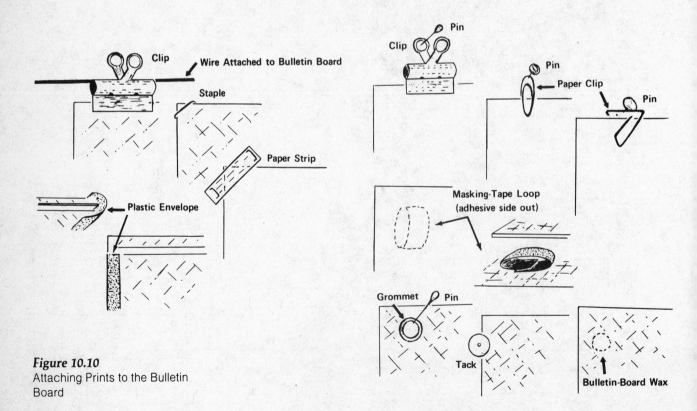

Figure 10.10
Attaching Prints to the Bulletin Board

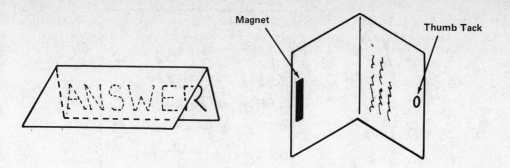

Figure 10.11
Folded Card

Magnet   Thumb Tack

to the appropriate place on the display. To keep the flap closed, lift it and push a thumbtack into the bottom of the card. Glue a small magnet to the inside of the flap so it comes in contact with the tack when closed.

Answer Back

Place a question on the front of a card and the answer on the back of the same card (see Figure 10.12). The card may have a special shape like the leaves in the "Balance" bulletin board example (page 160), or the card may be folded over a string as shown in the "Contrast" bulletin board example (page 161).

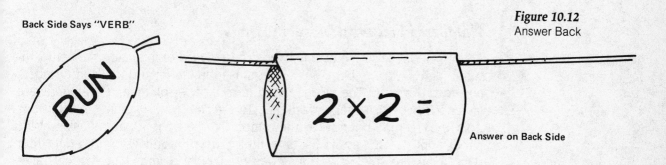

Back Side Says "VERB"

Figure 10.12
Answer Back

Answer on Back Side

Disclosure Pocket

An envelope such as a book card pocket works well on bulletin boards (see Figure 10.13). Place a question on the board, and put the answer in the pocket. When the student pulls the card out of the pocket, the answer is revealed.

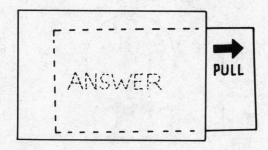

ANSWER   PULL

Figure 10.13
Disclosure Pocket

Figure 10.14
Electric Question-Board

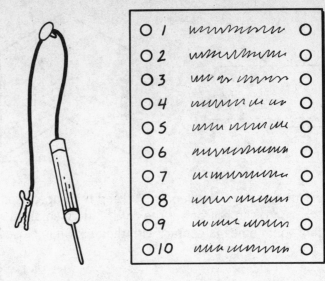

Electric Question-Board

Use the electric question-board with a bulletin board (see Figure 10.14). Simply number items on the board that you want students to identify. Then make an electric question-board that allows students to match the number on the bulletin board to the answer on the electric question-board. The "Proportion" bulletin board example illustrates the use of an electric board (page 161).

Numbered Face with Movable Hands

A numbered face with movable hands can be used to indicate time, temperature, quantity, or weight. The device is used in Figure 10.15 to add numbers and record weight. The face is made from a paper plate, and the hands are fastened on with a paper fastener. The scale shows weight designations from zero to nine pounds, by the ounce. On the right, a paper basket holds paper apples. Each apple has a weight written in ounces. On the left, four paper bags are labeled with a certain number of pounds. The student takes apples from the basket, puts them on the scale, and adds the ounces by moving the arm on the scale to record the weight of each apple. When the weight necessary to fill a bag is reached, the student moves the apples from the scale to the bag. The student tries to fill all of the bags.

Figure 10.15
Numbered Face with
Movable Hands

Chalkboard and Charting Tools

XI

By investing a little time in preparing basic chalkboard tools to fit your instructional needs, you will save time and be more effective in presenting material accurately. This chapter presents some tested chalkboard tools and techniques that teachers have found useful.

Four ways of using the chalkboard are described below: chalkboard templates, chalkboard stencils, projected negative drawings, and hidden chalkboards. This section also includes a short discussion of special chalkboard inks. Two methods for enlarging drawings, applicable to chalkboards and to paper charts, are also presented: the grid method and the projection method.

11.1 Templates and Stencils

Chalkboard Templates

Chalkboard templates are outlines of basic shapes and are useful for making uniform and accurate chalkboard drawings. Permanent templates are cut from plywood or masonite. They may include shapes such as triangles, circles, parallelograms, trapezoids, flasks, beakers, burners, animals, plants, people, states, continents, and any other shapes that need to be drawn repeatedly on the chalkboard.

Materials and Equipment
- sharpened pencil
- carbon paper
- drawing paper
- masonite or plywood sheets larger than the template size (cardboard can be used for temporary templates)

- brace and bit; or drill
- drawer pull or empty thread spool
- flat-headed wood screw
- sandpaper
- saw (for wood templates)
- scissors (for cardboard templates)
- felt
- counter sink
- glue

Procedure (Figure 11.1)

1. Outline the desired shape in pencil on a sheet of paper. Using carbon paper, transfer the completed outline to a piece of cardboard, masonite, or plywood.
2. Cut the shape from cardboard with scissors; or from plywood or masonite with a saw. Allow for the thickness of the chalk; cut any indentations larger than you wish to have them in the chalkboard drawing. Smooth any rough edges with sandpaper.
3. Fasten a knob to the center of a plywood or masonite template so that you can hold it more firmly and easily in position on the board. Drawer pulls or empty spools work nicely for this purpose. Use glue or screws to fasten the knob in place. Be sure to sink the head of the screw into the template so that the screw will not damage the chalkboard when the template is used. Glue two or three ¾″ squares of felt to the back of the template to keep it from slipping on the chalkboard.
4. Drill a hole near one edge of the template. Make the hole large enough to hang the template on a finishing nail beneath the chalk tray. If you hang templates below the chalk and eraser tray, they will be readily available when needed.

Chalkboard Stencils

Accurate chalkboard outlines may be made easily by the stencil method. Chalkboard stencils provide a faint outline on the chalkboard to be filled in as the lesson progresses.

Materials and Equipment

- a window shade (or a sheet of heavy paper or light cardboard)
- pencil
- leather spacer (or hammer and saddle punch)
- board
- 3″-wide board, slightly longer than the window shade is wide
- window-shade hangers and movable rack mounts for holding the board
- chalk and eraser

Procedure (Figure 11.2)

1. Draw or trace the outline of a figure on the window shade. An opaque projector may be used to make the drawing. Use a leather spacer (or a hammer and saddle punch) to produce evenly spaced

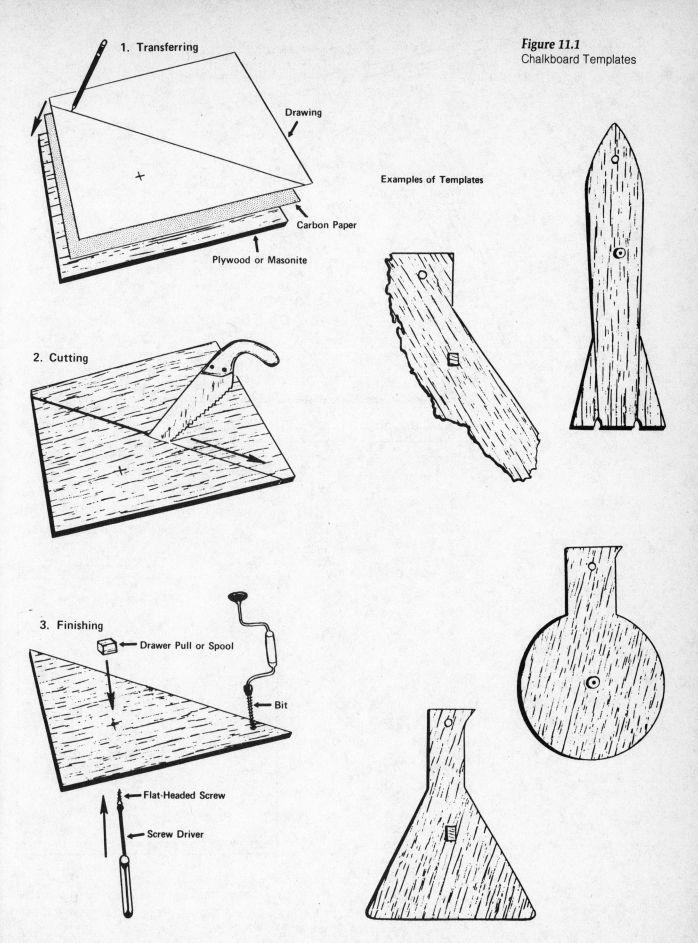

1. Transferring

Drawing

Carbon Paper

Plywood or Masonite

2. Cutting

3. Finishing

Drawer Pull or Spool

Bit

Flat-Headed Screw

Screw Driver

Figure 11.1
Chalkboard Templates

Examples of Templates

Chalkboard and Charting Tools

Figure 11.2
Chalkboard Stencils

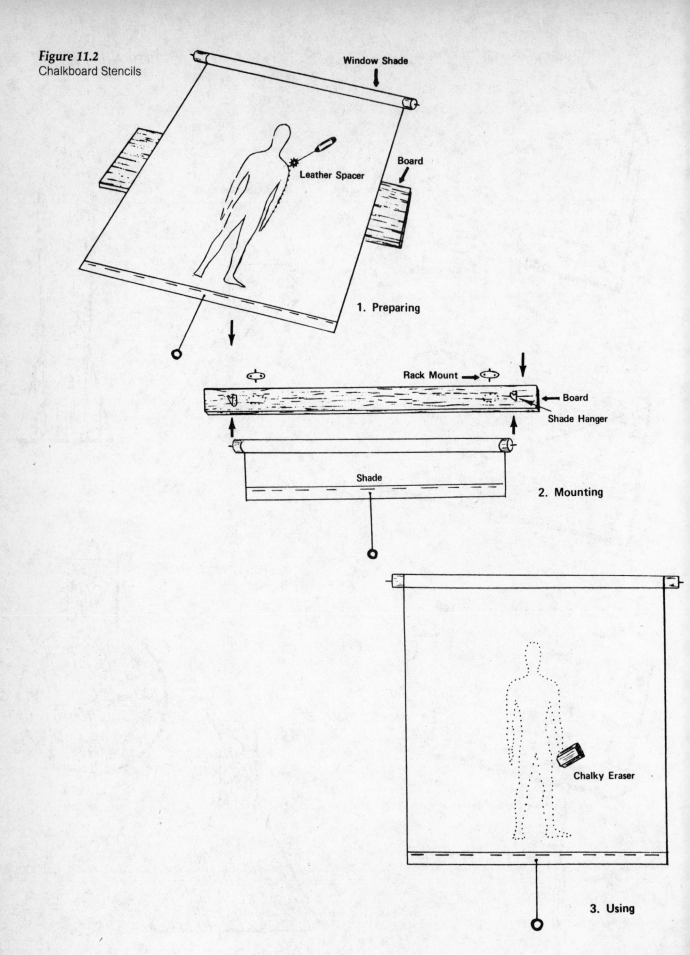

Window Shade

Leather Spacer

Board

1. Preparing

Rack Mount

Board

Shade Hanger

Shade

2. Mounting

Chalky Eraser

3. Using

perforations along the outline drawn on the shade. Be sure to use a board underneath the drawing as perforations are made.

2. To make sure that all holes are cut cleanly, hold the stencil up to the light to check the size as you progress. Mount the board in the rack at the top of the chalkboard. Fasten window-shade hangers to the board, and mount the window shade on the hangers as illustrated.

3. Pull the shade down, hold it against the chalkboard, and pat a chalk-covered eraser along the perforations. Release the window shade so that it will roll up.

4. Fill in the spaces between the chalk spots by quickly sketching over the dotted outline with a sharp piece of chalk. If additional identical outlines are needed, simply move the stencil along the rack to a new position and repeat the process. (Note: You may also use heavy paper or cardboard to make the stencils. Prepare paper or cardboard stencils by using the same procedure.)

11.2   *Projected Negative Drawings*

A 2″ × 2″ slide in negative form, projected on the chalkboard, may be helpful as a basis for supplemental chalk drawings (see Figure 11.3). Schematic

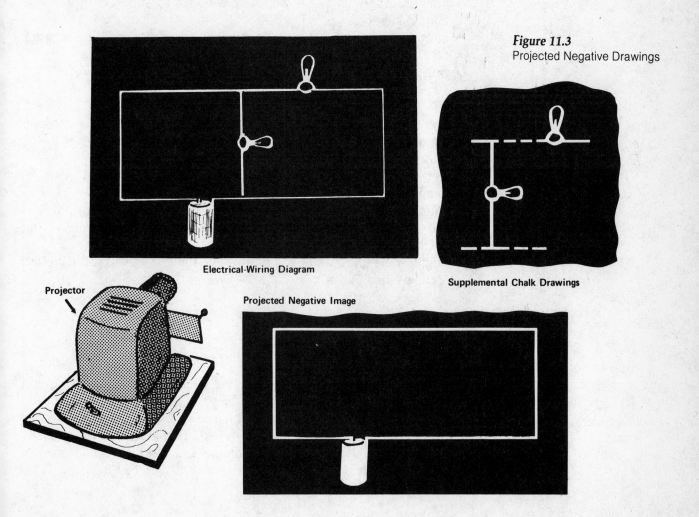

Figure 11.3
Projected Negative Drawings

Electrical-Wiring Diagram

Supplemental Chalk Drawings

Projector

Projected Negative Image

drawings or diagrams used in this way should be done on white paper with black ink and should be photographically copied with a 35mm camera. Process the film through the negative stage, and mount the negative between glass for projection. Negatives of this sort may be projected in a dimly lit room. Add any supplemental information to the projected image with chalk, and erase and modify as needed while projecting the slide.

11.3   Hidden Chalkboard

Materials prepared in advance will have special dramatic effect if they are hidden from view until needed to illustrate a point. Hide prepared materials on the back of a map, or behind a special movable curtain which hangs to one side of the chalkboard when not in use. The instructions below explain how to construct and hang a permanent curtain for a hidden board.

Materials and Equipment
- cloth curtain, cut in two pieces, long enough to completely cover the chalkboard and board frame (the color should harmonize with the color scheme of the room)
- split plastic rings or shower-curtain hooks to slide along the wire curtain support
- strong wire, slightly longer than the chalkboard and chalkboard frame
- screw eyes to hold each end of the wire
- one or two turnbuckles to tighten the wire

Procedure   (Figure 11.4)
1. Set the screw eyes into the board frame above and slightly to one side of the chalkboard.
2. Fasten the turnbuckles to the ends of the wire.
3. Sew the plastic rings to the curtain, evenly spacing them. Thread the wire through the rings and hang the curtains.
4. Attach a turnbuckle to one of the screw eyes. Pull the wire tight, and fasten the other end of the wire (or the other turnbuckle) to the second screw eye.
5. Tighten the turnbuckles to pull the wire tight. The chalkboard curtain is now ready to use.

11.4   Chalkboard Inks

At times you may want to keep an outline on the chalkboard for several days, making additions to it as you introduce new materials. By using chalkboard inks, you can place an outline on the chalkboard that cannot be accidentally erased, one that will allow the addition and deletion of chalk-drawn materials. Chalkboard inks are soluble and can be cleaned off with solvents at the conclusion of a unit of work.

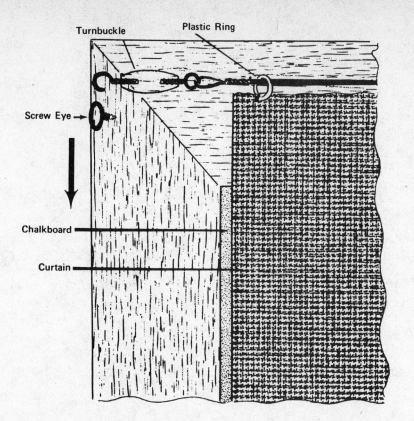

Figure 11.4
Hidden Chalkboard

Turnbuckle

Plastic Ring

Screw Eye →

Chalkboard

Curtain

11.5   *Enlarging Drawings*

The two processes described below, the grid method and the projection method, are excellent ways to produce enlarged drawings on chalkboards or on charts.

Grid Method

Use the grid method to enlarge small drawings on the chalkboard or on charts. This method requires little artistic skill and produces accurate, attractive drawings.

Materials and Equipment
- sharpened, soft lead pencil
- ruler
- yardstick
- sharpened chalk
- eraser
- picture to be transferred
- poster board

Procedure (Figure 11.5)
1. Using a ruler and soft lead pencil, draw a grid on the picture to be transferred. Or, to avoid damaging the picture, draw the grid on a sheet of tracing paper, place the tracing paper on the top of the

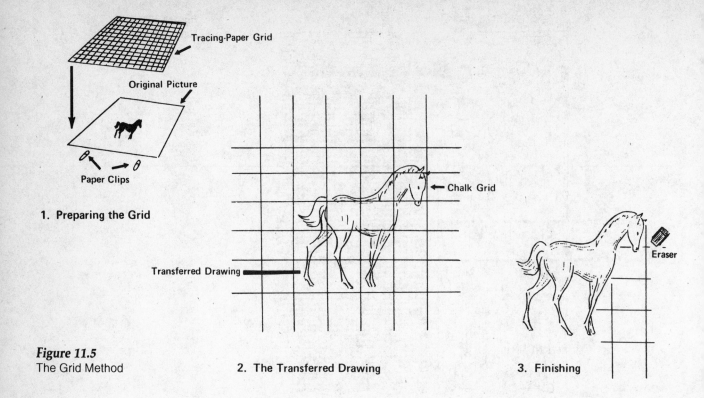

Figure 11.5
The Grid Method

1. Preparing the Grid

2. The Transferred Drawing

3. Finishing

drawing or print, and fasten it with paper clips. The grid should have from ¼" to 1" between lines, depending on the size of the picture.

2. Using a yardstick and a sharpened piece of chalk, draw a grid on the chalkboard (or chart), using a greater distance between the lines. A 2" to 4" space between lines is usually required. Draw the picture on the enlarged grid, one square at a time, starting at one corner. The grid on the original picture serves as an excellent reference for accurately transferring the lines to the chalk grid.

3. After the drawing is complete, remove the grid lines with an eraser and touch up your picture if necessary. You can achieve very good results with this technique if you follow the steps outlined above.

Projection Method

Teachers who wish to enlarge small drawings or pictures can use the projector method to create an acceptable chart or chalkboard enlargement. By using the projector, teachers with little artistic know-how can transfer pictures easily and accurately from books, slides, or filmstrips.

Materials and Equipment
- projector
- picture to transfer
- sharpened piece of white chalk
- pencil for chart enlargements
- poster board

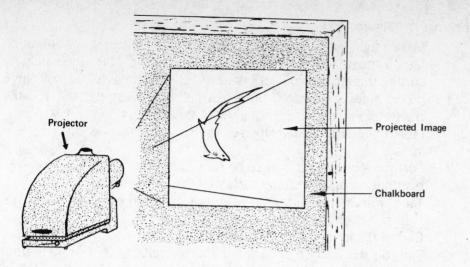

Figure 11.6
Opaque Projection Drawing

Procedure (Figure 11.6)

1. Place the picture, slide, or filmstrip in the projector and turn on the switch.
2. Adjust the size of the image on the chalkboard or chart by moving the machine toward or away from the board. To achieve a sharp focus, move the focusing lens into or out of the lens housing as needed.
3. Using chalk, outline the projected figure on the chalkboard. Use a pencil to outline the image on a chart.
4. As you progress, make periodic checks of your tracing to see if needed detail has been omitted from the chalkboard drawing. You can check the drawing easily by turning on the room's lights, for this will blot out the projected image and reveal any undrawn details. Continue tracing until your picture is complete.

11.6   Reducing Drawings

Visuals may be reduced to a small size by reverse projection. Reverse projection permits bright light reflected off a large visual to enter the objective lens of an overhead projector and produce a reduced image of the large visual on the stage of the overhead projector.

Materials and Equipment

- overhead projector
- two bright light sources
- large visual
- pencil
- white paper
- masking tape
- push pins
- cardboard, three 12" × 12" pieces
- paper cutter

Procedure (Figure 11.7)

1. Make a light shield out of cardboard. The light shield keeps unwanted light from striking the visual you are producing. Make the shield by cutting three pieces of cardboard to 12" × 12" in size. Place all three pieces side by side on a table leaving ¼" between pieces. Tape the pieces together.
2. Mount the large visual upside down with push pins on a vertical surface.
3. Position a bright light source on each side of the large visual for even distribution of light on the surface of the large visual.
4. Tape white paper to the stage of the overhead projector. Place the light shield on the projector.
5. Darken the room as much as possible.
6. Turn on the light sources. Move the projector toward or away from the large visual until the image appears on your white paper. Adjust the focus knob for a sharp image. Again, move the projector toward or away from the large visual, focusing as you do so until you get the image size you need.
7. Trace the image, leaving out any unwanted details.

Figure 11.7
Reducing Drawings

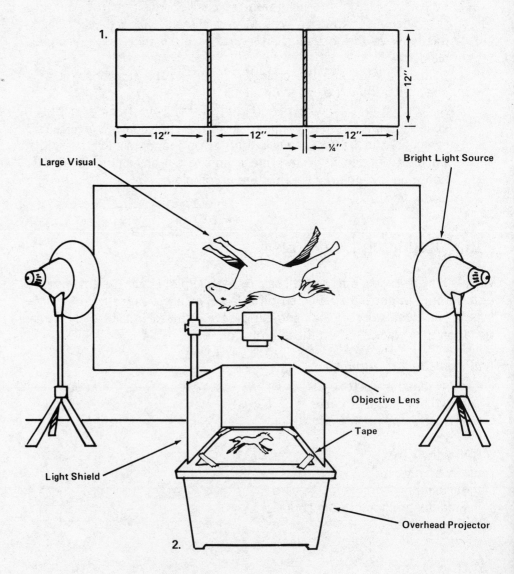

Chalkboard and Charting Tools

Tape Recording for Instruction

XII

Tapes that accompany pictorial presentations, such as opaque-projected pictures, slide sets, and study prints, often require special sound effects. This chapter describes how to produce an audio tape lesson, how to duplicate tapes, duplicate disc recordings on tape, record voice and music simultaneously, and make special sound effects on tape. (For basic operation of a tape recorder, consult the appropriate user's manual.)

12.1   Producing Audio Tape Lessons

An audio tape recording may provide personal attention to the individual needs, problems, personalities, and interests of learners. The recording's level of sophistication can vary from simple (prepared on a household recorder) to complex (prepared on studio equipment). But all levels require that you write a script of what will be presented, including sound effects, before recording the lesson; keep the lesson to about 15 to 20 minutes in length, depending on your students' listening abilities; and personalize the lesson by addressing your words to the student. Consider the following guidelines for making individualized learning tapes.

Guidelines for Making Audio Tape Lessons

Introduction
Your tape recording should start with its title and a description or list of the materials that will be needed to carry out the learning tasks.

Students should understand what is expected of them; so be sure to include a description of what the tape, center, or assignment is about and what the student is expected to learn.

Learning Pattern

Make sure the students are fully aware of what they are supposed to be doing and what to do next. Is there a clear pattern for using the materials, books, worksheets, or other items? Are there page turning instructions? Are there clear verbal commands, special sounds, or musical notes used as transition signals? Consider these questions carefully to help focus on the learning pattern.

Pacing

Design the tape so that learners can proceed at their own pace. Provide opportunities for the student to stop the tape and reflect on what has happened or partake in some activity. Use reading assignments, worksheets, or puzzles for a listening break.

An example might be, "Turn off the player and complete problem number two. When you are finished with problem number two, turn the player back on." Five to six seconds of music may be used as a pause or transition so the student is aware of when to stop and start the tape.

Reinforcement

Reinforcement is a teaching technique used to build the learner's confidence. Try to incorporate reinforcement in the tape. Periodic testing is one way of reinforcing learning. For example, you might say, "Answer question number five on your worksheet (pause) . . . If your answer was Robin Hood, good. Now continue with the next portion of this tape."

Motivation

Provide some motivation for learning. If activities are part of your tape, then verbally predict the student's enjoyment. Suggest that the student may enjoy acquiring a new, useful skill; or, offer a specific reward for the successful completion of the required objectives.

Personalization

Programmed materials, computer-assisted instruction, and other technological advances have been available for several years, yet they have not replaced teachers. Students want and enjoy interaction with other people.

Make the students feel they are learning from a person, not from a machine. Interject feelings into your tapes. Some examples might include, "I hope you have enjoyed this story so far. It is one of my favorites." "If you are having trouble with a part of the lesson raise your hand, and I will be happy to explain it to you."

Conclusion

Let the student know what to do when the tape and the lesson have been completed. Instructions might include directions for rewinding the tape, placing materials back into a box, taking a posttest, turning in assignments, or moving on to the next activity.

Use these seven guidelines—introduction, learning patterns, pacing, reinforcement, motivation, personalization, and conclusion—as a checklist for creating good tapes. Not every item will be appropriate for each tape you do, but each item should be considered.

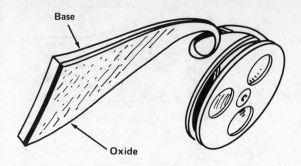

Figure 12.1
Audio Tape

Figure 12.2
Knockout Tabs

12.2 Selecting the Tape

Audio tape is composed of two basic elements: a base material, such as polyester or acetate, and a coating of iron oxide (Figure 12.1). The oxide is what gives the tape its color. Polyester tape is stronger than acetate tape and is recommended for classroom use. Some tapes are better than others. Consider the following questions before selecting a tape: (1) Is the base of the tape durable? Does it stretch easily? (2) Does the oxide used on the tape come off on the tape recorder heads (the parts that rub against the tape)? (3) Are the mechanical parts of the cassette of suitable quality?

Playing time length will depend on the length of tape on a reel or in a cassette, as well as on the thickness of the tape.

Cassettes have knockout tabs to prevent accidental erasing. In Figure 12.2, you will notice that two tabs are located on the back side of the cassette. These tabs are designed to be knocked out with a nail file or other similar device. When the tabs are gone, it is impossible to record on the tape. If you wish to rerecord the tape, place tape over the holes to duplicate the effect of the tabs.

12.3 Recording

There are various types of microphones. *Crystal* microphones are the type that usually come with inexpensive machines and work best for recording voice. *Ceramic* and *dynamic* microphones are better for voice and music, but both are more expensive than crystal. Your microphone selection depends on your needs and the needs of your students. Make a trial recording with the microphone. If you like the result and you think your students will like it, then use it. If you want a better microphone, see your audio-visual department or consult an electronics supply house. Microphones are designed for specific recording purposes:

1. An omnidirectional microphone (Figure 12.3) is designed to pick up sound from all directions. Most crystal and ceramic microphones fit this category. This type of microphone works well for recording groups.

Figure 12.3
Omnidirectional Pick-Up

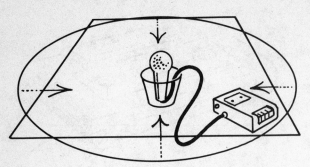

Figure 12.4
Unidirectional Pick-Up (Cardiod)

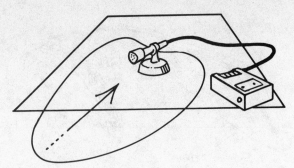

2. A unidirectional (cardiod) microphone (Figure 12.4) is designed to pick up sound from one direction only. This type of microphone is best for recording a single source, such as a story teller.

Automatic Gain Control (AGC)

Some microphones have automatic gain control (AGC) that compensates for low sounds by automatically making them louder on the recording. Sometimes the AGC is turned on and off by a switch on the microphone. At other times, it is built into the tape machine and is on at all times. The advantage of AGC is that all of the sound is automatically recorded. The disadvantage is that if you want to record only one sound and you try to keep out other sounds, such as street traffic, the AGC brings in the other sounds.

Mixer

The mixer is a device that allows you to insert two sources of sound, such as voice from a microphone and music from a record player. The mixer controls the volume of each source of sound and can help produce a very professional sounding lesson.

Acoustics and Recording Techniques

1. Keep the microphone 6" away from the person talking.
2. Do not wear jewelry or other items that might make noise.
3. Move people rather than the microphone.
4. Don't place the microphone on the same surface as the tape recorder unless the microphone is cushioned. Otherwise, you might pick up noise from the tape recorder motor.
5. Use a *pause* control to eliminate the click sound that may be produced every time the machine is turned off and on while recording.
6. Pick a quiet area to record in. For small groups, use a small room. A simple recording booth can be made by draping a blanket over a table and using the space beneath the table as a recording booth.
7. Set your recording level before you make your final tape. Practice recording your voice with the music or sound effects you intend to use.

12.4 Copying Recorded Sound

Tape Duplication

An original tape, or portions of several tapes, may be duplicated easily if two tape recorders and an appropriate connecting cord (a cord with a male plug on each end) are available. An electric company or school shop should be able to provide the appropriate cord for connecting the recorders.

Materials and Equipment
- two tape recorders
- blank tape
- original recording(s)
- appropriate connecting cord (a cord with a male plug on each end)
- sheet of paper and a pencil

Procedure (Figure 12.5)

Set up and turn on the power for both tape recorders. Place the original tape in one of the machines, set the counter at 000, and begin playing the tape. As the tape is played, jot down the counter setting for the beginning and ending of various selections to be used in duplication; then, rewind the tape and reset the counter at 000. The written references will help you skip over unwanted material quickly by using the fast-forward speed on the recorder containing the original tape.

1. Connect the two tape recorders by plugging one end of the connecting cord into the external speaker *output* of the recorder containing the original tape, and by plugging the other end into the radio-phono *input* of the other recorder. Insert a blank cassette into the second recorder.
2. Set the volume control on the machine containing the blank cassette to about one-third the full range, and press the *record* switch. Begin playing the original cassette recording, and adjust the volume control on the machine containing the original until the record-level indicator on the machine doing the duplication is responding as desired.

Figure 12.5
Tape Duplication

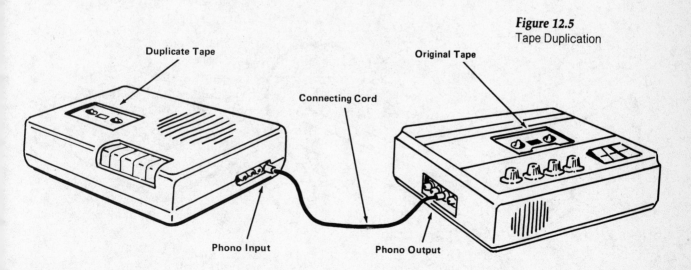

Duplicate Tape

Connecting Cord

Original Tape

Phono Input

Phono Output

3. Rewind the original cassette, start the duplicating cassette recorder, and then start the recorder containing the original cassette. Continue taping as desired.

Disc Duplication on Tape

Selected readings, portions of musical works, and other materials on records often need to be edited and pulled together from various sources in order to meet specific needs. By using a tape recorder, record player, and special connecting cord (prepared by a school shop or electrical company), you may be able to construct a tape containing all the needed sections.

Materials and Equipment
- blank tape
- record(s)
- record player
- tape recorder
- special connecting cords

Procedure (Figure 12.6)
1. Plug in and turn on both the record player and the cassette recorder. Connect the two machines by plugging one end of the special connecting cord into the speaker output of the record player, and the other end into the phono input of the cassette recorder (*direct method*). Or, using a cord that has alligator clips on one end and a plug on the other, attach the clips to the speaker terminals of the record player, and plug the other end into the phono input of the cassette recorder (*indirect method*). The *direct method* provides higher-fidelity recordings.
2. Place a record on the turntable, adjust the tonearm weight and the record speed, and make the correct needle selection. Turn the volume

Figure 12.6
Disc Duplication on Tape

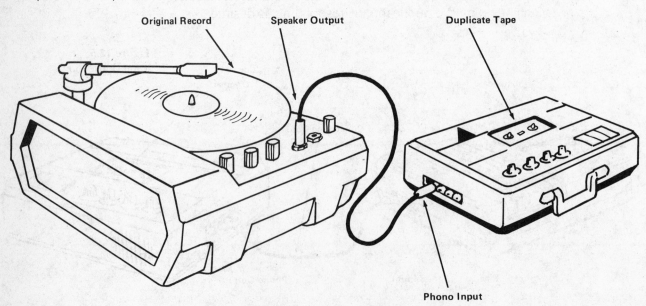

Original Record   Speaker Output   Duplicate Tape

Phono Input

Tape Recording for Instruction

on the *cassette recorder* to about one-third of the full range. Play the record, adjusting the volume by turning the volume control on the *record player* until a desirable volume setting has been attained on the cassette recorder volume indicator. Press the *record* switch on the cassette recorder, and record the sound.

Tape Radio and Television Sound

Often teachers have difficulty taping radio and television programs because of room noises or other interference in the area where the recording is made. By using a connecting cord with alligator clips on one end and a male plug on the other, you may record without picking up room noises. Attach the alligator clips to the speaker terminals of the radio or to the television speaker. Plug the other end of the cord into the phono or high-level input of the cassette recorder. Turn on the record player or television, adjust the volume control until the desired volume is attained on the cassette recorder volume indicator, and start recording.

12.5 Combined Recordings

Simultaneous Recording of Voice and Music

Dramatic renditions, oral interpretations, and spoken presentations to accompany visual presentations may be enhanced by a well-selected musical accompaniment. When planning sound tapes to go with visual presentation, write a script. Allow enough time for any changes in projections. Keep the music in the background while the narration is presented, and increase the music's volume between projection changes. The musical background should be continuous and smooth throughout the presentation to give unity to the lesson.

Materials and Equipment
- blank tape
- appropriate recording(s)
- special connecting cord (same as for record duplication on tape)
- script or other written material
- microphone
- tape recorder
- record player with microphone input jack

Procedure (Figure 12.7)
1. Plug in and turn on the tape recorder and the record player. Connect the two machines by plugging one end of the special cord into the speaker output of the record player, and the other end into the phono input of the tape recorder (*direct method*). Or, using a cord that has alligator clips on one end and a plug on the other end, attach the clips to the speaker terminals of the record player, and plug the other end into the phono input of the tape recorder (*indirect method*).

Figure 12.7
Simultaneous Recording of Voice and Music

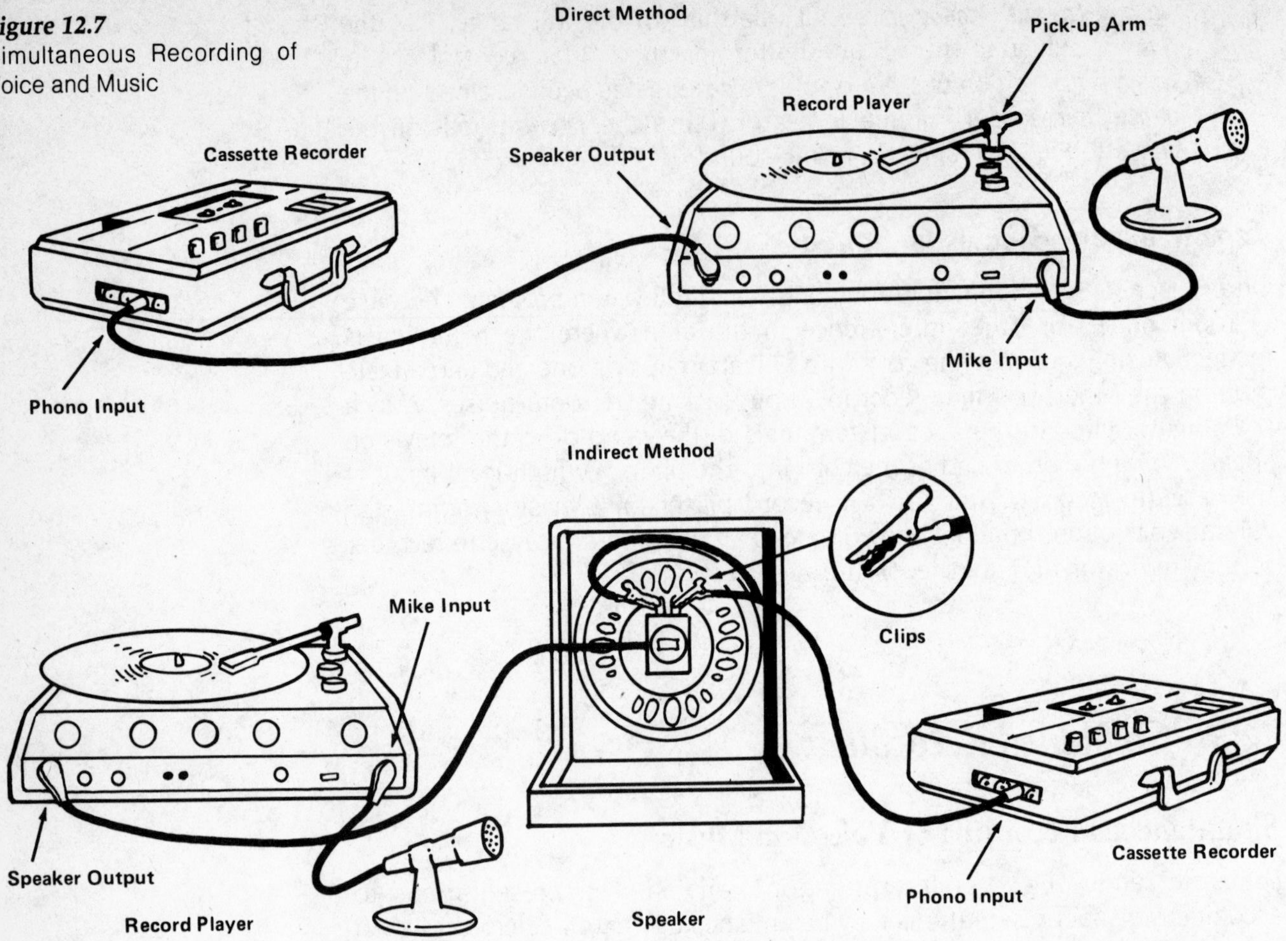

Higher-fidelity recordings are possible using the *direct* method of connection.

2. Place a record on the turntable, adjust the tonearm weight and the record speed, and make the correct needle selection. Turn the volume on the *cassette recorder* to about one-third of the full range. Play the record, adjusting the volume by turning the volume control on the *record player* until a desirable volume setting is attained on the cassette recorder volume indicator. Lift the needle off the record, and place to one side.

3. Plug the microphone into the microphone input of the *record player*. While talking into the microphone, turn up the volume control on the *record player* until the volume indicator on the cassette recorder attains an appropriate volume. Note the volume setting for voice and record.

4. If the recording is to begin with music, turn the *voice volume* control on the record player *off*, turn the cassette recorder *on*, and begin playing the record. When voice is desired, turn the music volume *down*, turn the *voice* volume *up*, and speak into the microphone. To eliminate unnecessary room noises, turn off the microphone, except when you are recording the voice.

5. Several trial runs may be necessary before the tape is finished. With a little practice, you can obtain professional results.

Tape Recording for Instruction

Sound Effects

Capture certain sounds, such as a train passing, a car starting, or an airplane leaving the ground, as these sounds occur in real situations. For plays and dramatic recordings at school, you may wish to create special sound effects. The sound effects listed here are easy to produce, seem realistic, and require no expensive equipment, other than a tape recorder and microphone. All other necessary materials are readily available, usually at no cost to the teacher.

- *Airplane motor or electric saw:* Hold electric hair clippers against mike, or hold a stiff piece of cardboard against the revolving blades of a fan.
- *Arrow flying through the air and impacting:* Whip a willow branch or a limber rod through the air near the mike; then strike the base of the branch or the rod against the table near the mike to simulate impact.
- *Boat with motor:* Run a popsicle stick back and forth over corrugated cardboard.
- *Boat being rowed:* Alternate between blowing through a straw into a pan of water, and working a rusty hinge back and forth.
- *Chains rattling:* Pour steel washers from one hand to another.
- *Fire:* Crumple a sheet of cellophane; increase proximity to the fire by moving closer to the mike. Diminish intensity by moving away from the mike.
- *Gun shot:* Place a pillow on a table, and strike sharply with a yardstick or ruler.
- *Horses' hooves:* Drum fingers on an inverted cigar box placed over a mike. For a horse passing over a bridge, click clam shells together near mike.
- *Rain falling:* Slowly roll a ball of cellophane between the hands.
- *Shutters in a storm:* Follow working of a rusty hinge back and forth with the impact of wood on wood.
- *Steamship whistle:* Blow across a partially filled pop bottle.
- *Stream or brook:* Blow lightly through a straw into a pan of water.
- *Surf:* Roll dried beans back and forth in a cake pan.
- *Telephone voice:* Hold a small can to one side of the face, with the opening toward the lips, while recording.
- *Thunder:* Rattle a large, limber cookie sheet near the mike.
- *Train engine:* Rub the face of the mike over flannel clothing.
- *Waterfall:* Roll cellophane or tissue paper between hands.

Photography for Instruction   XIII

Visuals represent a language, a method of communicating. At times, only visuals are needed to tell a story. Teachers and students can produce visual presentations that are educational by following the suggestions in this chapter. Slides and prints are common formats for presentations in educational settings.

13.1   Slides

Slides are usually in color and measure 2″ × 2″. They are simple to prepare, relatively inexpensive, and easy to rearrange as the need arises.

13.2   Prints

Prints, color or black and white, provide an inexpensive method to produce a series of images. The print series can be fastened together so that the images will remain in sequence. To mount prints on standard 8½″ × 11″ paper and place them in a three-hole binder is one easy method to arrange them in sequence.

13.3   Materials and Equipment

Simple and advanced cameras have many parts in common. A basic camera (Figure 13.1) consists of the following:

Figure 13.1
Basic Camera

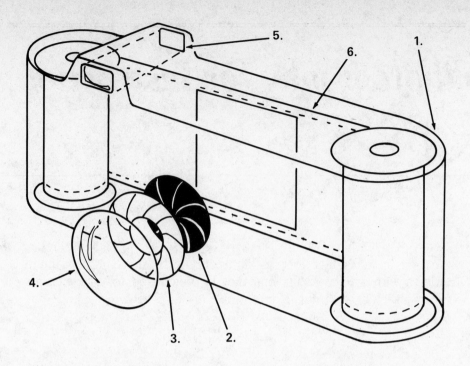

1. A *lighttight box* holds the film and the parts of the camera.
2. The *shutter* controls the length of time the light strikes the film. Simple cameras have only one or two speeds at which the shutter opens and closes. Advanced cameras have many more speed adjustments. Speeds are indicated in seconds or fractions of a second. Figure 13.2

Figure 13.2
Shutter Speed Settings

B	1	2	4	8	15	30	60	125	250	500	1000

shows the range of shutter speeds on an advanced camera. The "B" means bulb and is used for time exposures or flash exposures. On "B" the shutter remains open as long as you hold down the shutter button: "1" is one second, "2" is ½ second, "4" is ¼ second, "8" is ⅛ second, and so on. The faster speeds allow you to photograph moving subjects.

3. The *aperture* is the lens opening, which controls the amount of light that enters the camera. Simple cameras have one opening size; advanced cameras have many more opening size options. Figure 13.3

Figure 13.3
Aperture Settings

shows the range of opening sizes of an advanced camera. The openings are called "F" stops with the smallest number "F" stop being the largest opening. You may compensate for a wide variety of photographic conditions by using various combinations of lens openings with matching shutter speeds.

Photography for Instruction

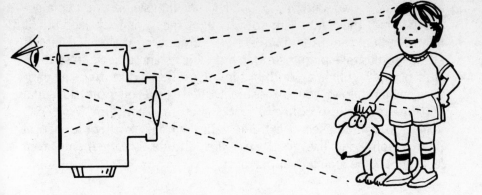

Figure 13.4
Simple Camera Viewfinder

4. The *lens* collects and focuses light on the film. A simple camera comes with a fixed-focus lens that is prefocused to take pictures from a distance of four feet or more. More advanced cameras may have lens options for focusing down to within a few inches of the subject.

5. The *viewfinder* is used to compose or "frame" the scene you wish to photograph. Figure 13.4 illustrates a simple camera viewfinder which allows the photographer to view the subject on a line parallel to the light entering the lens of the camera. When taking pictures close to the subject, you do not fully see what will be in the picture when the film is developed, because you are looking at the subject through a viewer that is placed in a different position than the lens. A more advanced camera uses a single-lens reflex viewing system (Figure 13.5). This allows the viewer to look through the lens of the camera prior to taking the picture. Thus, the photographer sees exactly the composition of the scene as it will appear on the developed film, whether taking pictures at a distance or close to the subject.

6. The film's sensitivity to light is called film speed and is measured by the ASA (American Standards Association) or the ISO (International Standards Association) rating. The higher the ASA or ISO rating, the less light the film requires to produce an image; and the grainier (less detailed) the produced image. Slow film (ASA/ISO 20–50) is

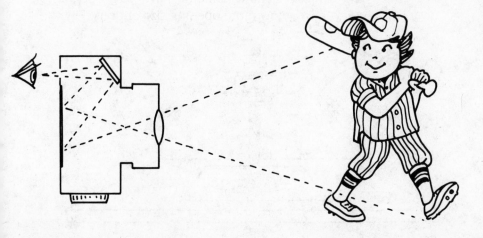

Figure 13.5
Advanced (Single-Lens Reflex)
Camera Viewfinder

Photography for Instruction   **189**

appropriate for working with detail, and it will make excellent enlargements. Since these films are not very light sensitive, they need bright light. Medium film (ASA/ISO 100–200) produces excellent results. It allows you to take pictures of moving objects and objects in shadow with bright highlights. Medium film also offers good exposure latitude, which allows your exposure to be a little off from the ideal setting and still produce a good picture. Fast film (ASA/ISO 400–1250) can be used in extremely dim light, is excellent for action photography, and has good exposure latitude. Enlargements from fast film will be grainy in appearance.

13.4   *Light*

Available Light

In general, it is best to take pictures when you can use available light. A sunny day, when the light strikes the subject directly, is usually best for taking pictures in natural light. However, to show the features of three-dimensional objects, it is preferable to have the light strike the subject from a 45-degree angle. If you are taking pictures indoors, the available light may not be strong enough to expose the film you have selected. Therefore, choose the film according to the light conditions under which the pictures will be taken.

Artificial Light

You may also take photographs with artificial light. Flash lighting provides instant light anytime and anywhere. Many cameras flash automatically, but distance is an important factor with flash pictures. If you are too close to your subject, you can "wash out" the subject by providing too much light. If you are too far from the subject, the flash will no longer be effective. Generally three to twenty feet is a workable range for flash photography. Consult your camera's instruction book for your camera's workable distance.

A copy stand that includes artificial lights, a flat surface on which to place the objects being photographed, and an adjustable stand to hold the

Figure 13.6
Copy Stand

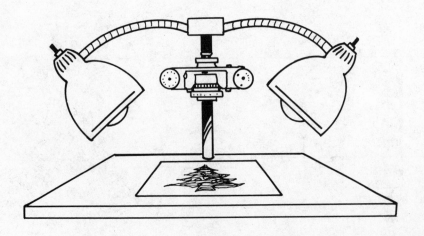

camera, is often used for precise photographic work (Figure 13.6). When using a copy stand, it is important to select a camera and a lens which will focus clearly within a few inches of the subject. The camera must have a threaded hole on its base to attach it to the adjustable stand. A 35mm single-lens reflex camera is usually used for copy stand photography. A self-contained portable slide or print production kit that simplifies copy work is the Kodak Visualmaker (Figure 13.7). Although easy to use, it is limited to two format sizes and does not allow for a wide range of adjustments. If you don't have a copy stand and lights, place the item to be copied on a sunlit outside wall (Figure 13.8) or on a windowsill where enough light is still available (Figure 13.9).

Figure 13.7
Kodak Visualmaker

Figure 13.8
Light Source: Sunlit Outside Wall

Figure 13.9
Light Source: Window

Figure 13.10
Object in Foreground Shows
Distance

Figure 13.11
Placing the Center of Interest

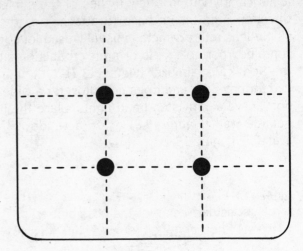

13.5 *Hints for Better Pictures*

1. Keep the picture simple.
2. Don't have subjects look at the camera; keep them busy.
3. For distance subjects, include a foreground object to help show depth (Figure 13.10).
4. Composition is important. Imagine your viewfinder divided into thirds, vertically and horizontally (Figure 13.11). Place the center of interest at any of the intersecting lines.

13.6 *Planning the Presentation*

1. Decide what you want your students to be able to do or know after they have finished viewing your photographic series. Write this down as an objective. One major objective is enough for one photographic series; do not overdo it. Once you know what the student should learn from the presentation, decide on the visual steps and the sequence of visual steps that the students must follow to meet the objective. At this point, you have invested little time and no money in the presentation. Planning it on paper first will save you time and money, and will produce better results.
2. Use 4" × 6" cards to list the visual steps (Figure 13.12). List one step per card. In the left corner of the card, draw a large box. In the box, sketch what the visual should look like when completed. If narration will accompany the presentation, it may be added to the card. Narration normally lasts from three to thirty seconds per visual. When all the cards are complete, place them in the correct sequence and ask someone to help you evaluate your presentation. After you have agreed upon the presentation sequence, number the cards in the upper right-hand corner.

Figure 13.12
Card for Presentation Planning

3. Titles are easy to produce, and they add interest to the presentation. Consider the following possibilities:
   a. Photograph a prepared sign (Figure 13.13).
   b. Photograph a chalkboard with the title in chalk (Figure 13.14).
   c. Use a photograph, and, with prepared letters, add a title over it (Figure 13.15).
   d. Use prepared letters or draw letters freehand on paper. Make a photocopy on colored paper, or prepare the title directly on colored paper (Figure 13.16).

Figure 13.13
Prepared Sign

Figure 13.14
Chalkboard with Title in Chalk

Figure 13.15
Photograph with Prepared
Letters

Figure 13.16
Prepared Letters or Freehand
Letters

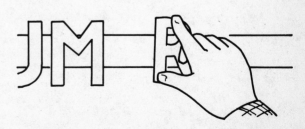

Individualized Learning and Interest Centers XIV

14.1 Developing Individualized Learning and Interest Centers

Learning and interest centers may offer effective, individualized instruction. You can design center activities to encourage problem solving, develop individual responsibility, and promote peer group learning through appropriate media.

The following steps may help you develop and organize individualized learning activities and centers for your students:

1. Identify the topic by assessing the learning objectives and the students' needs.
2. Select a programming style that is suited to your professional ability and the students' needs.
3. Arrange facilities for individualized learning.
4. Design record-keeping methods.
5. Select methods for making assignments.
6. Select learning activities, media, and equipment.
7. Select methods to control materials, equipment, and noise levels.
8. Provide evaluation methods for the program.

Although you should carefully consider all eight steps, they are flexible and can be altered to meet your objectives and the students' needs.

14.2 Step 1: Identify the Topic

Consider the following variables before you select your topic.

- *Assess your students' needs*, because your time and finances are limited. What student needs can be filled through center activities?

- *Assess your time.* How much time do you have to develop materials? How much time will you spend on program development? How much time will be required by the student to complete the individualized program? How will you schedule time for student involvement in center activities?
- *Assess your facilities.* Do you have facilities in which to set up the program? Do you need tables, electrical outlets, a bulletin board, or display space?
- *Consider your students.* Will their parents object to individualized learning as a method of learning or teaching? Are your students able to cope with the freedom they will have? Will your materials be suited to your students' backgrounds? Will your materials be relevant to the needs of your students? Do your students have prior experience with individualized learning? If they don't, you must be *very* detailed in your introduction to this new learning method.
- *Consider your geographic location.* If you are teaching a unit on sea life, do you live in a desert community or on a sea coast? Do your students have prior knowledge of the subject?
- *Consider the resources available to you.* Can the community help you by providing some learning experiences, such as field trips, speakers, or materials? Library services, media center services, and other services may be available to you through your school. Use them in planning your program.
- *Get help from your students.* Are they able to contribute in some way—cleaning up, making materials, monitoring materials, or keeping records? Do you have community volunteers or friends who will help you make materials?

Now that you have considered your own teaching situation, select your topic.

14.3 *Step 2: Select a Programming Style*

Individually Prescribed Style

This approach requires that the teacher pretest and prescribe a program for each student. The teacher needs to have the experience and time to give to each student. Ideally, this is an excellent system. If you do not have the time to work effectively with each student, however, consider selecting one of the less demanding individualized learning approaches.

The individually prescribed programming style involves:

1. Stating objectives that all students are expected to meet.
2. Providing a series of learning activities that range from the simple to the complex to enable students to meet the objectives.
3. Providing activities so that students may work at their own pace individually, in groups, or in teams.
4. Assigning students learning activities at the appropriate level.
5. Evaluating student competency.

Self-Directed Style

This approach is the most useful for the teacher who is just starting to develop individualized learning programs. The self-directed programming style involves:

1. Stating objectives that all students are expected to meet.
2. Having students meet the objectives by completing activities they select from a variety of learning assignments.
3. Evaluating student competency.

Personalized Style

In this approach, the student, with the approval of the teacher, selects an objective from a list and meets this objective by completing various activities. This approach gives the student freedom, but it requires a good deal of effort on the part of the teacher because the student will need personal attention. In this approach, the *student* does the selecting and the teacher approves, whereas in the individually prescribed style, the teacher does the selecting.

The personalized programming style involves:

1. Permitting the student to choose objectives from a provided list.
2. Providing students with contracts to meet the chosen objectives. The contracts should include enabling objectives and activities.
3. Scheduling time and activities for completing the personalized contract.
4. Evaluating student competency.

Independent Study Style

In this approach, the student, with the teacher's approval, chooses or writes the objectives to be met. Under the teacher's guidance, the student selects the activities to complete the objectives. The student works at his or her own pace, meeting with the teacher on a regular schedule, or as needed. The teacher determines when the objectives have been met.

The independent study programming style involves:

1. Students selecting or writing objectives to be met.
2. Students choosing the learning activities.
3. Scheduling time for completing the activities.
4. Evaluating student competency.

14.4   Step 3: Arrange Facilities for Individualized Learning

You may wish to arrange the desks into groups to provide a place for large groups, small groups, and individual learning (Figure 14.1). Consider locating stations in various places in the room. Stations can be arranged by media (film station or game station) or by topic (art station, science station, or

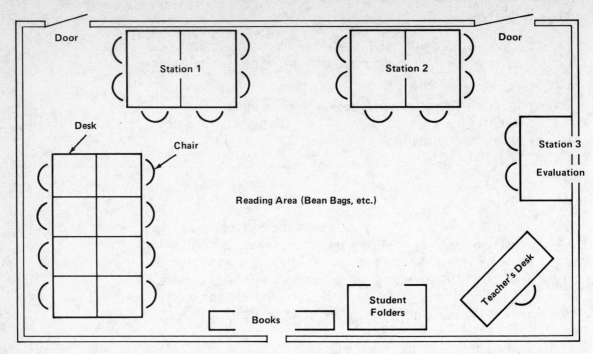

Figure 14.1
Facility Arranged for Instructional Modes

reading station). One station may be an entire learning center with all the tasks to meet the objectives at the station. Stations may also be arranged so that students can take materials to other areas of the room or work on them outside the room. When you design a room arrangement, remember that the teacher's area should be in a quiet place where you can meet with students.

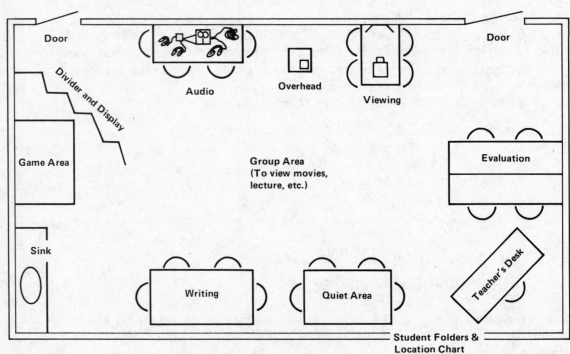

Figure 14.2
Facility Arranged for Stations Only

Individualized Learning and Interest Centers

Also, provide a quiet area for students who want to get away and just read or work by themselves.

Another possible room arrangement consists of stations only (Figure 14.2). Use dividers to separate stations and provide personal areas for students. This arrangement keeps all equipment and materials for a specific activity together. Students may move from station to station to complete assigned activities.

You may also choose to locate centers or stations on tables, on top of book cases, or even on the floor. Students may take learning center materials from the centers to their desks if necessary.

14.5   Step 4: Establish a Record-Keeping System

Student Location Chart

Keep a student location chart on the wall close to your desk (see Figure 14.3). Divide the chart into sections to correspond to the learning stations, and place a hook in the section for each position in that station. Have students move their name tags to the station positions at which they are working. You can tell at a glance where each student is, and the students

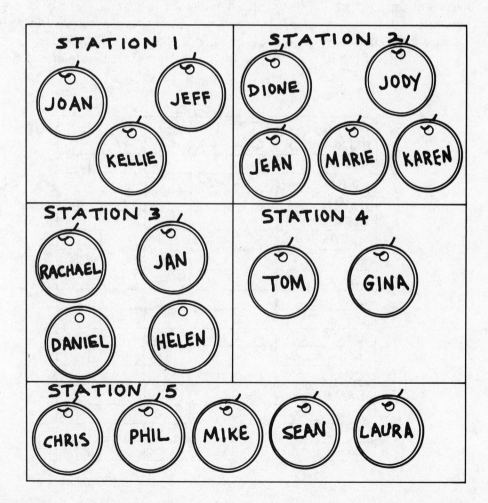

Figure 14.3
Student Location Chart

Individualized Learning and Interest Centers

can see where there are vacant positions. Make the chart out of cardboard and color each station a different color. At the station, color code each piece of material or equipment to match the station color.

Student Progress Chart

Make a student progress chart out of cardboard and cover it with clear acetate or clear adhesive shelf paper (see Figure 14.4). Suspend a grease pencil from the chart by a string.

After completing a station, have the students check off their names under the appropriate station heading. At a glance, you can tell who has completed a station and can put another check mark next to the student's check mark to signify approval, or erase the student's check mark to indicate that you want to meet with him or her.

Each station can have more than one task. For example, Station 5 on Figure 14.4 has four different tasks; each task can be completed and recorded separately. Keep this type of progress chart, or a variation of it, in a folder or grade book.

Student Folders

Give each student a folder large enough to hold 8½″ × 11″ paper (see Figure 14.5). The student should put his or her name on the folder and keep all the learning center work inside. Keep all folders in a box. If more than one group of students uses the learning center, then you can color code your folders and boxes. The left side of the folder contains work to be done, and the right side of the folder contains the completed work. By organizing this

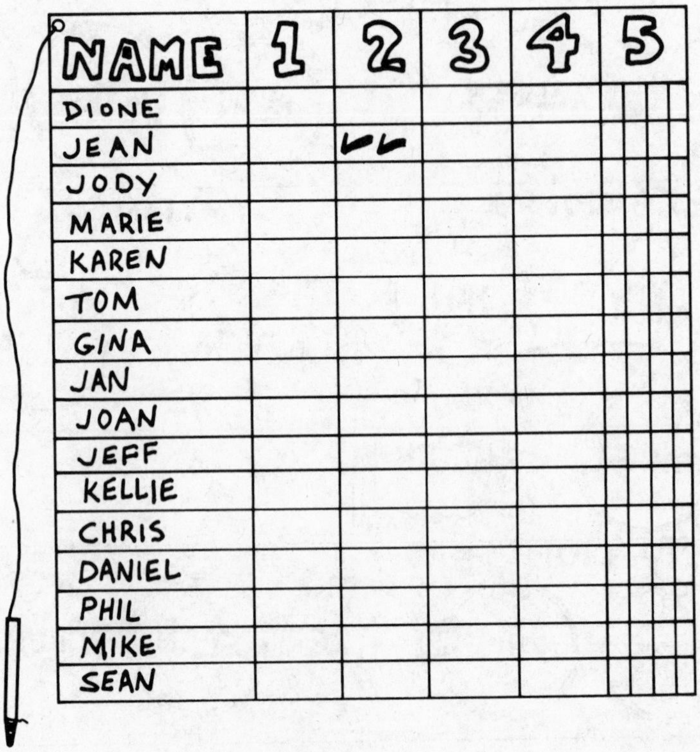

Figure 14.4
Student Progress Chart

NAME	1	2	3	4	5
DIONE					
JEAN		✔✔			
JODY					
MARIE					
KAREN					
TOM					
GINA					
JAN					
JOAN					
JEFF					
KELLIE					
CHRIS					
DANIEL					
PHIL					
MIKE					
SEAN					

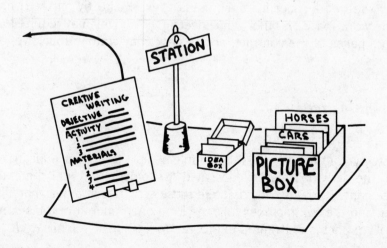

Figure 14.5
Student Folders

way, you can easily find the completed work. Use the message pocket as a personal mailbox between teacher and student.

14.6   Step 5: Select Assignment Methods

Task Cards

Write all the activities required to complete the assignment on one card, called a *task card*, and display it at the station. Place all the materials needed to complete the assignment at the station as well. For example, the content of the task card in Figure 14.6 is:

Creative writing

Objective: Write a one paragraph composition describing the feeling you get from viewing the picture.

Figure 14.6
Learning Center Station

Individualized Learning and Interest Centers

Activity:
1. Select one picture from the picture box.
2. Select an idea card that corresponds to the number on the back of the picture you selected.
3. When you have finished writing, put your completed composition in the "completed work" section of your folder.

Materials needed:
- Ballpoint pen
- Lined 8½" × 11" paper
- Picture
- Idea card

Contracts

The contract as used here is a student-teacher agreement that states how and what the student will learn. It is not a legally binding document. The format of the contract depends upon the needs, interests, and abilities of the student and the objectives of the teacher. Listed below are twelve items to include when you design a contract.

1. The student's name and any other necessary identification.
2. The date the contract is assigned.
3. The date the contract is to be completed.
4. A space for the teacher's initial, to verify that the contract is assigned.
5. A space for the student's signature, to verify that the student understands and approves.
6. Objective(s) the contract is designed to cover.
7. The location where the activity will take place, such as learning center, library, home, or playground.
8. A list of activities to meet the objective.
9. A list of materials for the activity.
10. A space for noting when the objective has been mastered.
11. A space for noting when the activity is complete.
12. A space for the student's comments about the contract after it has been completed.

Provide work space for the student to work directly on the contract, or include work space on other work sheets. One activity may require four, five, or more pages of the contract; or one page may contain four, five, or more activities.

Types of Contracts

ACTIVITY CONTRACT
An activity contract (Figure 14.7) supplements the regular educational program. The activities may be designed for remediation, enrichment, or reinforcement. Students can complete these activities at a designated activity center, and the contract may take the form of a handout or a task card. This type of contract is well suited to Programming Style II—*Self-Directed.*

Figure 14.7
Self-Directed Activity Contract
Example: Electricity

ELECTRICITY

Student _____

Date Assigned _____

Date Completed _____

Teacher _____

OBJECTIVE: To feel and see the power of the permanent magnet.

EXPERIMENT NO. 1

MATERIALS: Iron filings, acetate, magnet

PROCEDURE
1. Place acetate over the magnet and sprinkle iron filings over acetate.
2. Complete report one.

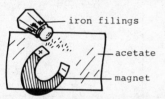

iron filings

acetate

magnet

REPORT ONE

What happened to the iron filings sprinkled on the acetate? In the space below, draw a picture of what happened.

EXPERIMENT NO. 2

MATERIALS: Two bar magnets with polarity marked

PROCEDURE
1. Touch the negative end of one magnet to the positive end of the other magnet.
2. Touch the positive end of one magnet to the positive end of the other magnet.
3. Complete report two.

REPORT TWO

1. What happened in step one? Why?

2. What happened in step two? Why?

DID YOU ENJOY THIS ASSIGNMENT?   YES   NO   If you answered no, please suggest how it can be improved. Use the reverse side of the contract.

SINGLE-SUBJECT CONTRACT

A single-subject contract (Figure 14.8) covers one subject. All of the activities can take place at a learning center, and the learning center's materials and equipment may be coded according to a theme related to the subject. For a science center, the theme might be a microscope; each station sign, contract, etc., might have a picture of a microscope on it. Having a theme helps you keep track of equipment and materials, makes the program more attractive, and helps students find the materials and equipment easily. Single-subject contracts may also include activities that do not take place at learning centers. This type of contract is well suited to Programming Style I—*Individually Prescribed*.

ELECTRICITY

OBJECTIVE: When you complete this contract you will be able to list the six sources of electricity.

NAME _____

DATE ASSIGNED _____

DATE TO BE COMPLETED _____

TEACHER _____ STUDENT _____

Activity	Activity Location	Activity	Materials Needed	Complete
1.	Station One	Work with a partner. Do Example 3 in electricity book. Take electric board test No. 6.	Paper, pencil, battery, bulb, textbook	
2.	School or Public Library	Write a one page report on a book or article in a journal that reports on the use of one or more of the six sources of electricity. Type or use ink and illustrate if necessary.	Paper, ink pen, access to library	
3.	Home	Read your electricity textbook pages 36-48.	Electricity text	
4.	Station Two	See filmstrip, "Sources of Electricity." Take electric board test No. 7. If you miss two or more, view filmstrip again.	Filmstrip, projector, screen, worksheet #1, mini center	
5.	Station Three	In a group of two to six, view motion picture, "Where Does Electricity Come From?" Allow 25 minutes.	Film, projector, screen	
6.	Testing Station	Take the final test then hand it in to the teacher.	Test, pencil	

FINAL GRADE _____   DATE COMPLETED _____   TEACHER _____

MULTIPLE-SUBJECT CONTRACT

This type of contract covers more than one subject and can include inside or outside learning centers. A multiple-subject contract is suited to Programming Style I—*Individually Prescribed*, and Style III—*Personalized*.

INDEPENDENT STUDY CONTRACT

This type of contract provides the student with a list of objectives and activities from which he or she chooses what to learn. This method is suited to Programming Style III—*Personalized* and Style IV—*Independent Study*.

14.7 Step 6: Select Learning Activities, Media, and Equipment

Select learning activities, media, and equipment that will provide your students with the experiences necessary to meet your performance objectives. (See Guidelines for Designing Instruction, p. 2.)

14.8 Step 7: Determine Management Methods

Noise level can be a problem for teacher and students alike. Determine the noise level you will allow and select a way to maintain it. One of the most effective ways to manage the noise level is to discontinue the learning center activity when the noise reaches the predetermined level. Or, flick the lights off and on as a signal that the noise level is too high.

Materials and equipment should be easy to inventory visually. One student or several students may be responsible for this task. You may code all the equipment and materials that belong to each station, learning center, or module, in one of the following ways:

- Label each item, indicating where the item belongs.
- Color code items that go together. As an example, Station 1 could be the green station and each item could be covered with green shelf adhesive paper or have a green spot attached to it.
- Use cartoon characters, flowers, cars, animals, etc., as a theme and code each item of a center, station or module with the theme symbol.

Keep an inventory list that includes each item in the center, station, or module. If items are housed in a box, attach the list to the box. If the items are left at the station, the list should be available to the person responsible for the inventory.

14.9 Step 8: Evaluate the Program

1. Test your program before implementing it. Ask a friend or a few students to go through the activities.
2. Introduce your program to your students as it will be introduced in the center. Be sure each student understands what is expected.
3. After the program is completed, analyze the results. Ask your students to evaluate the program and give you suggestions for improvement. Analyze the comments the students made on the contracts.
4. Revise your program as needed, and then try it again.

14.10 *Instructional Module*

An instructional module contains:

1. Objectives
2. Pretest
3. Programming system
4. Learning activities
5. Posttest

Once you have selected a programming style (see Step 2, page 196), develop it. Design and construct instructional modules that will provide the experiences necessary for your students to meet the objectives.

If you design the module in a kit format, place all materials in containers, and code each item to the kit by a color, number, or graphic symbol. Each time the kit is used, have the user check that all of the parts are in the kit when he or she is finished with it. An effective way to do this is to list the kit's contents and place the list where it may be easily seen. Students may then compare coded items to the inventory list. (Figure 14.9).

Figure 14.9
Kit

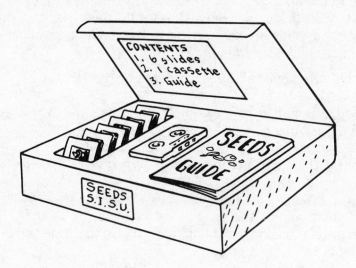

When the individualized program requires more than one instruction module, code each one individually (Figure 14.10).

The module's learning activities can be as simple or as complex as you wish. An example of a sophisticated and complex activity is a sound-filmstrip presentation with an automatic filmstrip advance (Figure 14.11). Another presentation might include black and white pictures, rubber cemented to cardboard and held in sequence with a ring or a three-hole binder, accompanied by an audio cassette. Or, you might type captions directly under the pictures (Figure 14.12).

An essential factor in designing a learning module is understanding your students' preparation. You must state exactly what you want your students to know when they have successfully completed the learning module. You must also provide sequential steps of learning activities to enable each student to reach the learning objective(s).

Individualized Learning and Interest Centers

Figure 14.10
Interest Centers

Figure 14.11
Sound Filmstrip

Figure 14.12
Sequenced Pictures

You may place modules in the classroom at special tables or at the student's desk. Consider making a module available to check out for home use or placing one in the school or public library for supervised use.

To design an effective instructional module, carefully consider how the learning will take place. Keep in mind that learning is usually the result of a sequence of experiences that change the behavior of the student.

Bibliography

AV Instructional Technology Manual for Independent Study. 6th ed. Edited by Brown, James W., and Lewis, Richard B. New York: McGraw-Hill, 1983.

Anderson, Ronald H. Selecting and Developing Media for Instruction. 2nd ed. New York: Van Nostrand, Reinhold, 1983.

Blake, Howard E. Creating a Learning-Centered Classroom: A Practical Guide for Teachers. New York: Hart, 1977.

Bloom, Benjamin S., et al. A Taxonomy of Educational Objectives; Handbook I: Cognitive Domain, New York: Longmans, Green, 1956.

Brown, James W.; Lewis, Richard B.; and Harcleroad, Fred F. AV Instruction: Technology, Media, and Methods. 6th ed. New York: McGraw-Hill, 1983.

Bullough, Robert V. Creating Instructional Materials. 2nd ed. Westerville, OH: Merrill, 1978.

Coloroso, Barbara. Media for Kids. Denver: Love Publishing Co., 1982.

Coplan, Kate. Poster Ideas and Bulletin Board Techniques for Libraries and Schools. 2nd ed. New York: Oceana Publications, 1981.

Espinosa, Leonard J. "Classroom Learning Centers. What Good Are They?" In Planning and Operating Media Centers: Readings from Audiovisual Instruction II. Edited by Association for Educational Communications and Technology. Washington DC: Association for Educational Communications and Technology, 1975.

Espinosa, Leonard J. Learning Centers. A Set of 18 Transparencies and Teacher's Guide. San Jose, CA: Lansford Publishing Company, 1974.

Fleming, Malcolm, and Levie, W. Howard. Instructional Message Design: Principles from the Behavioral Sciences. Englewood Cliffs, NJ: Educational Technology Publications, 1978.

Heinich, Robert; Molenda, Michael; and Russell, James D. Instructional Media and the New Technologies of Instruction. 2nd ed. New York: John Wiley & Sons, 1985.

Johnson, Rita B., and Johnson, Stuart R. Toward Individualized Learning: A Developer's Guide to Self-Instruction. Reading, MA: Addison-Wesley, 1975.

Kemp, Jerrold E. The Instructional Design Process. New York: Harper & Row, 1985.

Kemp, Jerrold E., and Dayton, Deane K. Planning and Producing Instructional Media. 5th ed. New York: Harper & Row, 1985.

Locatis, Craig N., and Atkinson, Frances D. Media and Technology for Education and Training. Westerville, OH: Merrill, 1984.

Mager, Robert F. Preparing Instructional Objectives. Revised 2nd ed. Belmont, CA: David S. Lake Publishers, 1984.

Minor, Edward O. Handbook for Preparing Visual Media. 2nd ed. New York: McGraw-Hill, 1978.

Minor, Edward O. and Frye, Harvey R. Technologies for Producing Visual Instructional Media. 2nd ed. New York: McGraw-Hill, 1977.

Morlan, John E.; Espinosa, Leonard J.; Friebel, Allen C.; Parker, Weldon W.; and Ramonda, Robert J. Classroom Learning Centers. Belmont, CA: David S. Lake Publishers, 1974.

Satterthwaite, Les. Audiovisual: Utilization, Production, and Design. Dubuque, IA: Kendall/Hunt, 1983.

Satterthwaite, Les. Graphics: Skills, Media and Materials. 3rd ed. Dubuque, IA: Kendall/Hunt, 1977.

Shannon, Claude E., and Weaver, Warren. The Mathematical Theory of Communication. Urbana, IL: University of Illinois Press, 1949.

Simonson, Michael R., and Volker, Roger P. Media Planning and Production. Westerville, OH: Merrill, 1984.

Turnbull, Arthur T., and Baird, Russell N. The Graphics of Communications: Typography, Layout, Design, Production. 4th ed. New York: Holt, Rinehart and Winston, 1980.

Sources of
Equipment
and Materials

Most of the equipment and materials needed for the projects in this book should be available in your school or at your local art, stationery, photography, hardware, teacher's supply house, or audio-visual store. If you cannot find the materials—or equipment locally, write for a catalog from the companies listed below.

ART SUPPLIES AND EQUIPMENT

General catalog

Alvin
P.O. Box 188
Windsor, CT 06095

Arthur Brown and Bro., Inc.
2 West 46th Street
New York, NY 10036

Dick Blick
P.O. Box 1267
Galesburg, IL 61401

Eberhard Faber, Inc.
Crestwood Industrial Park
Mountaintop, PA 18773

Graphic Products Corporation
Rolling Meadow, IL 60008

Lettering

Koh-I-Noor Rapidograph, Inc.
100 North Street
Bloomsbury, NJ 08804-0068

Kroy Inc.
Corporate Headquarters
P.O. Box C-4300
Scottsdale, AZ 85261

Letterguide Inc.
P.O. Box 30202
Lincoln, NE 68503

R.S. Beller Co.
3080-B McMillan Road
San Luis Obispo, CA 93401

Unimark System
Uniline Corporation
33450 Western Avenue
Union City, CA 94587

Prepared Art

Dynamic Graphics, Inc.
6000 N. Forest Park Drive
Peoria, IL 61614-3592

Volk Clip Art
1401 Main Street
Pleasantville, NJ 08232

Mounting and Laminating

Graphic Laminating, Inc.
5122 St. Clair Avenue
Cleveland, OH 44103

Laminex, Inc.
Subsidiary of Rexham
  Corporation
P.O. Box 240655
Charlotte, NC 28224

Seal Products Inc.
550 Spring Street
Naugatuck, CT 06770-9985

Display

Labelon Corporation
10 Chaphin Street
Canandaigua, NY 14424

AUDIO-VISUAL SUPPLIES AND EQUIPMENT

General catalog

Photo and Sound Company
116 Natoma Street
San Francisco, CA 94105-3704

Visual Horizons
180 Metro Park
Rochester, NY 14623

The Sourcebook
General Binding Corporation
One GBC Plaza
Northbrook, IL 60062-4195

Overhead Projector

Arkwright, Inc.
Main Street
Fiskeville, RI 02803

AVCOM Systems, Inc.
P.O. Box 977
Cutchogue, NY 11935

Audio-Visual Division/3M
225-3NE 3M Company
St. Paul, MN 55144-1000

Dorfman Products
23813 Archwood Street
Canoga Park, CA 91340

COMPUTER SUPPLIES AND EQUIPMENT

General catalog

Global
Computer Supplies
24218 East Del Amo Blvd.
  Dept. 66
Compton, CA 90220

Tandy Computer Catalog
Tandy Corporation
1801 Tandy Center
Fort Worth, TX 76102

Radio Shack Software
  Reference Guide
Tandy Corporation
1801 Tandy Center
Fort Worth, TX 76102

Sources of Equipment and Materials

Equipment

Apple Computer, Inc.
10280 Bandley Drive
Cupertino, CA 95014

Atari, Inc.
1265 Borregas
Sunnyvale, CA 94086

Bell & Howell Co.
7100 McCormic Road
Chicago, IL 60645

Commodore Business Machines
901 California Avenue
Palo Alto, CA 93404

IBM Corporation
1133 Westchester Avenue
White Plains, NY 10604

Texas Instruments, Inc.
8600 Commerce Park Drive
Houston, TX 77036

Materials

Color Me
Versa Computing, Inc.
3541 Old Conejo Road
Newbury Park, CA 91320

MacDraft
Innovative Data Design, Inc.
1975 Willow Pass Road, Suite 8
Concord, CA 94520

MacDraw
Apple Computer, Inc.
20525 Mariani Avenue
Cupertino, CA 95014

MacPaint
Apple Computer, Inc.
20525 Mariani Avenue
Cupertino, CA 95014

MacPublish
Boston Software
1260 Boylston Street
Boston, MA 02215

Page Maker
Aldus Corporation
610 First Avenue, Suite 400
Seattle, WA 98104

Paint Brush
HesWare
150 N. Hill Street
Brisbane, CA 94005

Ready Set Go
Manhattan Graphics Corporation
163 Varick Street
New York, NY 10013

Glossary

Accordion fold Mounted prints or flat materials fastened together, side by side, with tape.

Adhesive lamination A method of adhering a transparent self-sticking plastic film to a flat cardboard or graphic to protect the surface of the paper.

Adhesive pictorial art Symbols backed with adhesive, printed on white paper, and used to symbolize numerical quality for comparative purposes in chart work.

Anemometer A wind gauge used to estimate wind speed.

Animal cage A screened-in container in which to house and feed an animal.

Ant vivarium An enclosure for raising and viewing ant colonies.

Aquarium A container for keeping and viewing water animals and plants.

Audio mixer A device that allows you to simultaneously record from two or more sources of sound, such as voice from a microphone and music from a tape recorder. An audio mixer allows for separate control of the volume of each source during recording.

Automatic Gain Control (AGC) The ability of an audio reproduction system to compensate for low volume sounds by automatically making them louder.

Barometer A device used to indicate weather pressure-system changes.

Cellophane mounting A method of preserving plant specimens for display with cellophane or clear polyethylene film.

Chalkboard inks Inks used to draw an outline on the chalkboard that will not erase, one that allows for addition and deletion of chalk-drawn materials without effecting the ink outline. Chalkboard inks can be cleaned off with a solvent.

Chalkboard stencil Chalkboard stencils are outlines made of tiny holes in materials such as plywood, card-

board, or window shade fabric. The outline is placed against the chalkboard, and chalk is forced through the tiny holes with a chalkboard eraser, producing a faint outline. The outline is filled in as the lesson progresses.

Chalkboard template A shape cut from wood or cardboard to be used as a guide for tracing a chalk outline onto a chalkboard.

Charting tape Self-adhesive tape that can be used to line in colors and patterns.

Comprehensive layout An exact replica of what the finished product will look like. If the product is not to be reproduced (for example, a single poster) the comprehensive layout may also be the finished product.

Diazo transparency An overhead projection transparency that has been produced on a special acetate sensitive to ammonia. Wherever an opaque area on the transparency master prevents ultraviolet light from striking the acetate, an image is produced when the acetate is exposed to ammonia.

Diorama stage A device used to place objects in realistic, three-dimensional surroundings.

Dry-mount A method to adhere cardboard, photographs or other flat items to cardboard using an adhesive sensitive to heat and pressure.

Dry-transfer lettering Lettering printed on clear plastic sheets that will transfer to a dry surface when rubbed with a blunt pencil or similar object.

Electric question-board A teaching device that provides feedback to the learner by activating a light when the user touches one wire to the question terminal and another wire to the answer terminal.

Enabling objective The knowledge or understanding you expect your students to demonstrate before reaching the terminal objective.

Felt-tipped or nylon-tipped pen—permanent ink A pen usually made of plastic or metal that may have one of a variety of points. The ink is permanent but may be removed with a solvent when used on a nonporous, hard surface such as acetate.

Felt-tipped or nylon-tipped pen—water base ink A pen usually made of plastic or metal that may have one of a variety of points. The ink is water-based and may be removed with water when used on a nonporous, hard, surface such as acetate.

Film speed Film's sensitivity to light, measured by the ASA (American Standards Association) or the ISO (International Standards Association) rating. The higher the ASA or ISO number, the less light is needed to expose the film.

Flannel board Flannel fabric attached to a flat surface that serves as a display board. Items used on the display board are made of flannel or other textured materials that will adhere to the board. The top of the display board should slant back slightly when used.

Flip chart A prepared set of visuals, usually in a fixed sequential order, used in front of an audience or group.

Graphic layout and design Graphic elements arranged within a given space to attract attention, create interest, and convey a message.

Grid enlargement A process in which a clear plastic or tracing paper grid is placed over the drawing to be enlarged. The grid is then enlarged to the desired size on paper or on the chalkboard. Each line in each square of the clear plastic or tracing paper grid is reproduced by hand in the enlarged grid. When finished, the hand-drawn grid is erased and the enlarged image remains.

Hand-drawn transparencies An overhead projection transparency prepared by drawing and/or lettering on clear or frosted acetate.

Hand puppet A puppet that fits over or in the hand of the user.

Heat lamination A method of adhering a transparent or matte-surfaced acetate film that has a heat-sensitive coating on one side to paper, cardboard, or other flat material, using heat and pressure. This protects the paper surface.

Horizontal-Roll Theater A device used to present pictures and drawings rolled into view horizontally.

Hygrometer A device used to measure humidity.

Individualized learning and interest centers Individualized instruction to encourage problem-solving, develop responsibility, and promote peer group learning through the use of appropriate media.

Insect cage A device used to keep live specimens available for student observation.

Instructional module A complete unit of instruction that is usually designed for individualized study.

Layout A pattern, roughly or carefully drawn, to show the placement of the design elements on a visual.

Lift transparency An overhead projection transparency that has been produced by lifting the ink from a clay-coated printed page.

Magnetic chalkboard A metal-backed chalkboard that will allow magnet-backed visuals to adhere to it.

Mechanical lettering system A system of lettering that includes the use of an ink pen, drawing inks, and a lettering guide.

Omnidirectional microphone A microphone designed to pick up sound from all directions.

Opaque projection enlargement The projected image from an object placed in the opaque projector, hand-copied on the chalkboard paper or cardboard.

Opaque projector A machine that projects images of any flat opaque material, such as student papers; magazine or book materials; and small, real objects.

Overhead projection transparency Transparent or translucent sheets with information on them that can be projected by an overhead projector onto a screen.

Paste-up The use of an adhesive, such as rubber cement, to adhere the copy, art, and lettering to the layout surface.

Penny teaching machine An inexpensive teaching device that can be made by the student or teacher and is used for peer or independent learning.

Portable mini-center A portable display used to package materials such as directions, illustrations, and worksheets.

Prepared art Professionally drawn, copyright-free art that is printed on white paper. Such art is often called "clip-art."

Prepared letters Letters that have been die cut and are available in various sizes, styles, and colors. Some prepared letters are self-adhering.

Pressure lettering A system by which an image is transferred to a clear self-sticking plastic tape by the pressure of a template against a carbon ribbon.

Progressive disclosure A process by which opaque material such as light cardboard is attached to an overhead projection transparency to show selected parts of a transparency as needed.

Projected negative drawings A process by which a negative 35mm slide (black background and white image) is projected in a dimly lit room onto the chalkboard. Material may be added or deleted from the projected image with chalk during a presentation.

Reverse projection A process used to reduce drawings by reflecting bright light off a large visual through the objective lens of an overhead projector. A reduced image of the large visual is then reproduced on the stage of the overhead projector.

Riker mounting A technique for displaying specimens by placing them on cotton in a box and covering the box with clear plastic.

Rough layout A complete drawing of the best thumbnail sketch(es), where headlines and illustrations are placed approximately where they will be in the finished piece. See thumbnail sketch layout.

Rubber cement mount A method to adhere cardboard, paper, photographs, or other flat items to cardboard with rubber cement, a quick-drying glue.

Scroll theater Pictures mounted or drawn on long strips of paper and rolled into view, one at a time, when needed.

Seed-germination case A boxlike structure, open at the top, which is used to view seed germination and growth.

Self-adhesive lettering Lettering printed on clear adhesive-backed plastic sheets. The adhesive is covered by a protective sheet that can be removed after the letters are cut out.

Shadow screen A transparent screen that allows students to present a story or dramatization by projecting a light behind any cutout figure pressed against the screen.

Silhouette Projection The projection of opaque objects in silhouette on an overhead projector.

Spirit-duplicator transparency An overhead projection transparency produced by transferring an image from a spirit duplication master to a frosted acetate sheet run through the spirit duplicator.

Stencil A flat sheet of material in which letters, numbers or figures have been cut out. New letters, numbers or figures can be produced by tracing the cutout outlines with a pencil or other marker.

Terminal objective The behavior you expect your students to demonstrate after successfully completing each lesson.

Terrarium An enclosure for housing and displaying small plants or animals.

Thermal spirit master A master sheet to which carbon-based ink marks made on ordinary paper can be transferred by a thermal copy machine.

Thermal transparency An overhead projection transparency produced on a special heat-sensitive acetate that, when exposed to heat, will produce an image wherever carbon markings are made on the transparency master.

Thumbnail sketch layout Miniature drawings used to determine the placement of items in a rough layout.

Unidirectional microphone A microphone designed to pick up sound from one direction.

Visograph A transparent-faced display pocket with one open edge.

Visograph accordion fold A series of transparent-faced display pockets taped together, with the visograph opening at the top when the fold is placed in position for use.

Wet-mounting A method that uses paste to attach paper materials to a cloth backing.

Wind vane A device used to determine the direction the wind is blowing.